W9-BYH-052

Chicken Soup for the Soul®

Dreams and Premonitions

Chicken Soup for the Soul: Dreams and Premonitions
101 Amazing Stories of Miracles, Divine Intervention, and Insight
Amy Newmark and Kelly Sullivan Walden.

Published by Chicken Soup for the Soul Publishing, LLC www.chickensoup.com
Copyright © 2015 by Chicken Soup for the Soul Publishing, LLC. All Rights
Reserved.

The publisher gratefully acknowledges the many publishers and individuals who
granted Chicken Soup for the Soul permission to reprint the cited material.

Front cover moon image courtesy of istockphoto.com/portfolio/Eerik (© Eerik);
Front cover clouds image courtesy of istockphoto.com/portfolio/StanRohrer (©
StanRoher); Interior photo of woman in clouds courtesy of istockphoto.com/portfolio/
Vizerskaya (© Virerskaya); Photo of Amy Newmark courtesy of Susan Morrow at
SwickPix; Photos of Kelly Sullivan Walden courtesy of Carl Studna.

Cover design by Brian Taylor, Pneuma Books, LLC; Interior design by Daniel Zaccari

Distributed to the booktrade by Simon & Schuster. SAN: 200-2442

Publisher's Cataloging-In-Publication Data
(Prepared by The Donohue Group, Inc.)

Chicken soup for the soul : dreams and premonitions : 101 amazing stories
  of miracles, divine intervention, and insight / [compiled by] Amy
  Newmark [and] Kelly Sullivan Walden.

  pages ; cm

  ISBN: 978-1-61159-950-3

  1. Precognition--Literary collections. 2. Precognition--Anecdotes.
  3. Extrasensory perception--Literary collections. 4. Extrasensory
  perception--Anecdotes. 5. Dreams--Literary collections. 6. Dreams--
  Anecdotes. 7. Anecdotes. I. Newmark, Amy. II. Walden, Kelly Sullivan.
  III. Title: Dreams and premonitions : 101 amazing stories of miracles, divine
  intervention, and insight

  BF1341 .C45 2015
  133.8/6   2015946342

PRINTED IN THE UNITED STATES OF AMERICA
on acid∞free paper

25 24 23 22 21 20 19 18 17 16 15   01 02 03 04 05 06 07 08 09 10 11

Chicken Soup for the Soul®

Dreams and Premonitions

101 Amazing Stories of Miracles, Divine Intervention, and Insight

Amy Newmark
Kelly Sullivan Walden

CSS

Chicken Soup for the Soul Publishing, LLC
Cos Cob, CT

Chicken Soup for the Soul

Changing your life one story at a time®

www.chickensoup.com

Contents

❸

~Facing Fears~

❹

~Early Warnings~

❺

~The Next Generation~

8
~True Love~

9
~Personal Transformation~

10
~Love Doesn't Die~

Introduction

I'm in the future, married to the tall, dark, handsome man I am dating at the time. I think he is the perfect man for me — yet, in my dream that is showing me the future, I'm perfectly miserable. I'm bumping into furniture as I walk mindlessly through my picturesque house, with a soul-less dead stare. I'm a zombie Stepford wife.

I woke up from this dream feeling sick... because I really liked this guy. On paper he was ideal: He adored me, he had a great sense of humor, he had a thriving business, and my family and friends loved him. Yet, I couldn't deny what I'd seen (and felt) in my dream. I knew that even though the relationship was "perfect" on the outside, he and I would not be happy on the inside... down the line. A few days later, armed with nothing but the guidance from my dream, I called the relationship quits.

Years later, I met Dana, a music producer with whom I instantly developed a profound friendship/working relationship. For years we worked side-by-side on fulfilling, creative ventures. From time to time I'd wonder if he was the guy for me. But I'd shove the thought out of my head as quickly as it came in so as to not jinx this special friendship that had become so important to me.

Besides, there were many circumstantial reasons that made him light years away from being my "perfect" guy on paper. He had two grown kids from a recently ended relationship and he was many years my senior. Not only would my parents take issue with this relationship but so would many of my friends. The people pleaser extraordinaire that I was could never be with him. That was my firm conviction... until I had this dream:

There are two dragonflies in a cage, one that is perfect and one that has a broken wing. A woman in the dream desperately wants the perfect dragonfly — which I also want. But she is so adamant that I begrudgingly let her take it. I'm disappointed, but console myself: "A broken-winged dragonfly is better than no dragonfly at all."

I take my broken-winged dragonfly from its cage and watch it perch like a bird on my finger. As I connect with the energy of this dragonfly I begin to feel so much love for this amazing creature.

Suddenly, this dragonfly changes form and becomes a fleecy, white, little pig. (In waking reality I don't like pigs, but in my dream I love this pig.) I touch it, and my soul melts like butter. The pig feels like Dana... his soul. I cry tears of joy — so grateful to be connected, soul to soul, with this animal.

Just then, the pig transforms into a thousand dragonflies flying in circles around my head. I'm in awe, enchanted, thrilled beyond belief, and I hear myself exclaim, "I'm soooo glad I didn't insist on having the perfect dragonfly, because I would have missed out on the thousands of dragonflies in disguise!"

I woke up knowing that Dana was the broken-winged dragon-fly (a magical being with complicated personal issues that kept him from flying at full capacity), the pig (substantial, grounded), and the thousand dragonflies (more magic than I could possibly imagine that would take flight if we were together). I shared the dream with Dana (deliberately omitting the part about the pig, because I didn't think it was the kind of thing that would flatter a man's ego), and soon after that dream we began to tentatively tiptoe toward the possibility of being more than friends.

Fast-forward fourteen years (at this point we'd been married for twelve), and we emerged from a deep meditation together. Dana was uncharacteristically speechless, with the strangest look on his face. When I asked him what was going on he refused to tell me. He said he was afraid I'd think he was crazy. Finally, I convinced him to spill the beans. He confessed sheepishly:

"In my meditation there was this little white, fuzzy, cute pig. I kept trying to ignore him and direct my attention to something more spiritual... but he was so persistent and compelling. I finally just accepted him being there, and gave him my full attention... and when

I did I was filled with such bliss. As much as my ego doesn't want to admit this, I feel like this pig is more than an animal… it felt like it represented my soul."

I burst into tears and told Dana about the part of the dream I had omitted years before — the dream that flipped my switch from thinking of him as my beloved friend to knowing he was my "Beloved."

I heard the author Caroline Myss say, "When it's this bizarre you know it's the hand of God. A telltale sign of a relationship being a soulful one is if it's a little (or a lot) bizarre." So if you come to our house and see photos of a cute little pig intermingled with photos of family and friends, you'll know why!

Needless to say, I love dreams, premonitions, and dream-related synchronicities for the absolutely unconventional, ridiculously creative, and highly personal ways that they inform, guide, and heal us. They let us know when we're in the right place, at the right time, with the right people (our people), as imperfectly perfect for us as they may be.

I've lived in my own dream/premonition laboratory for more than forty years, having recorded thousands of my own dreams, and having received and worked with thousands of dreams sent to me by others via e-mail, Facebook, Twitter, radio, or on national TV. And I never cease to be blown away by their bizarre navigational power. I hope the stories in this book will inspire you to pay even more attention to your own dreams and premonitions. Whether you think they are sent to you by an outside force, or whether they come from within you and reveal knowledge you didn't even know you had, you can use your dreams and premonitions. They can provide you with unconventional — yet genius-level — guidance, and help you navigate your way into a more magical life than you could ever dream possible.

Thousands of stories about dreams and premonitions were submitted to Chicken Soup for the Soul for this book, enabling us to put together a powerful and diverse collection for you. I can't imagine you'll walk away from this book without being profoundly changed. Let me give you a little tour of what we have in store for you!

In Chapter 1, about "Navigating Life," you'll read about dreams and premonitions that helped change the direction of our writers' lives.

Mark Rickerby, for example, tells us about his brother Paul, who died of a drug overdose. When Paul came to Mark in a dream and told him to stop acting out his grief, which had resulted in road rage and other uncharacteristic behavior, it was a wake-up call for Mark, who snapped back to his normal patient, peaceful self.

Like Mark's dream, many of our dreams involve guidance from our departed loved ones, and Chapter 2 is all about these "Messages from Heaven." Sometimes those messages can be life-changing, and other times they may just provide a much-needed, but simple, piece of advice, as when Connie Pullen's late husband appeared in a dream to advise their son Chris on how to fix a broken bulldozer. Chris had struggled for hours the day before, trying to replace the clutch in his dad's old bulldozer. After his father told him during his dream that there was a hard-to-find bolt under the transmission that had to be removed, Chris quickly and easily finished the job.

Sometimes we teach ourselves something in our dreams, and you'll find great examples of that in Chapter 3, which is all about "Facing Fears." Dream expert Walter Berry describes how he always feared death in real life, even though he worked with death in dreams professionally. He was so afraid of death in real, "waking" life that he even was relieved to be 3,000 miles away when his dog had to make its final visit to the vet. Then Walter had a couple of dreams that repositioned death for him, erasing his fear. When his second dog died, Walter was right there by his side.

Speaking of death, we were overwhelmed by the multitude of fabulous stories that we received about dreams and premonitions that provided warnings about accidents, illnesses, or other disasters. We present you with many fine examples of this kind of dream in Chapter 4, called "Early Warnings," including one by Kathleen O'Keefe-Kanavos that will amaze you. She had to talk her doctor into doing a biopsy on her breast after she was guided in a dream to force the issue. Sure enough, there was cancer exactly where her dream had indicated, a cancer that did not show up using any conventional diagnostic means. Kathleen went on to survive cancer three times, each one prophesied in dreams and then validated by pathology reports. She is alive and well, and helping others advocate for themselves in the face of opposition.

You'll be smiling as you read the stories in Chapter 5, "The Next Generation." Who doesn't love a story about infertile women becoming pregnant or prospective adoptive mothers "seeing" their coming babies in their dreams, and learning later that their new babies were conceived right around the same date as their dreams? Dr. Sam Collins relates her own awesome story about how she visualized a future in which a beautiful young African woman named Grace was calling her "Mama." Sam told her husband they were going to adopt a little girl from Africa and her name would be Grace. Sure enough, six months later, they got an e-mail about a five-year-old girl in the Democratic Republic of the Congo who needed a family. Her name? Not a common one in Africa: Grace.

There is nothing like an intense dream to steer you in a new direction, and that's why Chapter 6 is all about "Waking Up to a New Life Path." Since I am a writer as well as a dreamer, I love Val Muller's story about how she was unhappy, stressed, and unfulfilled in her job as a teacher. When her late grandfather came to her in a dream one night, they talked about it, and he helped her realize that she actually wanted to be a writer, and then pointed out that she could "go to school each day, teach your students, and then go home and write. It's as simple as that. If you want to be a writer, then write." Even in death, Val's grandfather was a great mentor.

Dreams and premonitions change lives, and they save lives too. Chapter 7, called "Life Savers," will certainly make you pay attention to your dreams. You'll read stories about saving friends from committing suicide, getting the jump on cancer treatment before doctors would have caught it, and avoiding car accidents and other danger. Dream expert and bestselling author Robert Moss shares his own story about a vivid dream in which he died on a road near his home when a double-parked truck forced him out of his lane into the path of an oncoming, speeding eighteen-wheeler. The next day, in waking life, Robert was driving on that same road, in the same spot, when he discovered that his view was blocked by a parked delivery truck. He slowed almost to a stop instead of doing what he normally would have done, which was pull into the center of the road and pass the parked truck. Because he paused, he missed a head-on collision with an eighteen-wheeler barreling down the hill at sixty miles per hour, exactly as in his dream the night before!

Listen to your dreams; pay attention to your premonitions; and make sure you tell someone! These are constant themes in this book. You'll smile when you read Chapter 8, "True Love," about the rewards of doing just that. Rebecca Guernsey might have never met her husband Lyle if she hadn't confessed her dream to a friend, a dream about a man she had never met, with "deep blue eyes and a smile that could melt your heart. He loves the outdoors, hunting, fishing, hiking, camping, anything outdoors. He has something to do with Colorado." Her friend knew that exact man, but would never have thought they were right for each other if Rebecca hadn't shared her dream, since Rebecca says, "I don't have an athletic muscle in my body."

Those of us who specialize in dreams often talk about "transformative" dreams. It is remarkable how one dream can cause an epiphany, resulting in huge positive changes in our lives. You'll read about many such changes in Chapter 9, stories about "Personal Transformation." With bullying in the schools such an important topic these days, I was pleased to have a story from my mentee, Mariah Reyes, who had a dream in which she realized that she had reacted to *being* bullied by *becoming* a bully herself. She woke up and resolved to apologize to everyone she had hurt and she says, "That dream changed me. I've learned to be compassionate, to open my heart and to put myself in other people's shoes before I speak, to consider how they may feel." She has also become an advocate for young people, fighting against bullying and for positive change.

When the people we love pass on, we miss their support and their love. Sometimes we also are filled with regret that we didn't have a final conversation. But Chapter 10, "Love Doesn't Die," is filled with stories about our continuing connection with our loved ones, and about getting closure, too. You'll read Amy Schoenfeld Hunt's story about how her late father came to see her in a dream, to have the final conversation they never got to have when he lay dying in the hospital.

After he reassured her that everything between them really was okay, she clung to him in relief. But then he had to "go back" and she woke up sobbing, only to find her alarmed husband, also awake, exclaiming that he had just seen a bright white light glowing over her head.

"Miracles Happen" is the theme for Chapter 11, which is filled with stories about the weird ways in which dreams can make good things happen in the most unexpected ways. Kristi Woods had a rather amusing dream that she recounts to us: She was pulled over for a Breathalyzer test for no apparent reason. When the police officer announced the results of her test, instead of admitting her sobriety, he declared, "You are most definitely lactose intolerant," a condition that had never occurred to Kristi. Sure enough, in waking life Kristi stopped consuming dairy products and the numerous symptoms she had endured over the years quietly disappeared.

As I finish writing this introduction, I'm on a flight from California to Boston, my heart feels full, and I have tears running down my face. The lady in the seat next to me just asked if I was okay. I smiled and said, "Yes... more than okay... these are very happy tears." As I look out the window at the world below I marvel at how, from this sky-high perspective, all aspects of life seem clear, uncomplicated, and beautiful. This is the way dreams and premonitions make us feel — a blessed opportunity to rise above the clouds of stress and worry, and see things from a higher (more divine) perspective.

My coauthor Amy Newmark and I pray that reading this book will enhance your ability to pay attention to the miracle of your dreams and premonitions. We enjoyed collecting, selecting, and editing these extraordinary stories for you. Now we wish we could be there to see firsthand how you like them, and to hear how they change your lives, too. I suppose we can... in our dreams... or at least via social media!

Until then, keep dreaming and listening to that still, small voice within. Thank you for reading, and may all your wildest and most wonderful dreams come true!

~Kelly Sullivan Walden

Chapter 1

Dreams and Premonitions

Navigating Life

Mosaic

*There are very human beings who receive the truth,
complete and staggering, by instant illumination. Most
of them acquire it fragment by fragment, on a small
scale, by successive developments, cellularly, like a
laborious mosaic.*

~Anaïs Nin

t was hours past midnight and a young tennis pro, Brian Newcomer, was on the road heading to work. He was going to drop off his girlfriend along the way. Earlier that night the two of them had been celebrating their new commitment to each other and their future plans. Jessica was the love of his life. Thanksgiving had been wonderful and one great experience seemed to lead to another for the happy couple.

With no warning, the red gas light came on at the same time as Brian's car motor suddenly stopped running and sputtered to a stop in the middle of the freeway... between off ramps... with no shoulder available to pull over. They were hit from behind, killing Brian, age twenty-seven, and seriously injuring Jessica.

The more than 800 people at the funeral acknowledged Brian for the person he had become, or spoke of Brian as their best friend or remembered a "Brian moment" and referenced how Brian had become a light in the life of their child. To say Brian's death was a loss is the understatement of the century.

Several days after Brian's death, his sister Katherine called and booked a counseling session with me. Through sobs she told me the devastating news. Over the years Katherine had shared so many stories about Brian that even though I'd never met him I felt I knew him. At the end of her session she asked if I would be willing to provide sessions for her mom, dad, and brother, as well as Jessica.

I told her my specialty was not grief counseling, but the Newcomer family opted for me to work with them. The night before I was to have my first session with Margarita, Brian's mother, I fretted—what could I possibly do or say that would help her? "God help me help her!" was the prayer I said as I fell asleep.

Disappointingly, I awoke with no elaborate dream. Only one thing stood out from the jumble of incoherent images… the word "MOSAIC."

As had become my practice over the past three decades I dutifully wrote it down in my dream journal. I'd become habituated to not evaluate, but to take dictation and write my dream down, like a dutiful secretary, even if the dream didn't make sense… even if it was ridiculous… and even if it seemed like an accident that had nothing to do with my life. I was so frustrated that I had no clear image of what I wanted to say. I traced that word over and over on the page in my journal, so many times that you could see the imprint of the word MOSAIC on the next page. However, I couldn't help but look at this random word, MOSAIC, and think, *Really, God, that's the best you could do?*

I approached my session with Margarita carefully, tenderly, and with the intention of providing a space where she could feel safe enough to fully express herself. In our session she did just that. She shared feelings that ran the gamut from anger to devastation to shock to gratitude for the time she spent being Brian's mother, and for all the wonderful people who showed up at the funeral.

In the final moments of our session, as an afterthought, Margarita shared that though she'd received mountains of flowers and cards, there was one very special present she would treasure the rest of her life: a mosaic that one of Brian's best friends created. From afar it looked like a poster of Brian smiling, but viewed up close it was apparent that this one picture was comprised of hundreds of tiny Brian pictures.

I asked Margarita, "Did you say 'Mosaic'?"

"Yes, this mosaic of Brian is beautiful. It shows what an incredible life Brian lived. I've been looking at it the whole time we've been talking."

Then it was time for my tears. I couldn't believe the beautiful synchronicity.

After I told Margarita my "Mosaic" dream we shared a stunned silence as a tremendous blessing began to reveal itself.

We both interpreted this dream as communication from Brian letting her know he had survived death, and though he was no longer in the body, he was intact and the individual pieces of the Brian mosaic would live on as they connected everyone who loved him.

• • •

Later that same day, my mother called to tell me about her and my dad's dream to move to the heart of vibrant Los Angeles from the sleepy suburbs. They had found a place to live. I'd been advising them not to move downtown. "City life is no place for retirees," I cautioned. I was worried about them and strongly suggested they consider a quiet place by the ocean, maybe even a retirement villa with other folks their age. However, they were acting like rebellious teenagers lusting for a fast-paced, metropolitan lifestyle.

I was getting ready to make my case when my mom told me the name of the apartment complex she'd fallen in love with. "It's called the Mosaic."

What?

In one second flat I went from being against their life-changing agenda to becoming their biggest cheerleader.

It's been a few years now and the move to the Mosaic, in the center of art and commerce, has given my folks an exciting new lease on life. They've both lost weight, look ten years younger, and couldn't be happier.

I hear regularly from Brian's family, and although they still miss him tremendously, the mosaic dream became the beginning of innumerable messages from Brian through dreams and "coincidences." Margarita said that even though losing Brian broke her heart into a million tiny pieces, the Brian mosaic has become a symbolic road map of a peace filled heart and mind.

Later I spoke to Brian's dad, and he sent me this note:

One individual photo does not represent a person's life. But, this mosaic of Brian gives the 360-degree view, as it's comprised of little individual moments that together make the whole. A mosaic is such a perfect symbol to represent my "B-man's" life, because in this one mosaic you can see how we are all part of a larger serendipitous work that includes moments and people instead of brushes and paint. This mosaic of Brian is special for us because Brian was the glue that bonded us, and so many communities of people, together — in such a joyous way. Also, he was not one to get caught in any of the small stuff; he had a knack for keeping the larger picture (mosaic) in mind at all times.

~Kelly Sullivan Walden

The Warning

I sought my soul, but my soul I could not see.
I sought my God, but my God eluded me.
I sought my brother and I found all three.
~William Blake

My brother Paul started out in life with great potential. He was a gifted storyteller and an amazing athlete. I idolized him and followed him everywhere. We got along very well until he became a teenager. He changed drastically and I couldn't understand why.

It was 1973 when he turned thirteen, and our Southern California neighborhood was awash in illicit drugs — mostly marijuana, but also harder drugs like LSD. Paul became a stranger to me, and I became an annoyance to him and his friends. I internalized this rejection until I realized they didn't want me around in case I "finked" on them about their drug use.

Most teenagers laugh at adults who tell them marijuana is a gateway drug that will lead to harder drugs, but in my brother's case it was absolutely true. He went right up the ladder from pot to heroin, spent eight years of his life in jail for drug-related offenses, and died of an overdose at the age of thirty-seven.

His death was devastating to my parents and me after so many years of hoping and praying that he would get his life together. By the time he died, he was covered with menacing tattoos, had lost most of his teeth, and no longer resembled the sun-kissed big brother I played with as a child. The athlete was gone and the only stories he told were lies to the police.

Mothers always suffer most for their children's mistakes. My father told me that when the police called at 3 a.m. to tell them Paul had died, she walked away from the phone crying "no" over and over. Their worst nightmare had come true. She took prescription drugs for years afterward just to avoid being driven insane by grief. She slept a lot and my father buried himself in work. I was so angry and resentful toward Paul for dying in such a preventable way, and for the misery he caused our family, I couldn't even cry. Anger and hatred were easier to handle than sadness.

I moved back in with my parents for a few months and found that I had to hide my grief to help them through theirs. The accumulated weight of their pain and my own was so overwhelming, I felt numb inside. Grief at its worst is a kind of walking death. Eventually, this numbness started to get me into trouble.

I was driving on a freeway one night when another driver started tailgating me, even though I was traveling ten miles per hour faster than the speed limit. I ignored him until he got closer and flashed his brights. A disproportionate rage started building in me.

Earlier that day, I had stood with my mother under an umbrella in a cold cemetery, trying to find a gravesite for my brother. I felt a kind of righteous indignation toward the tailgater for adding to the unbearable load of pain I was already carrying. In that moment, he became more than just some jerk on the road. He became a symbol of the chaos in life that attacks us without warning. He also became a target for my anger, which, until then, had been unfocused.

I slammed on my brakes. He went into a skid, then caught up with me and yelled at me to pull over. I did. He stopped behind me. We got out of our cars and walked toward each other. My grief had removed all fear. I had never been aggressive before, but that night, I wanted to fight. I couldn't fight the bitter reality of my brother's death, or the avalanche of pain my parents were buried under, or the dark labyrinth of despair my life had become. But I could fight this man. This was tangible. I suspect most violence is that way — an outward expression of deep inner torment and helplessness. People don't punch each other; they punch their own misery.

He continued to curse at me, but I said nothing. As we got closer, he looked at my face in the headlights of oncoming traffic and saw my eyes, which had been rendered lifeless by sorrow. I wasn't angry, scared, or even slightly agitated. I just didn't care anymore. He stopped and asked, "What's wrong with you?" I kept walking toward him. When I had almost reached him, he turned, ran back to his car, cursed me one last time and drove away. It was terribly reckless of me. If he had a gun, I could have been killed. Part of me must have wanted to die so the pain could finally stop.

The next night, I dreamed I was driving on the same freeway with the same tailgater behind me. Everything happened the same way, but as I walked toward him and his face became clear, I saw it was my brother. Shocked, I ran to him and hugged him tightly, crying with relief that he was still alive.

I said, "Paul, you've got to let me take you to see Mom and Dad. They miss you so much."

"I can't. I have a new home now," he replied.

I asked him where it was. He looked up, and then smiled at me. It was a smile full of the peace and joy he had lost long ago in life. The teeth that were rotted out by drug use were fully restored. I knew what and where he meant when he looked up, but I kept begging him to come home, desperate to keep him from leaving again.

He said, "Mark, listen. I came to tell you to stop doing things like this. Your sadness is making you crazy. Don't die in some stupid way like I did. Mom and Dad need you now more than ever."

I promised I wouldn't and hugged him again, as if I could make him live again by not letting go. But then he was gone.

I awoke in bed and lay there thinking about the dream, trying to remember and feel every part of it again.

The psychologist Sigmund Freud said one of the purposes of dreams is wish fulfillment. My deepest wish was to talk to my brother again, so that may be true, but I still think Freud was too cynical. The fulfillment of a wish doesn't make the dream untrue. I didn't dream that my brother was alive again. He was physically dead in my dream and he knew that he was.

Maybe those we've lost can't get through the wall of our conscious minds, but our unconscious minds are just porous enough for them to find a way in. Surely they're just as desperate as we are to talk again, especially if they see us behaving foolishly and need to warn us off a dangerous path.

Since I had that dream, I have honored my brother's request. I allow myself to feel sad, and I don't let it become rage. Aside from all the other gifts I might receive from being a patient, peaceful person, it is also the fulfillment of his dying wish for me, a wish delivered in a most mysterious and liberating dream.

~Mark Rickerby

3

The "R" Factor

All our dreams can come true, if we have
the courage to pursue them.
~Walt Disney

Over the years I've come to realize that premonitions are more a matter of recognition than anything else — at least for me. In fact, it's so obvious I've come to call it the "R Factor."

The first time I really grasped the nature of the premonition process was back in the early 1990's. I was driving an aging dark blue Chevy van that needed a good tune-up. A nearby mechanic did inexpensive work out of his yard, so I made an appointment.

Pulling up to the nondescript dark brown house I was surprised. I'd been driving past the place almost every day for two years, but it was so hidden in the trees I'd never noticed it before.

Kurt poked at the engine. It was a pretty summer day and rather warm for the Pacific Northwest. After a while I asked if I could get some water. "Sure," he said. "Grab a glass for me. Kitchen's just inside the door."

I went inside, filled two glasses at the sink and turned around. The house smacked me a psychic blow so strong I almost dropped the water. *This is my house!* I inwardly gasped, shocked. The recognition was inescapable. *Oh my God, this is my house!*

Astonished, I took in the polished cedar paneled ceilings, the roughhewn tree trunks supporting the staircase and upper floor, and the faux flagstone painted floors. I soaked in the rustic ambience that was at once totally known and totally new. Eventually I gathered my wits and went back outside.

"So," I began, "I don't suppose you want to sell your house?"

What was I doing? I barely had the cash to pay for the tune-up. Kurt put down his socket wrench and scratched his head. "Funny you should ask. Linda and I just decided this week that we're going to sell."

Excitement rippled through me. Before I knew it, I was making an offer. "So, how about $100 down and $100 a month for the next 100 years?" It was a joke and yet it wasn't a joke. If, for some strange reason, he had said "yes," that would've been that. Never mind I'd only seen two downstairs rooms. Never mind that car parts littered the driveway and I hadn't seen the land, the gardens or the barn. Never mind I didn't have the hundred bucks. This was my house and I knew it.

He laughed and went back to work. For the next year I drove past the house, gazing fixedly at the black and white For Sale By Owner sign. When it came down, my heart sank. I was no closer to having a down payment or the wherewithal to get a mortgage than I had been the year before. Then a Century 21 sign went up and I breathed a sigh of relief. A year later it came down and I panicked again. Then a Remax sign went up. Six months later it came down only to be replaced with another For Sale By Owner sign.

And then my beloved mother died unexpectedly, leaving me just enough money to buy my own place.

"We were wondering when we were going to hear from you again," Kurt said when I called them. "We were talking the other night and realized this house has been waiting for you."

We drew up a contract and I handed them a cashier's check. We transferred the title and that was that. Three days after I called, I started moving in and they started moving out.

I had very little in the way of personal possessions. After all, I'd been living in a one-room cabin for years. But as I was sorting through old papers I ran across a picture of a "dream" house that I'd drawn four years earlier — and the hair on the back of my neck rose. Except for the fact that I'd sketched the house in turquoise blue crayon, it was the exact house I'd just bought!

I showed the picture to Linda. "Oh my God," she said. "It's this house!"

"I know. Isn't it amazing? But what's so weird is, I was absolutely compelled to draw it in turquoise blue."

Linda laughed. "When we first bought the house six years ago it was painted turquoise blue inside. Everything was turquoise. Even the toilet."

We stared at the drawing, amazed.

Since then I've recalled other major events in my life that were preceded by an instantaneous "recognition" of both the object/person and what was to come — including my first husband. If only I'd been given the whole picture! Oh, well.

But if time isn't linear — if there is no past and no future and all there is is NOW — the recognition thing makes total sense. The house was already part of my life years before I pulled in the driveway. The man — as lover, husband and ex — was "known" to me even as I played as a child. Of course I recognized these potent places and faces when they finally showed up in the stream of time. How not?

And they, I think, also recognized me. At least the house did!

~Cate Montana

The Courage to Listen

Sometimes you're not given what you want because
something you need has been planned for you instead.
~Author Unknown

I sat straight up in bed. It was still dark outside. I was distinctly aware of the silence around me. The air on my nose felt cold, but there was a warmth inside my body. I felt the softness of the blanket on my legs, and the world felt cozy, still, and calm. I rubbed my eyes to ensure I was indeed awake.

"But my dreams are never that clear and straightforward," I remember thinking to myself. "What do I do now?"

I wanted to bury my head under the covers and pretend the dream never happened.

Listening to the guidance in the dream was going to demand a lot of courage, not to mention create a logistical nightmare. "Maybe if I fall back asleep I will wake up with more insight, or just forget it happened altogether," I said to myself.

But I lay awake, eyes wide open, staring into the darkness, unable to erase his voice from my mind.

In the dream, he was sitting across from me. I did not see his face. I sat quietly on a single bed across from him. It was a simple room. We were facing one another. I felt very comfortable with his presence. I knew him, but not from my waking life. I listened attentively, not saying anything myself. He spoke in a calm and direct voice: "Go to South Africa before you go to India. Doors will then open for you to go to India and you will meet someone who is meant to be a teacher for you."

That is when I awoke.

As I stared at the ceiling, recalling his voice, I began a flustered inner dialogue with this mystery man.

"Really? You're telling me this now? Now, after I have been planning this trip for months, have booked my flights and set everything up? And who are you anyway? Maybe you are just trying to trick me. Why should I trust you?"

But as I argued with an "invisible" man in my head in the middle of the night, something deep within me felt drawn to him. He was direct and calm. I liked him. The soft stillness I had sensed upon waking was still lingering around and within me. And, for some reason, I trusted him.

A few months earlier, I had graduated a semester early from Cornell University and had decided to embark on an extensive journey overseas. For at least a year.

From a young age, I had longed to explore the sacred, to align my life in some way with a higher purpose, and to follow the pull of my soul regardless of what people thought.

At the time, my friends and boyfriend could not understand why I would want to be absent during our final semester at college. This was the time to celebrate, to party, to enjoy the final months of college life, carefree and laidback. But, it was not something I could explain. I just knew I needed to go.

I had planned to visit two destinations for six months each — India and South Africa, which is the land of my heritage. In South Africa I had arranged to volunteer at an HIV/AIDS orphanage for abandoned and abused children for six months.

To prepare for such a daunting task, my plan was to travel around India first. India had always enthralled me. I prepared to visit various meditation and yoga centers, and yearned to make a pilgrimage of self-exploration.

Everything had been booked and planned carefully.

The dream could not have come at a more difficult time. I was booked to leave in ten days. If I obeyed the dream I would have to change my flights, my bookings, everything. Not to mention, I would have to call the orphanage in South Africa and inquire if I could come six months early!

It was a massive disruption to my schedule, and not one I wanted to make based purely on some weird dream.

But the guidance was so clear.

I sat with the dream all day. During breakfast, I was withdrawn and quiet. My mother asked why. I told her about the dream.

"Wow. See if it stays with you throughout the day, my angel. If so, maybe you should listen."

This is a classic response from my mother, who has always encouraged my exploration of spirituality and mysticism. She is a warm and highly intuitive woman who often trusts aspects of our existence outside of logic and rational thought.

Throughout the entire day, the mysterious man never left my psyche. On the surface, I wanted to ignore him. But in some hidden corner of my heart, I knew he had come for a reason, and I liked him.

And so I changed everything.

I traveled first to South Africa. During my six months at the orphanage, I was told about a course in Pranic Healing — a systematic form of energetic medicine based on the ancient Chinese, Indian, and Tibetan healing arts. Without knowing anything about the course, I knew I had to be there.

The instructor was a lovely Indian man. He saw my raw enthusiasm and passion for the material. He encouraged me to travel to India to meet the founder of this system of healing, who was a Chinese-Filipino man by the name of Master Choa Kok Sui.

At that moment, time stood still. I remembered the voice in my dream. Here was the door to India. Opening.

I booked my flight and left a month later. I spent three incredibly formative years learning healing and meditation under the master's direct guidance. They were three years that greatly altered the direction of my life. I now teach healing, yoga, and meditation all over the world, and I write for various publications on these topics. I have been able to touch and transform many lives through this work, including my own.

I cannot imagine what my life would be like had I not found the courage to listen to the kind, faceless man in my dream.

~Deborah Anne Quibell

House Call

*A dream which is not interpreted is like a letter
which is not read.*
~The Talmud

A cancer diagnosis messes with your head, especially in the middle of the night. I would lie awake worrying about the future. The surgery was successful, the healing had begun, but I was still panicking. What made it worse was that my sister also was diagnosed, and she died six weeks later.

One night, as I lay down to sleep, I said a prayer to the angels asking for their guidance in my dreams.

I wanted to live. So, I asked them for answers, to give me a clear dream — not one of those wild and cryptic ones that leaves you questioning your sanity in the morning.

What followed next was more than amazing. It literally was the answer to a prayer in the form of a dream.

The scene opened up in a blood-work lab. There were many technicians at lab tables and many people of all ages and degrees of ill health walking around.

A technician inserted a needle attached to a very thin tube into my arm and instructed me to walk around until the thin tubing was full of blood.

As I did this I looked at the people around me; every one of them would be recognizable if I saw them on the street the next day. It was all so vivid.

There were drops of bright red blood on the floors, on the techs' gloves, aprons… the dream was obviously focused on blood. I needed to pay attention to this information.

When it was my turn to have the blood work tested I approached the technician and he spotted one drop of gleaming red blood on the immaculate white lab table from the person before me. He said the most intriguing thing, as if in slow motion: "Let me wipe up this drop of acid."

It was as if he was saying that acidic blood makes illness.

After he wiped it up, he turned to me and said, "Did you know people who eat tapioca never have a trace of cancer in their bloodstream?"

I had no idea, until I woke up and called a herbalist friend, that tapioca is made from the root of a plant in South America known for its medicinal properties. The friend said it alkalizes the blood. I have been eating it — warm and in moderation — since then, and loving it.

Then the technician said, "The trouble is you sit in front of your computer as if you are a monk cloistered in a cave. You need to walk three to four miles a day." I am a pet columnist and author and I was indeed sitting at the computer for eight to ten hours a day.

Well, that message was very clear! Get up and move the fluids in my body.

Then the dream ended. My panic abated and a new life began. My dream had indeed brought me the desired, clear information and direction to rebuild my strength and health.

The next week, I asked for another dream "message." *During the night, I had a dream in which a pretty young angelic woman with shoulder-length copper/brown hair, who looked to be about twenty-two years old, came and stood in front of me. She said, "You know some people can see into other's bodies and energy fields. I can, and you have no trace of cancer anywhere in your body. You must believe this."*

She was right. I had let fear hinder my recovery. So, whenever I dropped into the fear rut, I said, "I believe. I believe."

Twelve years have passed since those dreams and I'm still happily eating tapioca pudding!

~Mary Ellen Angelscribe

Ten-Dollar Blessing

The measure of a man's real character is what he
would do if he knew he never would be found out.
~Thomas Babington Macaulay

As the janitor continued to dump the popcorn she had swept off the floor into the trashcan, I kept reaching in for more. I couldn't help myself. It was so fluffy, buttery, and crunchy. As the woman emptied the dustpan, I grabbed another handful from the top of the garbage pile. It was the best popcorn I'd ever had. A piece was melting in my mouth when a faint beep caught my attention. It seemed far away at first, but then got louder and louder, irritating me.

I opened my eyes and realized I was in bed. My cellphone alarm was going off on my nightstand. I reached for the phone and swiped the screen, turning off the high-pitched sound. What a weird dream that had been.

Outside, the grass and pavement were wet. Twigs and branches littered the streets and puddles splashed high with every passing car. I pulled into the school parking lot and rushed through the muddy playground and into the old building. The halls rang with laughter and conversations. Lockers slammed, kids lined up. I made my way to the office and swiped in. My third-grade classroom was out in the mobiles on a lot adjacent to the main building. I rushed back outside toward my classroom trailer, hoping to get in before my students came in from breakfast in the cafeteria. Dodging most of the puddles, I made my way up the metal steps of the trailer. When I got to the top, I noticed a folded and very wet ten-dollar bill stuck to the metal landing. I looked around and didn't see anyone. Putting the wet cash in my pocket, I looked up and smiled. God was treating me to lunch.

I always return things to their rightful owner, but how do you find the owner of a wet ten-dollar bill sitting outside a classroom trailer after a storm? Finder's keepers, I thought.

I walked two blocks to the closest Mexican restaurant for lunch that day. As I was getting ready to pay, I reached for the ten-dollar bill. It was still a bit wet. Unfolding it, I realized it was wrapped around a Target receipt. The receipt was also damp, but totally legible. I looked at the time and date on the receipt and the address of the store. Maybe I could find out who went to Target two days ago. I decided that would be the right thing to do, so instead of paying with the damp bill, I handed the cashier my debit card. There was a mystery to be solved.

I returned to work and asked two co-workers who had classrooms in the mobiles if they had been to Target lately. They both replied "no." It couldn't have been one of the students because they hadn't yet arrived when I found the money outside my door.

That evening I went home and took another look at the receipt. This time, instead of just looking at the date and address, I read the whole thing. The person who dropped the money had bought two items: iced tea and popcorn. I stared at the word. Popcorn.

My kitchen seemed extra quiet. I was lost in my thoughts. I replayed the events of the day in my mind: I dreamt of a janitor cleaning up popcorn that morning before leaving for work, I found the wet bill, the receipt indicated that the person who lost the money had bought popcorn. How strange.

When my husband got home I told him about my dream, the money, and the receipt. He agreed that it was strange and called it a coincidence. I didn't think it was a coincidence. I had to decipher my dream.

The next morning I arrived at work a bit earlier than usual. I unlocked my classroom door and realized that my room had already been cleaned. Our school janitor was out on vacation but someone was covering his regular morning shift. As I walked over to the corridor between my classroom and the other room in the mobile, I heard some shuffling in the next room. Peering in through the tiny door window, I saw the substitute janitor sweeping the room.

I slowly turned the doorknob and stepped in. "Good morning," I said. She looked up at me.

"Good morning. Is this your classroom?" she asked.

"No, I'm in the next room. Room 316."

"Oh, okay," she smiled. "How's your room look? Does it look okay?"

"It looks great. Thank you," I said. "I wanted to ask you something. Did you happen to lose any money recently?"

"I don't know," she responded. "I think I might have had ten dollars in my back pocket the other day, but I'm not sure."

"When was this?" I asked.

"I'm not sure. A few days ago, I guess."

Maybe it was her ten-dollar bill. "I found some money the other day. There was a store receipt with it," I said. "Have you gone to Target lately?"

"Um… I don't know," she replied. "Wait. You know what? I think I did."

"What did you buy there?"

She paused for a moment as she thought. "I think I bought some iced tea," she responded. "Oh, and some popcorn."

I couldn't believe it. My dream had helped me find the rightful owner of the money, a female janitor, just like in my dream. "I have your money," I said smiling. It felt so good to hand her the bill.

When I first found the money, I thought it was something God had placed in my path for my personal benefit. In hindsight, I have realized that finding that money was an even bigger blessing. The feeling that came over me when I returned the money was amazing — even better than the feeling I got eating the popcorn in my dream!

~Daisy Franco

Finding My Family

We may not want to think about our ancestors, but our
ancestors are thinking about us.
~Robert Moss, Dreaming the Soul Back Home

I was puttering around at home when I heard the voice. "Go to Ancestry.com." What? "Go to Ancestry.com." My inner voice was insistent. I ignored it.

"Go to Ancestry.com."

The nudges continued as I attempted to go about my day. Clearly this voice would not give up until I gave it my full attention. I stopped what I was doing and said, out loud, maybe even a bit annoyed, "Okay! I'll go to Ancestry.com!"

I'd heard this voice before on several notable occasions in my life. I can't call it up at will, though I've often wished I could. It is a non-gender, calm, clear voice without emotion, delivering short messages of guidance. Once, when I was alone on an elevator heading up to work, feeling exhausted and distraught during the early stages of a divorce, I thought, "How will I ever make it alone? I'm so lonely...." The voice surprised me with, "You always have yourself." Startled and looking around the elevator for the source of these words, I was reminded of how much strength I have. That powerful thought healed something in me in that moment, and it has stayed with me since.

I went online to Ancestry.com. Peeking into a bulletin board devoted to my family name, I saw a request seeking family information that seemed to refer to my late father. It was puzzling though, because the name was slightly different, but it was my father's actual birthdate. I answered the posting and that is how I met my father's first wife and her family, including my half-brother, whom I had not met in person and didn't know existed until long after I had become an adult. I didn't know my father had changed his name.

My meeting with Helen shifted something fundamental in my life. Suddenly, without realizing the important healing it would bring, I had embarked on a genealogical treasure hunt. In e-mails to Helen I shared a few stories, a few clues my father had dropped along the way, and she took the ball and ran with it. My ancestors began to appear in Helen's e-mails, and that was the beginning of something vital for me: a connection to my roots.

I had grown up feeling I didn't belong to any community. I felt like I had no foundation. When asked where my hometown was, I felt a vague unacknowledged sadness and a bit of shame. My father was in the military and my family moved frequently. Our isolated nuclear family, which consisted of my parents, my two brothers and me, had little exposure to extended relatives, and I had no concept that family was so important.

My father grew up without parents on the streets of Boston, a child of many foster homes. He was listed as a boarder at the age of five in the 1930 United States census. He had been abandoned by his parents, like many children of the Great Depression, and never felt the safety of trust again. He was a warrior and a survivor.

My mother was a refugee from Silesia at the end of World War II, from a region that was German and then became Polish after the war. One night in the final months of the war my Polish grandmother fled from the Russians with her five children. My mother was nine years old. After many months of danger, abuse, and starvation, they found their way to Bavaria, where the family lived for seven years in one room in what was left of a home that had been bombed. My mother is a survivor, too. When she left Germany with my father, a U.S. serviceman, she left her family behind.

I had no idea old family wounds were a part of my story, but my truth is I grew up without grandparents, aunts, uncles, and cousins in my life, and it was a loss, even though we had lovely Christmas boxes from my grandparents in Germany, filled to the brim with delicious chocolates and gingerbread, and occasional loving visits. To this day chocolate feels like love to me.

Helen uncovered interesting history on my father's side. We learned my grandmother was most likely part Mi'kmac First Nations people of Nova Scotia, and that I had two generations of great-grandparents who were missionaries in India, running a home for people with leprosy. I began to see the adventure and courage in my lineage instead of the weaknesses.

The distractions of life unfolded after my initial meeting with Helen, and genealogy was put away for a while. I was grateful to have had the chance to meet Helen and to be a long-distance member of her loving family. And not longer after, I met my lovely niece.

Then, in 2007, I had a dream:

I am sitting on a park bench in a forested place underneath an illuminated old-fashioned streetlight. Sitting next to me is a handsome young man who is my brother. He is supposed to be one of the brothers I grew up with, the one who was named after my grandfather, but it isn't his face. We are discussing what we would need to do to have a healthy relationship. He looks exotic, wearing dangly diamond earrings and he has glossy black hair and a rich olive complexion, perhaps like a person from South Asia.

As I woke, a voice prompted me to look up my paternal grandfather's name on Google. A group photo of a high school football team from 1913 appeared on the screen. One of these players was my grandfather, a freshman in high school. As I looked at the faces, I felt a blast of energy through my solar plexus and burst into tears as I recognized the very face I had dreamed. I dreamed my grandfather's face without ever seeing an image of him. The emotion I felt was remarkable.

This propelled a new surge of genealogical research. I found stories of my missionary relatives and learned my grandfather was born in India. I learned I have three generations of ancestors who lived in India. Some were born there and some died there, and several spent all of their adult lives in service to the poorest and most ill. I found my great-great-aunt, who was the first woman doctor in her region in the Himalayan foothills. She started a hospital for women that is still in service today. My sense of belonging and family pride healed the more I learned about my distant family.

Finally, during Christmas of 2011, I met my brother for the first time, and in 2014 I met my sister-in-law. The blessing of family continues with the birth of my grandniece this year. I never expected to know and love this part of my family, and never would have if I hadn't listened to a persistent voice and paid attention to a dream.

~Jane E. Carleton

The Branching Woman

Why not go out on a limb? Isn't that where the fruit is?
~Frank Scully

Have you ever awakened from a dream that left you feeling stunned? By stunned, I mean awed, astounded, marveling in wonder. You might have seen an unusual image and wondered what it could mean. If so, you have probably experienced what Jungians would call a numinous dream, the word numinous coming from the Latin word *numen*, which means divine will, divinity, deity, and is related to *nuere*, meaning "to nod or give assent." Ancient folk believed that when the gods approved of a mortal's behavior, they nodded to indicate the individual was on the right path.

On March 9, 1973, I had a remarkable dream. I titled it, "The Branching Woman." At the time of the dream I was thirty-seven years old and three years into a gloriously happy second marriage. I had already received my Ph.D. in Clinical Psychology and had been a full-time Psychology teacher at the university level. My husband, Zal, and I had just returned from two years living in Europe, culminating in a six-month trip around the world.

We had recently moved to San Francisco, a city we felt combined some of the best parts of the United States and Europe. I was again teaching, at what was then Sonoma State College, this time a course that I had devised called "The Creative Use of Dreams." I had also written and submitted a professional paper, entitled "Keeping a Longitudinal

Dream Journal," but it had not yet had a response from the editor of the journal. It had occurred to me that my course lectures might make an intriguing textbook, but I was still in the process of writing them. My entire life was about to change. The dream of the Branching Woman announced this lifetime shift.

In the dream, Zal and I were with a group of professionals at a conference discussing various aspects of dreaming. Several people had spoken earlier about the symbolism involved in "leaving," referring to leaves dropping from a tree. Zal and I were seated in chairs at the front. All of us were eating.

I stood up and said, "We've talked about 'leaving.' I'd like to discuss the concept of 'branching.' I've had several dreams in which there was a growth. There was a woman's head and from it grew branches, almost like antlers, each subdividing, until it grew very thick and dense."

I continued to describe the concept. I finished and there was a slight pause as the head person, to whom I'd mainly addressed the remarks, got up and ducked under a kind of tabletop to get more food. In the meantime, Zal said to me, "You did that really well," and kissed me on the cheek.

The dream continued with me going for food and eating, too, but not getting anything I especially wanted. Although everyone ignored my comments except Zal, I felt good in the dream for expressing myself.

The key image in this dream was the strange one of antler-like branches sprouting in every direction from a woman's head. In the dream I said I had had "several dreams" with the same image. Could that possibly be true? I didn't recall any similar images. I checked.

Looking back through my dream records it was easy to search for unusual images because I almost always sketch them in the left margin of my dream journal. At this point I have forty-nine binders of handwritten dream records, beginning in 1948, when I was thirteen-and-a-half until my present age, eighty.

I did not have to go back very far before locating images related to the Branching Woman. They just hadn't caught my full attention before.

I had sent inquiries to several large publishing houses asking whether they would be interested in a manuscript on the creative use of dreams. A number of them answered my query letter with, "Possibly. Let us see more." My manuscript samples seemed to hover between too academic for the popular market and too popular for the academic presses.

Eventually Zal and I went to New York City and met with a literary agent. He read the manuscript overnight and forwarded it to the editor-in-chief at a major publishing house, Simon & Schuster. The editor replied with an offer, all within three days. A week later he doubled the offer. I accepted. The editor wanted to hire a ghostwriter to make the book more appealing to a general audience. I asked to try it myself.

Up until then my role had been mainly that of a very good student. Even in teaching, although I created a couple of new courses, I was still mainly handing on to students the information I had been taught or what I had learned from doing my dissertation. Aside from my thesis, I had not done much that was truly original.

Now, confronting the possibility of someone else shaping my material, I knew I must try myself. I rewrote the manuscript in six weeks, telling stories to make the points clear, as I would in a classroom. Rather than writing for the academic audience, I translated the material I'd found into a form that any interested person could follow.

To my amazement, I loved doing it. No longer forced into a rigid academic format. I could let my imagination soar and still convey the facts. I could ride my passion and pass it onward. I could "branch out!"

Now I felt stunned, wide-awake. The Branching Woman dream image had shown this possibility to me. I reveled in enacting it. My attitude toward my professional role shifted totally, from good teacher to creative innovator. My activity stopped feeling like work and became playful and joyful.

Simon & Schuster loved the manuscript I produced and gave it full support, with an elegant hardcover edition. They sent me on a month-long publicity tour to seventeen cities. I hit all the major talk shows of the day and major newspapers ran stories about my book. *Harper's* did an excerpt; *People* ran a four-page spread. When the *San Francisco Chronicle* printed a two-page spread on *Creative Dreaming*, it included several photos. One of these was of a clay model I had made of the Branching Woman. Published in 1974, *Creative Dreaming* became a bestseller. It is considered a classic, has had several editions in fifteen languages and is still available. To this day, people tell me this book changed their lives for the better. I had taken a chance, "branched out," and my life blossomed into a career that continues to nourish me and untold numbers of others. We can all become our fullest selves."

~Patricia Garfield

The Dream Staircase

The truth is, unless you let go, unless you forgive
yourself, unless you forgive the situation, unless you
realize that the situation is over, you cannot
move forward.
~Steve Maraboli

We were hiking on a mountain trail that overlooked the ocean. It was a gorgeous summer day, and we stopped at an overlook to gaze at the sparkling blue water far below.

"I'm taking a neat class through the community college," my friend Tania said.

"Cool, what's it about?" I asked.

"Dream interpretation."

That sounded interesting. As a writer, I've always been interested in dreams — I see them as narratives that our subconscious selves weave about our lives. However, I had never done dream interpretation myself.

"Could I ask you a favor?" Tania continued. "I was wondering if I could analyze one of your dreams."

"I haven't remembered one in a while," I told her.

"Well," Tania said, "if you remember one of your dreams, let me know?"

I promised I would.

Less than a week later I jerked awake in my pitch-black bedroom, heart pounding. My clock numbers glowed 3:45. The dream — nightmare — still felt so real, so vivid, that I was afraid of sinking back down into it if I dared close my eyes. I ended up getting out of bed, turning on my light, and reading for half an hour to calm down.

The next morning, as I ate breakfast, the dream flashed through my mind. I briefly considered telling Tania, but that only seemed like I would be giving the dream more power, more attention, and more brain-space. I yearned for it to just fade away. I told myself I would let Tania analyze the next dream I remembered.

But I had the nightmare again. And again. And again.

By the fourth time, I knew in my gut that this was no coincidence. I was dreaming this dream for a reason. I needed to meet with Tania to figure out what it meant.

We met at her house on a weekday morning, settling down side-by-side on her comfy couch like this was any other visit. She had asked me to write a paragraph about what happened in the dream. I had written:

I wake up in my bedroom (but I am only dreaming about waking up) and I know immediately that someone is in my house. I see a strip of light under my bedroom door. Feeling uneasy, I get out of bed and open the door. Tim is standing there. Even though he doesn't say anything, I can tell he is angry and I feel afraid. I try to flee past him, down the stairs, but he is blocking my way. Then I wake up, for real this time.

When I finished reading it aloud, Tania looked at me with compassion and concern in her eyes. I knew I made the right decision to share this dream with her.

"Have you talked to Tim recently?" she asked.

"No, not for months. Not since I moved back home." Tim was my ex-fiancé; I had broken off our engagement earlier that spring for a variety of reasons, not the least of which was his temper.

"In the class I'm taking," Tania explained, "we are taught that every person and item you see in your dream is representative of you. For example, when you see 'Tim' in your dream, it's not actually Tim — it's you. The emotions you and he feel in the dream all stem from your own psyche."

I nodded, though I wasn't sure I agreed. Tim had seemed so clear in my dream—and so clearly himself.

Tania continued, "You have a recurring dream when your inner self is trying to work through something important. We unlock meaning by talking through the dream and making space for difficult conversations."

She asked me to imagine the various items from my dream "sitting" with us in the room: me, Tim, my darkened bedroom, the sliver of light under the door, and the staircase. Next, she instructed me to have a conversation with each item, speaking about the emotions I felt in the dream. I sat on the couch as "me" and then physically got up and moved around the room to speak as each object.

At first, I balked. It seemed silly, and I wasn't sure what to say. What emotions would my bedroom feel, for example? But with Tania's gentle, guiding questions, I began to relax and embrace the activity. I decided that my room was comforting and dark, like a cocoon. The sliver of light under the door was hopeful and bright. The stairs were sturdy and optimistic.

"What do they want?" Tania asked.

The sliver of light wanted to flood the darkness away. I closed my eyes and imagined my bedroom filling with light. The stairs wanted to take me onto the next chapter of my life. I imagined walking past Tim, down the stairs, and away.

The turning point came not when I spoke to "Tim" as myself—describing my dread, confusion, and fear—but when I sat down in the place I had designated as "Tim" and spoke as him in his voice. As Tim, I spoke about how devastated I felt about our breakup, and how frustrated and helpless the whole situation made me feel. "I don't understand why you called off our engagement," I said as Tim. "I am angry at you, Dallas, but I would never hurt you."

Tania instructed me to get up and sit in my own designated spot again. "What do you want to say to Tim?" she asked me.

"I want to tell him that I'm sorry," I said.

"So tell him that," Tania urged.

Gazing at the empty chair that symbolized my ex-fiancé, in that moment I could clearly imagine him sitting there. "Tim, I want you to know that I'm sorry," I said. "Even if you never understand my decision, I hope one day you can forgive me." Tears streamed down my face as I choked out, "Goodbye."

In real life, our breakup had been a complete mess. There had been so much rage and pain and fear that we had never talked like this. I hadn't been able to tell Tim I was sorry. I hadn't been able to say a real goodbye.

Still crying, I moved over to the chair and said, as Tim, "It's okay, Dallas. I forgive you."

In that moment, I felt a weight release inside me. I hadn't even realized I was holding on to that weight until it was gone. I felt so much lighter.

That night, I had another dream featuring Tim. Only this dream was different. Instead of night, it was bright daylight. Instead of feeling afraid, I felt hopeful. I was walking down a long staircase, and Tim was walking up the staircase toward me. As we squeezed by each other, I smiled and he nodded hello. Then he continued on his way up the stairs, and I continued on my way down.

At the bottom of the staircase, there was a door. I opened it, and stepped outside into the fresh air of a sunny morning.

~Dallas Woodburn

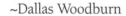

Inconceivable

*Life is what happens when you are busy
making other plans.*
~John Lennon

One night in early 1995, my wife, Nina, lay peacefully at rest, my arms and our warm covers there to stave off a chill Phoenix evening. We had closed our eyes that night warmed also by the joyous news that our daughter, Tracy, was engaged. As we lay there anticipating sleep, but unable to quite shake off the day, our discussions had revolved around the idea that with our daughter moving away and her brother, Craig, growing up and leaving in a few more years, perhaps being close to schools would no longer be an issue. Maybe it was time to begin planning our move closer into town where we could set up our "empty nest." Finally — blissfully — we succumbed to the need for sleep, and sank into peaceful slumber.

The old saying is that if you want to hear God laugh, tell Him your plans. I was startled awake that night to discover my wife moaning in her sleep, low at first but increasing in tone and volume. As had happened so many times over our many years of marriage, I took her gently back into my arms to rouse her just a little and then soothe her back to restful sleep, asking, "Are you okay?"

She said, "It was horrible — I had a nightmare. I dreamt that I was pregnant, and suddenly schools would be a factor for a long time." We both had a good laugh at that, knowing that first of all, we were in our mid-forties, and second, both of our children, born ten years apart, required liberal doses of fertility drugs to be conceived. We drifted back to sleep that morning, but that entire weekend the uncertainty of that dream and the emotions it elicited weighed heavily on my wife.

People speak of woman's intuition, a subconscious feeling that will neither release nor comfort them and which men are reluctant to admit or understand. By Monday morning, Nina's premonitions had grown very strong, reaching a point where she had to know for certain that the dream was just that — a dream. Stopping by the local grocery, she retrieved an over-the-counter home pregnancy test, hiding it under some other items so that our neighbors would not see it and possibly suspect it was for our newly engaged daughter; after all we wouldn't want to start any rumors.

The following morning I was once again startled awake to her voice, this time with a question: "Can you check this for me?" Now, in the past when we had used this particular product, the results were not truly clear. More often than not, it meant beginning another course of fertility drugs, followed by that long, long wait once again. This time, however, there was a perfect, unmistakable circle on the device, an indication that my wife might, in fact, be pregnant. But could we truly trust that? Fearing that our advanced age or something else more insidious had tainted the results, we scheduled an immediate appointment with our physician.

"You are SO pregnant…" The news was not entirely unwelcome — just not completely expected. My wife was forty-four at the time, and such things just don't often happen at that age. Unspoken thoughts of possible complications and health issues filled our minds, and then the doctor finished her revelation with, "We'll set up a procedure immediately." We had in no way even considered that as an option, but it was her normal recommendation in these situations. We looked at each other, and almost in unison said, "We don't do that." She proceeded to explain the potential challenges we would face, and then, just to be certain we were fully aware, she asked, "What do you want to do?" to which we responded, "We're going to have another baby."

We would, in fact, face challenges, none insurmountable, but the most difficult was the first — sharing the news. My wife sat our daughter down on the family room couch; we had already laughed together with her the previous weekend about the aforementioned dream, and yet before Nina could get a single word out, Tracy said, "You're not — YOU ARE!" That's all it took. Our daughter, wonderful as she is, was blessed with neither filters nor fear; she took the next challenge upon herself without trepidation. How do you share such news with the folks back home? It went something like this: "Hello, Nana? Yeah, it's Tracy. I just wanted to let you know that I'm engaged. Thank you! Oh, and Nana, if you like that, you're gonna love this — my Momma's pregnant."

Flash forward to a lovely family event under azure skies on the beautiful, windswept beaches of Coronado Island. Our daughter had moved up her church wedding by several months because we couldn't imagine finding a mother-of-the-bride dress with a built-in burp cloth. And exactly one week after her forty-fifth birthday, my beautiful bride of twenty-six years delivered a healthy, blond baby boy who has blessed our aging years and awakened us from an unbelievable dream to experience all the blessings a loving God can bestow when we allow Him to have a bit of a belly laugh at our expense.

~Rus Franklin

Dreams and Premonitions

Messages from Heaven

11

Service Call

Dad, your guiding hand on my shoulder will
remain with me forever.
~Author Unknown

"Darn it, I give up!" My youngest son threw the huge wrench in frustration.

"Looks like I didn't pick the best time to check on how things are going," I quipped.

Chris had been trying to replace the clutch in his dad's old bulldozer. It had broken down just before he finished clearing out some overgrown trees from the acreage.

"Dad always made working on the equipment look so easy," he said.

"Did you ever watch him put a clutch in this dozer?" I questioned.

"Yeah, when I was about six."

We had lost his dad to cancer a few years earlier, and Chris had taken over the duties on our Christmas tree farm. Of our five kids, he was the one who had always loved working outdoors with his father, especially on the heavy equipment. Following in his father's footsteps seemed to help ease the pain of his dad's untimely death.

"If you want to give it a rest for the night, I can start dinner while you take a shower," I offered. I knew that a hearty dinner and a good night's sleep always made things better.

The following morning, Chris ran down the stairs and flew past me as I was standing at the stove frying some bacon and eggs.

"Hey, what's the hurry?" I inquired. "No time for breakfast?"

"I'll be back in a minute, Mom," he said as he bounded out the back door and headed toward the broken-down dozer.

What a difference in attitude. Hopefully, he had figured something out.

I decided I'd leave him alone for an hour or so. I knew he'd be more frustrated if I were to go out there and stand over him while he was trying to work.

I ate my breakfast and cleaned up before going out to gather eggs and feed the chickens.

"Are things going better this morning?" I yelled to Chris when I saw his head poke out from under the dozer.

"Much better," he shouted. "I'll be up in a bit to tell you about it."

I was relieved to see his upbeat attitude.

About an hour later, I heard my son come in the back door. I hurried into the kitchen where he was pouring himself a cup of black coffee.

"Hey, take a break, Mom. I'll get you a cup of coffee," he suggested with a smile.

I took a seat at the weathered oak breakfast table as he made his way over and sat down across from me.

"So, why the happy smile? And why were you in such a hurry to get out back this morning?"

"I had to see if Dad was right!"

"I have no idea what you're talking about."

"I saw Dad last night!"

"You what?"

"Well, sometime during the night, I woke up and opened my eyes to see Dad lying on the couch in my bedroom. He was wearing his old blue and white plaid shirt, and his red Mack baseball cap was pulled down over his forehead.

"Dad just started talking as though nothing was unusual! He said, 'Chris, there's a hard-to-find bolt under the transmission that you have to remove in order to slide it out of the way.' He explained the entire repair job to me step by step in a way that made it perfectly easy for me to understand. I would never have figured it out if it hadn't been for his detailed instructions!"

"Did you have to tell him you were having a problem fixing the dozer?" I was truly captivated by what he was telling me.

"No, he seemed to already know. Actually, I didn't say anything. Dad did all the talking."

"Did he want to know anything about me?"

"No, all he did was tell me how to fix the dozer, and then I fell back to sleep. When I woke up, he was gone, and I knew exactly how to remove the tranny."

"Do you feel like he was really there?"

He pondered my question for a moment before answering. "I've never believed in seeing spirits or ghosts, but I know for a fact that I was awake! I also know that there is no way in the world that I would have had the knowledge to fix the dozer if Dad hadn't really been there! That bolt was so well hidden I would never have found it. But, I'm at a loss to explain what actually happened."

Neither of us could ever explain with certainty what had transpired. But, there's one thing I do know with every fiber of my being—if Chris needed help, there is nothing his dad wouldn't have done to make sure he got it.

~Connie Kaseweter Pullen

The Dream Dress

Dreams are road signs along the
nighttime highway of sleep.
~Terri Guillemets

While I spent my final year of high school partying, my best friend Katarina was laid up in a Brooklyn sanatorium, isolated from family and friends. It was just a few miles away from us in Long Island City, Queens, but it might as well have been across the ocean. She spent six months in quarantine after contracting tuberculosis.

The disease had put Kat's life on hold. The treatment and drugs for TB that became available later were nonexistent then. By the time she had recovered I had relocated to another state. She moved back to care for her ailing mother until her mom died.

Kat was not one to whine or complain. Dismissing the unexpected bumps in the road, she picked herself up, worked by day and obtained her high school diploma at night.

After I moved we didn't see each other often, but when we did the friendship was rekindled as if no time had passed. Meanwhile, she was only a phone call away.

One day my phone rang. I had a feeling it was her. "Hi, Kat!"

"How did you know it was me?"

I laughed. "Well, you always did say I was psychic."

It was true. I was intuitive and acted on instinct. She was the logical, sensible one.

"Then tell me why I called," she teased.

I had no idea, but since she sounded so bubbly, I took a guess. "You're getting married!"

"Yes! Can you believe it? You're amazing! A clairvoyant extraordinaire!"

Yes, I certainly could believe it. Katarina had lived through some setbacks, but I knew she would make a wonderful wife and mother. It was about time she got her life on track again.

Four weeks before the wedding, I went to visit her. We sat at the same kitchen table as we had years ago. Katarina was flipping through the family album. Pausing at the photo of her mother as a bride, her eyes filled with wonder and admiration.

"Wasn't she lovely?" she asked. "Mom and I had always dreamed I'd be married in her wedding gown."

I was delighted to see her in such high spirits.

"Where is that gown? I can't wait to see you in it."

"Well, that's the problem. It's here somewhere. But when Mom was dying she became so disoriented that she couldn't remember where she had put it. I didn't want to press her and then it was too late. Maybe you can help me find it."

She went through her mom's closets, opening boxes and trunks that had been shut for eons. We rummaged through the storeroom in the basement that had been shared by various tenants over the years and through boxes in the attic, where all the renters had been allocated some space.

No dress! Finally, we abandoned the search. In a building with many occupants, we surmised someone had walked off with it, intentionally or accidentally.

I wanted to leave her on a hopeful note. "Kat, don't give up. Miracles do happen."

I squinted as if envisioning an apparition. In an eerie voice I proclaimed: "In my mind's eye I see you walking down the aisle in your mom's wedding dress."

She managed a small smile. "If only that were true!"

An idea came to me. "Kat, you have four weeks. Why can't your mom's dress be duplicated?"

A glimmer of hope lit up her face.

"Well, my cousin has just opened a tailor shop on Steinway Street. Maybe if I take these photos to her…."

Three and a half weeks later I returned for the wedding. Disheartened, we sat on Kat's stoop staring at the pavement where years ago we had played hopscotch and skipped rope. The wedding was a few days away and the cousin/seamstress who was supposed to save the day had turned out to be an incompetent novice. It was a totally botched job. The dress was too tight here, too loose there, the zipper appeared to be in backwards, and the bodice had been torn and poorly patched up. Any resemblance to the dress in the wedding photos was only in the wild imagination of the seamstress. I tried to hide my true feelings.

"You'll look beautiful no matter what," I told Katarina, but this so-called dress just didn't cut it. If it weren't such a disaster, it would have been laughable!

"It's not perfect but it will do. It's not like it's life and death. It's just a dress!" Kat sighed bravely.

We parted with a hug and encouraging words neither of us believed.

I returned to the house next door where my mom still lived.

I couldn't get Kat out of my mind. I wasn't in the habit of praying every night, but that night I prayed with all my might for her and her future husband to have a rich, fulfilling life. Feeling just a little guilty asking for something so trivial, I prayed, "Dear God, let Katarina walk down the aisle in her mom's treasured wedding dress."

That night I tossed and turned, dreaming about my life and Katarina's — growing up next door, sharing happy memories until her life took a bad turn… first her illness, then losing her mom.

Suddenly, Katarina's mom appeared in my dream. She was standing on a staircase above me, wearing a graceful, willowy white dress — her wedding gown. Her face was as youthful as it had been in that photo album. She was staring straight into my eyes, mesmerizing me. Speaking so softly that I could barely hear, she whispered, "Under the top step."

Under the top step? What could that mean — if anything?

In the morning I woke before the sun came up. It was too early to call Kat, but I did anyway.

"Kat! Under the top step!"

"What?"

"Under the top step, Kat. Look under the top step going to the attic."

"One of your premonitions, Ms. Psychic?" I could envision her smirking.

I almost shouted, "Never mind! Just do it."

Twenty minutes later, as I looked out the kitchen window, I had another vision — Kat walking toward me with a big grin, wearing her mother's treasured wedding dress. Her fingers were gingerly grasping the skirt, raising it off the pavement, while exposing her pink bunny slippers.

There had been a secret compartment under the top step leading to the attic. The dress and the veil had been safely tucked away in there. All it took was for someone to give the step a slight pull.

The dress was taken to the cleaners and restored to its original splendor.

Two days later Katarina floated down the aisle, a vision of loveliness in her mother's wedding dress.

~Eva Carter

13

It's Time to Go Upstairs

I believe that there is an explanation for everything, so,
yes, I believe in miracles.
~Robert Brault, rbrault.blogspot.com

I was asleep in the Bay Area of California, but in my dream I was in my hometown in Bloomington, Indiana, more than 2,000 miles away. And I was walking up the street to see my friend Sally Granger.

During my childhood, my family lived two blocks away from the Grangers for several years. Visiting Sally was always an interesting experience, because her parents both had such strong personalities. Sally's father, Mr. Granger, was always fixing old cars, and by old I mean Model-T old. He would treat us kids to rides around the neighborhood. Mrs. Granger was fighting to get junk food out of schools, and wrote many letters to the editor on the subject. Her crusade did not exactly make her popular with us kids, but looking back I can see it was a good idea.

In the dream, as I approached the Grangers, I was greeted not by Sally, but by her parents who met me outside the front door. Mrs. Granger showed me the newest plants in her garden, while Mr. Granger showed me the autos in the garage.

Then, in my dream, we entered the house.

The outside of the dream house was not really different from the Granger house in reality, although it might have been a bit spruced up. The inside, however, was completely different.

Instead of the usual rooms and furniture, the inside was nothing but an enormous mahogany staircase. The three of us climbed up together, flight after flight. I was growing tired. Finally Mrs. Granger paused and said to her husband, "Veronica is here to see Sally. So you should say goodbye to her. Rick, it's time to go upstairs."

At that point, Mr. Granger continued climbing up the stairs. Mrs. Granger stayed where she was and I went back down. I located Sally, and in the dream we sat outside for a bit.

In the morning I awoke with the dream still strong in my mind, much stronger than my usual dreams, which were generally vague and quickly forgotten. I had not thought about the Grangers in a while — after all, they were in Indiana and I was in California. But the last time my father had mentioned them, several months before, he had told me that Mr. Granger had liver cancer.

I told my boyfriend about the dream and about Mr. Granger's cancer. "I think he must have died last night," I added.

A few hours later my father called me and told me that Mr. Granger had, indeed, died during the night. I was sorry and I reached out to Sally to express my condolences. I also felt rather peculiar, because it was as if Mr. Granger's spirit had made a point of visiting me during the night. I had liked him, but we were not exactly close. On the other hand, it had been a nice, rather comforting dream. So the next time I visited my father in Indiana I made a point of calling on Mrs. Granger and telling her about the dream.

When I described the staircase to her she became very still. "That's very strange," she said. "You see, a staircase was Rick's metaphor for leaving his body. The last words I said to him were, 'Rick, it's time to go upstairs.'"

~V. Grossack

14

A Knock at the Door

God pours life into death and death into life
without a drop being spilled.
~Author Unknown

When it comes to seemingly mystical events, I can almost always come up with a pragmatic explanation. However, every now and then something happens in my life that I cannot explain, and it strengthens my faith that there is more to this life than that which I can see and comprehend on a rational level. Such was the case the day my grandfather died and then came to me in a vivid dream.

I knew my grandfather was very ill but, unfortunately, I could not make the cross-country trip to be with him. Being a retired minister, my grandfather, whom I called Papu, loved gospel music. My boyfriend Tom, now my husband, was a musician, so he helped me make a CD for my grandfather that mixed Papu's favorite gospel songs in with recordings of me reminiscing about my best childhood memories. My dad later told me that when he arrived at Papu's home, Papu was listening to the gospel CD and softly singing along with it.

I spent the next few days telling Tom about what a wonderful man Papu was and how he was loved not only by his family but also by the communities he had lived in. I told him about the gentle, quiet way Papu would sit with people in nursing homes and hospitals, and how he was always up for a good chat at a potluck supper but also was not afraid to sit in silence when someone came to share their heartache and grief with him. He was more of a listener than a talker. And, though he was very devout, he was not judgmental.

My relationship with Tom was serious and I told him I deeply regretted that he would not have the chance to meet Papu.

During the last few days of Papu's physical decline, I would wake up wondering if he was still with us. I'd call my dad and he'd say Papu was not doing well but that hospice was making sure he was not in pain.

One night during this time, as I was sleeping, I heard a knock at the door. I thought, "Wow, it's really late for someone to be knocking." I looked at Tom but he was sound asleep so I got up, peeked out the door and saw Papu standing there. Papu and I both laughed and cried at the same time as I said, "Given that you live thousands of miles away, there's only one way you could be in Los Angeles right now." He nodded his head and said, "I can't stay long but I wanted to come in for a little while to meet Tom." I took Papu into the room where Tom was sleeping. Papu looked at him for a few minutes, then turned to me and said, "I can tell you're in good hands now, so I can go." I hugged Papu and then walked him to the door. I quietly lay back down, feeling a mixture of sorrow and peace.

A few hours later, the phone rang and my dad, choking back tears, said, "Papu died."

I whispered, "I know."

My dad asked how I knew and I told him about my dream. He said, "I had something strange happen, too. I'd been sitting by Papu's bedside all night and finally very early this morning I stepped outside to get a breath of fresh air. It was still dark outside but suddenly the sky lit up really brightly, and then went back to being dark. I assumed some sort of military aircraft was testing something so I went in to tell Papu about it. But when I walked back into his bedroom, he had passed away at the very moment I'd been outside and had seen the bright light."

A year later, Tom and I got engaged. I had always planned on Papu being the minister at my wedding, but since that was no longer possible, we decided we'd get married in one of his churches to honor his memory. We chose a beautiful little country church in rural South Georgia where Papu had preached when I was young.

The congregation, which over the years had dwindled to less than a dozen people, did everything they could to make our day special. They told me stories of how I'd often escape from my parents' arms as a toddler and run up to the pulpit to sit at Papu's feet while he preached. My parents would apologize to them and Papu for the disruption but no one seemed to mind. Papu would let me sit there while he finished his sermon. And there were lots of good stories about Papu and how he'd helped this person or gone to visit that person when they were sick and how they loved him and missed him to this day.

One of the church members said to me, "Now, did your grand-daddy actually get to meet Tom?" I wasn't sure how to answer so I simply said, "Yes."

~Rebecca Hill

The Little Voice

Intuition is a spiritual faculty and does not explain,
but simply points the way.
~Florence Scovel Shinn

I was at my prenatal checkup about six weeks before my delivery date. This entire pregnancy had been difficult. The doctor came into the tiny examination room where I was waiting with my five-year-old daughter, Emma.

The doctor looked at me, pulled my eyes open from below, and took my blood pressure. I know I looked a mess. I'd been sick since day one; my skin was sallow and there were great purple circles under my eyes all the time. I knew I wasn't well, that something was wrong. I'd been waiting for everyone else to realize it, too.

The doctor looked at me long and hard. "Do you have someone who can come pick up Emma?"

"Right now? No."

"Well, I suppose she can ride in the ambulance with you."

"The ambulance."

"Yes," she said. "You are going to the hospital now, and we are going to deliver this baby. Now." Another hard look. "Your blood pressure is 154/100. That is not good."

"Hmmm. I'll drive to the hospital so she doesn't worry," I said.

At this point Em finally looked up and asked me, "Worry about what?"

"We're going to the hospital to get your brother out, kiddo! You good with that?" Smiling.

"Yeah, let's go!" Emma was now very excited. I was remembering to breathe, slowly, deeply, relax my body, no stress.

As we left the doctor semi-jokingly said, "Don't have a stroke on the way over...."

Not funny.

We got to the hospital, and they started me on a magnesium drip of some kind to help with the toxins. I was in full-blown HELLP syndrome. My liver shut down, my kidneys shut down, and my body was flooded with toxins. My blood pressure was 200/135. I was in danger, plain and simple. I learned later that the mortality rate for HELLP is twenty-five percent.

They gave me drugs to intensify the contractions. I asked them to shut off the lights, play some Mozart, keep rotating the warm blankets, never to whisper — so annoying — anything I could think of to keep myself calm. I needed to focus on living through this birth. My nose bled. This was a good thing because it was relieving the pressure elsewhere. My heart fluttered and got "tachy." I set off the alarms every couple of minutes.

About ten hours later, the attending doctor entered the room, examined me, and decided to break my water to get the labor started in earnest. Two hours later, Isaac was born. He was oddly quiet.

They took him from the room. With Em, I told them no way could they take my baby out of the room. With Isaac, I needed him to be elsewhere so I could try to live. It was a struggle. My husband came into the room to sleep. Everyone else had gone home because it was about 2:30 a.m.

Then, a little voice spoke: "You've done everything you needed to do here. You can go now if you'd like."

"Oh, okay." I started to get warm, light, very comfortable. I was letting go of this life. It was all right. I could go.

Then a vision came to me. I saw Isaac, just seven weeks old, in the hospital with a respiratory infection. His father was asleep in the chair beside the crib. Isaac stopped breathing. The alarms went off, but no one heard. In a minute, Isaac was gone.

The vision continued with my husband dropping off Emma at her biological father's house three months later. He was returning to Olympia to live with his mother, a well-meaning social worker who put him on antidepressants. He would spend the rest of his life in anxiety and depression, mostly because the drugs were not what he needed—he needed to talk to someone and never did. Grief at the loss of his son consumed his life.

Next, I saw Emma, seventeen years later, dying of a heroin overdose. Her biological father was a drug dealer, and when Emma got to be a certain age, he started selling her to his friends. She didn't want to live.

I opened my eyes and pressed the call button for the nurse. She came in to see a pool at the end of the bed. She called for a team, STAT! The room became very bright. I was freezing and shivering. The team went to work. The little voice said, "You will suffer." I answered, "Better me than them."

Today, Emma is nearly twenty-one. She is happy and healthy. Isaac is fifteen and his little brother Matthew is thirteen. Their father is married to someone else now, and he has another baby on the way. I am happy for him.

And I am happy.

~Kate McCulloch

16

It's Okay

*Is solace anywhere more comforting than
in the arms of a sister.*
~Alice Walker

"Where is she?" I asked my mom as I entered the kitchen.

"In the bathroom."

I stood and waited in the kitchen until I heard the bathroom door open. As my sister walked, she grabbed onto doorways and leaned against walls. I went to help her but she slumped to her knees in the dining room doorway and began sobbing. I met her on the floor, tears streaming down my own cheeks.

"I'm checking out," she cried.

"You're what?" I asked.

"Checking out," she repeated. "Of life. Making all the final arrangements. Paying the final bill. Checking out."

"Oh God! No, Terri! You're not dying yet. Think positive. You're gonna be here a while yet."

"No. No, I'm not. I'm not going to make it till this day next week."

"How do you know that?" I asked.

"I just know." She returned to heavy sobs.

I held her as she cried, careful of her tender body, so frail and sickly thin. She was losing her battle with cervical cancer, one we thought she had won. Less than a year earlier we had celebrated her fifth year of remission on Thanksgiving.

"I don't want to go. I don't want to leave my girls," she cried.

"I don't want you to go either," I said, not letting go until she let go first.

"It will be okay," I told her.

"Okay? How is any of this okay? It's not okay!" she argued.

I got up for the box of tissues on the kitchen island. Terri and I both wiped our tears. "Well, you dying is not okay. It's awful. But our dad died when we were younger and we lived. We had our tough times, but we did okay."

"I don't want to die. I'm scared, Stephie. I'm so scared."

"Oh Terri," I comforted. "It will be okay. You will to go Heaven. You won't be sick anymore. Dad will be there to greet you."

"Heaven. Yeah, right. Heaven." She sounded doubtful.

"What? You don't believe in Heaven?"

"I don't know. I did once. But what kind of God of Heaven would let me die when I have two beautiful little girls to raise? I love them so much." Terri broke into sobs anew.

"Oh, I don't know why He would let you die. But I believe He loves you and doesn't want you to suffer. I believe that it will be okay," I tried to assure her.

"How do you know? I mean, really know."

"I guess I just have faith. I mean, I don't know it. But I'm pretty sure."

"Pretty sure," she laughed sarcastically.

"As sure as I can be. Do me a favor, if you can. When you die, let me know if it's okay or not. I would not want to go on living my whole life believing that in the end everything is okay if it's not. Can you do that for me?"

"How am I supposed to do that?" she asked.

"I don't know, exactly, but if there is a way, do it."

"It's almost three o'clock," Mom announced, popping her head up from the other side of the kitchen. "Are you going to get your girls from school?"

"Yeah. Stephie, will you take me? I can't drive anymore," Terri pleaded.

"Sure," I said. I popped up off the floor. I offered my sister a hand, but it took Mom and Merl, our stepdad, to assist her to her car.

The late afternoon sun peeked through the orange, red, yellow, and brown leaves and cast a warm glow of light on us as we drove. As the leaves gave up their hold on life, they rained gently onto the car. Then, it occurred to me that this would be the last time I saw my sister alive.

"This will be the last time I pick up my kids from school," Terri stated.

I was at home when I got the call less than a week later. Terri had been hospitalized earlier that day.

"There is no need to rush up here. She could be here a couple of days. You never know with these things," my sister Randee informed me. "Just stay home. Don't your kids have some program at school tonight? Just go do that and when John gets home from work you can come. He can stay with the kids."

"But I really want to be there," I protested. Adrenaline started pumping into my veins, a knot formed in my stomach, and my heart sank.

My three kids and I went to the school program as planned. An artist-in-residence had worked with students on some original art for the school, and they composed a song for the unveiling.

Fighting tears, I picked a spot to the far left of the stage in the middle of the risers. The principal started promptly and gave a brief overview of the program. The curtain was drawn and the artwork revealed. The musical piece was a ballad; I was listening intently to the lyrics.

"Stephie," someone called my name. I didn't see anyone looking in my direction so I blew it off. Then I heard it again, "Stephie? Stephie, where are you?" the voice, sounding like my sister Terri's, asked. I looked around to see if anyone else heard, then looked in the direction of the voice. There, in front of me, floating about four feet from the ceiling, I saw an odd-looking sphere, foggy with some shadows inside it.

"Here. Here I am," I whispered.

"It's okay. It's gonna be okay." I was sure now it was Terri's voice. Then the sphere faded and was gone. The clock near the sphere read 7:02 p.m. I made note of the time as though it were evidence. I fought off the gut wrenching sobs about to overwhelm me. I looked again to see if anyone was aware of what was happening, but they were absorbed in the performance.

Afterwards, we skipped refreshments in my anxiety to get home. As we pulled into the garage I heard the phone ringing. I dashed into the house to answer, even though I knew what I was about to hear.

"Hello?" I panted.

"Hello, Stephie." I recognized the voice.

"Dan?" I asked.

"Yeah. Um, Stephie, I hate to be the one to tell you, but they wanted me to keep trying to reach you…" he started but I interrupted. "I know. I already know. Terri is gone." I spared him. "Do you know what time she passed? It was 7:02, right?"

"Uh, I don't know. Hang on."

I heard commotion in the background, people entering the room. It seemed important to me that they knew I knew the time before they told me.

"Wait! Dan?" I tried to get his attention, twice.

"Here Stephie. Here's Randee," he said, passing the phone.

"It was 7:02!" I shouted.

"Yeah, Stephie."

"Terri died at 7:02, right?"

"Yes, she did. How did you know?" Randee asked.

"I know. Everything is going to be okay."

~Stephanie Sharpe

17

Connections: A True Story

People find meaning and redemption in the most unusual human connections.
~Khaled Hosseini

I moved to New York City and decided to find a job in a literary agency by cold-calling agents listed in the *Writer's Market*. I found one agency right in my new neighborhood. "Connie Clausen," announced a husky voice on the phone. I immediately felt lucky. The agent listened to three-quarters of my self-promotion spiel and then interrupted me: "Wait a minute. How did you know about the job when I haven't even placed my ad yet?"

I laughed. "I didn't know about any ad. I'm just cold-calling you from the *Writer's Market*. So you *are* looking for someone then?"

"Ha! Honey," she said, "you'd better get over here quick. I like the sound of you. How soon can you be here?"

I liked the sound of her, too. It still resonates in my mind: that deep Lauren Bacall voice that impatiently sliced through formalities, always punctuated by a distinctive throaty laugh. That voice alone made me get over there quickly. Living only a couple of blocks away from her, I arrived in about six minutes. Connie was laughing as she opened the door, displaying a Lauren Bacall face to match the voice. "Now that's what I call fast!" she exclaimed, waving me inward.

Her shining blue eyes, graced by soft wrinkles that showed decades of experience, mirrored her voice, as we talked like two new friends learning about each other rather than like an employer interviewing a job applicant. I found out I had the job when she answered an editor friend's phone call in my presence: "Oh, hi Diane! Honey, listen to this. You'll never believe it. I'm sitting here with this terrific girl who just walked into my office looking for a job — like it was meant to be — and I didn't even have a chance to place my ad yet. Just wait till you meet her…."

In a very short time a warm friendship developed between Connie and me. She inspired me with her brilliant self-taught editing skills and her confident assertion that she, without any college degree or "fancy credentials," knew more about writing and editing than most people with MFAs. "Look, I edit those MFAs now!" she laughed. Who could argue with a former book publicist who had climbed the corporate ladder by challenging her superiors' marketing decisions, turning herself into a V.P. of Publishing by launching two major bestsellers almost single-handedly?

Connie trusted me as an associate and as a friend, calling me "the daughter I never had." She gave me manuscripts to edit and rewrite and within just a few months assigned me my own clients as well. She showed her faith in me by answering my advice-seeking questions with a dismissive wave as she rushed off to appointments, calling over her shoulder, "You can handle it, Susan! I know you." But she sure had time to tell me stories, and I couldn't help but immerse myself in her compelling, comical tales. She was a gifted storyteller who, ironically, wrote only one book of her own — though she had at least ten in her — choosing to spend her life as a passionate midwife to authors rather than an author herself.

Driven by her passion, Connie pushed her way through obstacles, using humor as her shield, drama and style as her platform, and shrewd insight as her weapon. When she called me at my home in California, years later, to tell me about her serious eye problem and ask my eye doctor husband to refer her to a specialist in New York, my heart sank. Her prognosis, I knew, was not good. One good eye and all that reading? How would she cope with that obstacle?

"As long as I can read, I'm working!" she declared. "At least I look better than I see!"

We laughed together, miles apart, yet still connected by more than phone lines—I know that because of The Dream.

On the Thursday before Labor Day weekend in 1997, I was in the middle of other random dreams about mundane things when the screen in my brain faded to black. From the darkness came Connie's distinctive voice: "Susan! Honey, I need your help."

"Connie? Is that you?"

"Yes, honey. Can you please come here?"

I suddenly found myself, as a disembodied observer, in her home office. I saw everything in such vivid detail that I think of it as hyperrealism. The rooms we once worked in together were dimly lit. Dusty piles of unread manuscripts covered my old workspace. An ominous silence replaced the usually ringing phones. Around the corner, in the living room/meeting room, another tall stack of manuscripts stood on the wooden coffee table. A lipstick-stained coffee cup sat beside them, empty but for a drop, and beside it, a plate still smeared with butter and sprinkled with crumbs from Connie's daily bagel. I could hear her sigh as I viewed the bulletin board crammed with to-do lists and book auction lists, but I couldn't see her. Her voice merely emanated from around the corner, in front of the bathroom: "Susan, I can't run the agency anymore. I'm dying. I need you to get things in order."

"Dying? How do you know you're dying?"

"I just know. Now you've got to help me, honey. Clean up all this crap, make sure everything's handled fairly, make sure it's all done right...."

"Of course I'll help you, but how do you know—"

The dream dissolved as though she'd just issued one of her dismissive waves in reply to my question. I awoke sweaty and breathless. I nudged my husband awake and recounted my dream. He mumbled, "Why don't you call her if you're worried?"

So I did call, but only reached her answering machine. "Hi Connie, it's Susan. It's Friday morning, and I just wanted to say hi. I, uh, had a kind of weird dream and... well, I just want to hear your voice and know you're okay. Call me when you have a chance."

She didn't call back. I figured, with Labor Day weekend starting, she might have gone down to Florida to visit her sister. Although the dream haunted me all weekend, I dismissed it as some aberration from my writer's imagination and got back to my regular business after the weekend ended.

Three days later, a former author-client phoned to tell me that she had just called Connie's office and Connie's son had answered and said that his mother had passed away. I shuddered as a cold tingling spread over me.

I immediately phoned her son at her office/apartment in New York. He said she had fallen into a coma late Thursday night or early Friday morning — at the same time as my dream — and had been found on her floor, barely alive, by an employee on Monday. She died shortly after arriving at the hospital.

I blurted, "Michael, was she found in front of the bathroom?" That was the location of her voice in my dream.

"Well, yeah, she was. Why do you ask?"

I shared the dream. Michael was silent for a moment. Then he cleared his throat, "I thought you were calling about the will."

"The will?"

"You know how disorganized my mother always was. Well, the only will she left was the one she made back in 1989 — the one that leaves you in charge of overseeing the sale of the agency and the disposition of the assets."

I saw a flashback suddenly, as if watching a film: Connie and I discussing her surgery plans for a hysterectomy, and how my job requirements would expand during her six-week recovery period, and possibly beyond if the surgery were to reveal cancer. And how I was now named in her will as the manager of the agency in the event of her death.

"Clean up all this crap, make sure everything's handled fairly...."

Had Connie's soul left her body to call out to me in my sleep? Had I ignored her?

No, I had called her and left the phone message. In fact, she might have even heard the machine recording my voice as she lay paralyzed on the floor, knowing at least that I had received her communication.

I can imagine her relief at knowing that her message had been received. What I can't imagine is how she decided to contact me while she hovered between here and there. What an honor, what a gift, to have connected this way!

I wonder now whether sleep has certain layers of depth, like the comatose state, that create a kind of portal for the soul to cross back and forth between the body's world and another plane of existence. Just thinking about this event, and another similar one I've experienced, fills me with the utmost confidence that our souls move on after our bodies pass; it also erases any doubts about death and the afterlife in the minds of those to whom I've told this story.

In recounting this experience, I realize that Connie's parting gift to me was greater than her incredible visit. Her gift was the knowledge that death is a train stop for a soul, an exit to a new station and the beginning of the next leg of a journey. It's not only for the soul who passes, but also for the one left behind with the knowledge, who can now appreciate the journey without worrying about departure times or missed connections. I imagine that if the tracks can intersect as they did for Connie and me, they must continually offer points of intersection and opportunities for connection throughout our journeys.

~Susan L. Lipson

The Angel on the Door

*Pay attention to your dreams — God's angels often
speak directly to our hearts when we are asleep.*
~Eileen Elias Freeman, The Angels'
Little Instruction Book

"Lie back, honey," I said. "I'm going to lower the bed a little so you'll be more comfortable." My husband no longer had the strength to stay upright, so he was slumped to one side. I pushed the button to lower the head of the hospital bed that took up a large portion of our living room. It was late, nearly midnight, and Grover was having trouble settling down. I adjusted his pillow, moving his shoulders to the side so he was more evenly on it.

Grover reached up and touched my face. He said something I couldn't quite make out.

"What?" I asked.

"Goodbye," he said slowly, with difficulty.

Tears sprang to my eyes and my throat closed. I took his hand.

He put his arms up and I moved into them for the hug he wanted. He had said goodbye to me several times that day. Each time I had avoided returning the sentiment, instead saying things like, "It'll be okay," or "The kids are coming tomorrow." To speak those words out loud, I feared, would make them true.

A non-smoker, Grover had idiopathic pulmonary fibrosis, a lung disease of unknown origins. He'd been doing remarkably well with it for years, until the past spring when his health had taken a sudden, dramatic turn for the worse. In the months since then he'd gone from the strong, happy man I'd known for twenty years to someone who couldn't even hold his head up.

When it looked like he was finally dozing, I went to our bedroom to change into pajamas and get my bedding. Each night I made up a bed for myself on the living room sofa so I would hear him if he woke during the night. As weak as he was, his nights were restless.

As I left our bedroom, sheets and pillow in my arms, I glanced at the angel on the bedroom door.

Grover had pointed it out to me months before, when we'd still occupied our bedroom. "Have you seen the angel on the door?" he asked me one night. We were sitting up in bed, the open bedroom door directly in our line of vision. He pointed. "There, in the grain of the wood. You can see the wings there, pointing up to each corner. Below them is the robe, and there in the center—outstretched hands."

I looked. And I saw it. It really did look like an angel in the wood grain. But we'd been in this house for nearly two decades, in this same bedroom. How had I never noticed it before? "When did you first see that?" I asked.

"A couple of weeks ago. I didn't know if I should say anything."

Since then we'd talked about the angel several times, but once we moved into the living room it was in our thoughts less. Now I looked at it, and wondered if he might find comfort in the angel again. Maybe I could have the door removed and propped up in the living room, where he could see it.

When I finally settled down on the sofa and managed to fall asleep, I dreamed.

In my dream, Grover was healthy. We were walking on a beach, the waves lapping nearby. In our travels together over the years, what we'd loved most was visiting beaches. Grover's youngest daughter lived in Florida, and we'd been there several times. We had friends who wintered on the Gulf of Mexico and we usually managed to spend a few days with them there. We'd flown to the Turks and Caicos for a niece's wedding. We never passed up an opportunity to go somewhere with white sand and salt water.

We walked together along this beach in my dream, holding hands, the sun on our shoulders and sand between our toes. It was perfect, and it seemed perfectly natural.

Then Grover released my hand and lagged behind. I was picking up shells, examining them one at a time. He fell farther behind. When I looked, I saw that he'd stopped walking.

Grover stood at the edge of the ocean. He was looking not at me, but at an angel. It was a hazy, indistinct image that stood about a foot taller than my husband, and I knew immediately it was our angel from the bedroom door.

Turning, he started to walk away from me, accompanied by the angel. I wanted to call out to him to come back but I couldn't form the words. Then Grover paused, turning to look at me. "Goodbye," he said clearly.

This time I was able to say it. "Goodbye," I whispered. I watched until they faded from sight.

When I awoke on the sofa it was 4 a.m., still dark. The oxygen concentrator pumped loudly, the sound a constant presence in our home. Other than that, however, the house seemed too quiet. I got up and crossed the room to the hospital bed.

Grover was gone. He'd slipped away during the night.

I'd become such a light sleeper that it seemed impossible that this could have happened without my waking. I sat beside him and wept. I should have been with him. I should have been holding his hand, comforting him as he took his last breath.

Then I remembered — I *had* been with him. We'd walked together on the beach one last time. Though my tears continued, a sense of peace slowly settled over me. I'd watched him go, knowing he was in good hands, accompanied by the angel that had been watching over him these past months.

And I had, at last, been able to say the word he wanted: "Goodbye."

~Jean Tennant

Rooster and Toad

There is a connection between heaven and earth.
Finding that connection gives meaning to everything,
including death. Missing it makes everything
meaningless, including life.
~John H. Groberg, The Other Side of Heaven

The love of my life is a big, longhaired, tattooed biker. He is just the opposite, on the inside, from what he appears to be on the outside. He is the kindest and most sensitive soul you would ever meet. He is also a tattoo artist and this was where our paths intersected in this lifetime.

I had decided to get a Celtic Phoenix tattoo on my lower back and walked into this man's tattoo shop. He introduced himself to me as Dave and we began a multiple-session tattoo.

At our fourth session, Dave was very quiet, not his usual chatty self. He said his brother had passed away and to forgive him for his demeanor. I told him I was sorry for his loss and asked how many brothers and sisters he had. He said one of each, but this was his club brother.

"Club brother?" I was confused.

He smiled and said, "I'm a biker and he was my motorcycle club brother."

I said, "You are a biker?"

He smiled and said, "Yeah, does that change things?"

I laughed and said, "No, I guess not. What was his name?"

He said, "Rooster."

I said, "Rooster? Do you have a nickname?"

He got a slight grin and said, "Yeah. Toad."

As the months went on, he and I became very close and eventually, three years later, we moved in together. I had revealed the big "skeleton in my closet" to him, the fact that I was a psychic medium and dead people visited me in my dreams. He was a huge skeptic. He believed when you died, you were just gone and you became "worm meat," end of story. I had tried to assure him otherwise over the years, but to no avail. His mother, who had passed before I met him, had visited me several times with messages for him or about him and assured me that we would be together. He refused to believe any of the things I relayed to him, saying that anyone could find that stuff out. So, I just let it go and hoped that someday he would see things differently.

Then one night I had a dream.

I was at the tattoo shop and there was a man sitting in the mirror. For some reason, I knew it was Dave's club brother, Rooster.

I walked over to the mirror in my dream and said, "Are you Rooster?"

The man jumped out of the mirror and said, "You can see me?"

And I said, "Yes!"

He did a quick little two-step jig, arms out to his sides and said, "How do I look?"

I said, "Fine, if I didn't already know you were dead!"

He was dressed in dark denim jeans, biker boots and a 1970's-style brown suede vest. His hair was shoulder length and he had on glasses with brown tinted lenses.

I asked him, "Can you give me something to tell Dave that only he would know? Just to prove I am talking to you?"

He walked around a second and then he showed me, with his hands on the table, a small octagon that looked like a concrete model of something.

He pointed to a spot on it and said, "I got stuck right here, in the pit."

He walked back into the mirror.

I woke up and jostled Dave awake.

"Did Rooster ever work in a gravel pit?" I asked.

Dave said, "No, go back to sleep."

I said, "He was just in my dream and I asked him to give me some information that only you would know and he pointed to this octagon thing and said he got stuck 'right here.' Do you know what that means?"

Dave said, "Shhhh. No. Go back to sleep."

So I did. I let it go. A few days later, we were pulling up to the tattoo shop for Dave's next appointment and as we walked inside, I decided to give it another try.

I said, "That's the mirror that Rooster came out of."

Dave spun around and said, "What? What are you talking about?"

I said, "My dream I had the other night, remember?"

He looked at me like I had lost my mind. I told him, again, about the dream and what Rooster had said to me about getting stuck in the pit. Suddenly, Dave's eyes filled with tears.

He said, "How did you know that?"

I said, "Know what?"

He said, "Nobody knows that except me and maybe one other person that is still alive, Germ. He was there too."

I immediately got goose bumps and said, "Rooster told me! Now, explain it all to me, please!"

Dave took a deep breath and wiped the tears from his eyes.

He said, "Back in the 1980's our club used to take our bikes to the Menard Prison for bike shows. The whole place is shaped like an octagon and it was made out of stone from the quarry. Inside, in the middle, where we would ride our bikes, they called it "The Pit" and Rooster was showing off and gunned it and got his bike hung up on a concrete divider when we were pulling in and he laid his bike down. He was really embarrassed and, like I said, there were only two of us, besides him, that knew about it. It was in 1987. There is no way you would know that!"

I said, "Nope. You're right! In 1987, I was working at the bank and getting married for the first time. There is no way I would have known that!" I was totally excited because finally I had been given something to prove to him that our loved ones' souls lived on. It was extremely validating for me and I could see that it helped him heal from his friend's passing.

Dave will say that he is not as skeptical as he used to be and he is open to consideration of all that I relay to him, but he also will not go out on a limb and profess his total belief in the afterlife, either. That's okay, because I can't draw or tattoo, so he does what he does and I do what I do and we have reached a mutual understanding. Or I guess you could say we have found "a happy medium."

~Pamela Freeland

20

Let Me Hear His Voice Again

Perhaps they are not stars, but rather openings in heaven where the love of our lost ones pours through and shines down upon us to let us know they are happy.
~Eskimo Proverb

I had a vision about my seventeen-year-old son Jovan. It felt so real that I ran into his bedroom and felt his face, checked his pulse and felt his body for warmth. I started shaking him; Jovan struggled and rolled over. "Ma! Let me sleep!"

Thank You, God! He's alive. I have my son here with me, everything's okay. Tears streamed down my face as I left his bedroom. I called my mother.

"Mom, I need to tell you something. I saw Jovan and he was in heaven with Jesus. While lying on my bed I was looking up at the ceiling and it seemed to open up and was like a big cloud. They were looking down at me. Jovan was standing there in a sparkling white robe, smiling. He was saying, 'Ma, I'm okay. It's beautiful here. Don't worry, Ma. I love you.'"

I was increasingly worried about Jovan. He had wrestled with an emotional/chemical imbalance for most of his life. I was seeing some alarming signs with his behavior and knew that I needed to get help for him soon.

Two weeks after the vision, I tried to talk to him. "Mommy has to call the hospital because you are sick again. They will put you on medication."

"Ma, I'm not going back to that place," Jovan shouted as he grabbed his skateboard and slammed the door.

Before I could walk from the bedroom to the front door, my son was gone.

As evening arrived and Jovan had still not come home, I paced the floor. I had been praying all afternoon for him. We had a hard life, living in the middle of what might be called the projects. There was a lot of drug activity and I thought Jovan used marijuana when he had a few extra dollars on him. I rarely gave him money because I didn't want him to be able to buy drugs.

As a mom, though, I was street-smart and knew many people are out on the streets willing to fund drugs to get people addicted and under their control. I myself had come through much pain and many trials. I was just beginning to get some things together in my own life, taking some courses and leading a sane life. We still didn't have a car, though.

Where could Jovan be? Just as I was about to go ask the neighbor to take me to look for him, there was a knock on the door.

A policeman and a man who I soon learned was a detective stood there.

"Where is my son? What has he done?"

"May we come in?

"Of course."

"Do you have a picture of your son?"

I ran into my bedroom and brought out some pictures I had taken recently. They stepped aside to talk to each other, looking at a picture they had brought in a manila envelope.

What was going on? "Can you tell me, is he in jail? Can you take me to him?"

"I'm sorry ma'am; your son has passed. He was hit by the local train. Your son died on the way to the hospital."

My knees buckled as a wail of grief exploded from my mouth. I didn't even recognize my voice; it seemed like it had to be someone else piercing the air with her screams.

"No! No! Oh Jesus, no! Not my son. Not my baby, not my boy! Jovan! Jovan, I love you!" I ran into the kitchen and started punching the door, saying, "Why? What was he doing on the train track? Now I have no body left, no head, no toes, no fingers! He's completely crushed and run over. What do I have left to bury?"

"No," one of the men answered, as he tried to restrain me, "his body is intact. The train impact moved him over to the side; the skateboard was shattered but not your son's body."

The next few days were a blur of pain and despair. Only because of my faith could I pull myself together for the funeral. Jovan was very well loved in the skateboard community and over 160 kids made a profession of faith because of his death. Kids skateboarded to the cemetery behind the hearse.

After the funeral I went home and cried out to God. "Oh, please Lord, I know he is with you. Please Lord; just let me hear his voice one more time."

And then another vision came and it was so sweet, the most awesome moment in my life, as it seemed Jovan could hear me crying out to God.

I heard Jovan saying, "She can hear me? You shouldn't have told me that because I'm gonna talk to her all the time." I heard something that sounded like God was chuckling, laughing at Jovan as a father chuckles at his dear child. "Ma, Ma, I'm okay," Jovan said. "Ma, I'm okay. You were so right, Ma. Keep doing what you're doing, keep doing what you're doing."

I turned over in my bed and wept. I was so grateful that God gave me a chance to hear my son's voice one more time. I can face the future with peace because my son told me in his own words that he was with God. Though gone, he remains as near as this vision that was given to me.

~Gloria Marie Gonzalez

Dreams and Premonitions

Facing Fears

21

A Smiling Journey in Darkness

Live your dreams, not your fears!
~Albina Hume

I was scared to death of death. I suppose everyone is scared of death in some way, but I avoided thinking about it at all costs. When my significant other decided she wanted to get a dog, I loved the idea — except I knew that one day I would have to see it die, and so I resisted as long as I could. We ended up with two dogs, and when the first one died, I happened to be 3,000 miles away, which was a great relief to me. I felt like I had dodged a bullet. The thought of being there when this thing happened was anathema to me. When my grandmother died, I cried for days, and then I talked myself into not going back for the funeral. I couldn't deal with it.

I was a death-chicken. But I am also a dream worker: I explore individuals' nightly forays into the realm of the unconscious. I work extensively with people's nighttime dreams, run workshops at international conferences, have private clients, do occasional radio shows about dreams, and lecture on the subject.

When it comes to talking about death in the context of dreams, I am totally open to it and gung-ho about working with it. Death comes up often in dreams, and in my lexicon it is usually about transformation. Dreams speak a symbolic language, and death is an iconic symbol that may indicate change in one's life, often a radical change. We get shot, beheaded, flattened by an elephant, fall and go splat on the concrete, shoot others, suffocate, get struck by lightning, have our bodies ripped open and all the organs pulled out, and—two of the most common—we drown in a tsunami or we fall to our death off a cliff.

It's an old wives' tale that if you die in your dream, you will actually die. I have died countless times in my dreams. I have willfully plunged into a vat of acid and felt myself die, I have been shot through the heart with an arrow and turned to stone, I have ridden across the river Styx with the ferryman into Hades, I have been eaten by a bear and died, and then woken up inside the dream realizing that I was inside the smelly bear.

It is odd that I was perfectly fine dealing with death in dreams, but in the waking world, I shrank from that reality. I became numb and distracted and made jokes and excuses when the subject came up.

That was my world until I had a pair of dreams that changed the way I saw death forever.

In the first dream, it is a warm afternoon and I am cruising on the Ventura Freeway. I get off at my exit and I just miss the light at the bottom, so I am the first in line for the next light. There is a sign that says "No turn on red" so I wait, but I have this strange feeling—something is not quite right. The light turns green, but my foot won't step on the gas. The people behind me start beeping. I hesitate a second longer and then lurch forward. As I do so, a giant truck comes screaming at high speed across my path, blaring its horn and just missing me. "Oh my God, I would have been flattened for sure if I hadn't hesitated," I say out loud.

I woke up from that dream and didn't think much of it. After all, we spend a lot of time driving freeways in Los Angeles, so it stands to reason we'll dream about them.

Two months later, I was crawling east along the Ventura Freeway and I finally got to my exit and just missed the light at the bottom of the exit. I was first in line, and there was a sign that read "No turn on red."

"Hmm…" I thought. "This reminds me of that dream I had!" And there was a red car on my left, just like in that dream. How odd. "But wait," I told myself. "Big deal. I have been in this spot hundreds of times." However, the feeling persisted that this was exactly like that dream I had. The light turned green. I started forward, but stopped suddenly, and sure enough, the horns blared. I still hesitated. I looked and didn't see anything coming. I thought, "This is just silly. Go, you dummy!" I stepped on the gas, and a giant rumble shook my car as the exact same giant truck I dreamed about came screaming through the intersection. He missed me by inches! My heart was racing and I was yelling "Oh my God! Oh my God!" over and over.

I moved out into traffic, but suddenly an odd thing happened. My left arm started shaking uncontrollably, and so I pulled off the road into a parking space. Still shaking, I started talking to my body, as if I were working on a dream. "What's wrong with you? We have had close calls before and you have just shrugged and moved on. What's wrong with you?" And then my body really betrayed me — I started bawling. I sat there for twenty minutes, with NPR yammering on the radio in the background, as for some unknown reason I broke down in tears.

Then I really got it: "That dream saved my life! I would be dead right now if I hadn't had that dream." This was not like any close call I had ever had before, for a dream stepped in and saved me! But why all this crying? It slowly dawned on me that this had to do with the connection between dream death and real death. The easy but very deep, even comfortable, way I had dealt with death in the dream realm had suddenly come alive in waking life and smacked me hard across the face. If death in dreams was transformation, perhaps death in life was also transformation. This was a moment of epiphany. I knew that I had to use this to help me deal with my extreme fear of death.

After that, I started reading about death. I trudged through the *Tibetan Book of the Dead*, and various other texts about death — a real investigation into death. But more importantly, when death was mentioned around me, I turned my soul toward it instead of away from it. I let death in.

And then the second dream appeared.

In this one, I am at a seminar with the Dalai Lama. It is a lively discussion with great minds and great humor. We are in his living room, which is round, with a Tibetan feel. We finish the seminar, and I fall asleep standing in the doorway while I am waiting for the group to leave. I then have a dream while asleep (a dream within a dream) and when I wake, I ask the Dalai Lama if I can tell him my dream, and he says, "Sure, come to the temple with us and tell your dream there." The dream inside the dream is about my future. How cool that I might have the answer to what my life is about!

Now the strangest image appears. At the bottom of a path that leads to the high mountains sits an enormous vehicle that looks like one of those metal spinning tops that I had in my youth — the type with a handle that you pump up and down and the thing spins madly. Only this one is twenty feet across and has rockets on the sides. It is muted red and black and copper, and it has tassels and filigree work on the side, and gold Tibetan writing. The Dalai Lama and the group climb into this strange vehicle and it starts to spin as the rockets spray fire everywhere. As it whirls, there is a clanging and the sound of Tibetan horns. I am wide-eyed as the spinning top climbs the mountainside up to the temple.

I am going to go there also, but there is something I have to do before I go to the temple. I have to help a woman load a car. The car is a station wagon, much like the one my family used to take on summer vacations. The woman is both herself and at the same time she is also a child, a small child who is dressed like the Dalai Lama with those woolen striped clothes and a woolen striped hat with earflaps.

The child/woman is very hungry and she needs to eat before we go to the temple. She goes over to a taco truck and stands in line. While we are waiting for the food, I grab the child/woman and dance with her. "Holy, Holy…" We sing as I swing her about. This is fun and we both smile.

I notice that the spinning top vehicle is returning now, black and singed from the flames, returning empty to take its place for the next journey. It is late, and I am upset because we have probably missed the ceremony at the temple.

As I ponder this, a realization comes over me and shifts my whole mood. My body softens and relaxes. "The Dalai Lama wants to hear my dream and he will wait patiently at the temple. There is no rush to get there. It is totally guaranteed that my dream will be heard," I say to myself.

I am suddenly aware that there is another place that the Dalai Lama and his group have to go. They leave the temple at the top of the mountain and they go to the end place, the place of death — which doesn't feel like death at all. They are clearly going to death, but there is no fear and no dread. This is my answer, I think. Oh my God, this death thing is not death at all as we think of it! It is just a smiling journey in complete darkness that ends up at another temple. I mean, the Dalai Lama and his kin are headed there and it is no big deal. How cool is that? Death is just another place.

I woke up and recorded this dream, and when I got to the part about death being just another place, I had some sort of awakening that has stayed with me ever since. It is difficult to explain, but if you have ever had an experience like this you know how the soul can spend endless time searching for something and then the unexpected answer hits you upside the head like a huge truck. I live with death inside of me now, and it feels fine.

Oh, and when the second dog died? Well, I held him gently as they administered the drugs that caused his life to ebb from him. And I was fully present and tuned into what was going on. I saw his tiny spirit rise gently and leave the room. Some day mine will also, because I get it now. Death is just another place, a smiling journey in total darkness.

~Walter Berry

Flying at Fifty

*The reason birds can fly and we can't is simply because
they have perfect faith, for to have faith
is to have wings.*
~J.M. Barrie, The Little White Bird

All my life I've had flying dreams that ended badly. They always ended with flying that became falling and that terrible feeling of tumbling out of control toward the ground below. I've noticed that I have more of these flying and falling dreams when my life is in turmoil.

So I guess it's no surprise that I had a lot of these dreams in the year before I turned fifty, which was an intimidating milestone for me. I'd heard so much about how women become invisible at fifty, about all the physical and emotional difficulties that come with the age.

I tried to talk myself out of it. My career was in a good place, my family was doing well, and I felt great. So why worry?

But this kind of worry is rarely rational and it doesn't respond to a reasoned argument. I continued to fret, to look at myself in the mirror and wonder who I was at this age. Fortunately, I didn't have to rely on reasoning to pull me out of my anxiety. I was rescued, by my sister and my friends and by a dream.

For my fiftieth birthday, my sister and some of my friends threw me a party. They went all out, giving me beautiful silk scarves, new shoes, a massage, and, of course, a great deal of chocolate. My sister even bought me a Barbie doll, because we never had them when we were growing up and she knew I had always wanted one.

"It's about time," she told me, "that you have exactly what you want, just because you want it."

Then, one of my Jewish friends told me that in the Hebrew Scriptures, every fifty years is referred to as a Jubilee year. At that time, slaves were freed, debt was forgiven, and all old chains were broken. Fifty is a year of liberation.

That night, I dreamt I was at the beach with my husband. As we watched the sun play on the water, he took my hand and said, "Let's fly."

I was suddenly frightened. "I don't know if I can," I told him.

"Sure you can," he said. "Just go ahead."

I started moving my arms as if I was swimming, and sure enough, I began ascending toward the sky. I heard my husband laughing, and he joined me as we soared through clouds, dipped down toward the water, and then soared again. For the first time in my life, I was flying in my dream, and I wasn't at all afraid. In fact, I felt completely in control of the situation, as if I'd been doing this my whole life. The motion was gentle and soothing, and the vista was grand. I felt connected to the earth and water below me, and yet free of its gravitational constraints.

When it was time to land, we simply swam downward to a gentle landing.

Dreams are the stories our souls tell us when we're ready to hear them. That night, fifty years of falling ended and I understood that I'd accepted my personal power in a new way.

The next morning, I woke up and decided that fifty was indeed a Jubilee year after all.

~Barbara Chepaitis

23

Take the Leap

*I have been a seeker and I still am, but I stopped
asking the books and the stars. I started listening
to the teaching of my soul.*
~Rumi

n the summer of 2000 I found myself between homes, identities and careers. It had all started eighteen months earlier, when I quit my job in public radio news because it no longer suited me. After that I spent several months working freelance and temporary jobs in New York City before applying to a summer yoga studies program in the green hills of western Massachusetts.

At the yoga center, I found the atmosphere, teachings and community that my soul had been longing for. I stayed on for an additional year to soak up all I could learn about healing, nutrition, Eastern spirituality and personal growth. I cultivated deep and lasting friendships and trained to become a yoga teacher. It felt like being in graduate school, minus the tuition and research papers, and I loved it.

And that's where I was in August 2000 — finishing up my yoga training, knowing it was time to move on from my radio career, and yet scared to do so. I didn't really feel qualified or ready to teach the ancient science of yoga or make a living at it. I was eager to leave the countryside and return to the city, but going back to my old life didn't appeal to me and I didn't know where else to go. I needed help, so I gathered some friends who were also in transition and we met each week to support each other.

One night during this time I had a powerful dream:

I was determinedly making my way across tall rock formations in the Grand Canyon. As I'm not even much of a hiker in waking life, this was pretty strange, but there I was, boldly trekking. At one point in my journey across the canyon I came to a place where the next rock was too far away for a safe leap, and I froze. I somehow knew there was no going back, yet I was too afraid to take the next step.

Suddenly, part of me split off — like a cartoon character — and jumped, falling hundreds of feet to the ground with a splat. As I peered down in horror, I saw a crowd gathering around my fallen self. What happened next was even more bizarre. To everyone's amazement, the me who had fallen got up, brushed herself off, and walked away.

Up above, the frightened me was somewhat emboldened by this triumph. Very shakily, I stepped forward into the air. Immediately, a kind of magic carpet appeared under my feet and transported me to the next rock, Aladdin-style, where I safely landed.

And so it went, all across the Grand Canyon.

This vivid dream, which came to me during a time of great change and uncertainty, told me two important things: 1) You may fall (fail), and it may even happen in front of lots of people, but it won't kill you; 2) When you take a step forward, despite your fears, help will arrive.

A few months later, I left the yoga center and moved to Boston, where I began to teach yoga and personal transformation workshops. I'd landed there without a job, but I had a car, a new set of skills and generous friends with guest rooms. I also had colleagues who let me substitute-teach for them and referred me to places where yoga and workshop instructors were needed and welcomed.

Today I'm a writer, teacher and coach. It's a career I never could have foreseen from my news-anchor chair at the radio station, and it came about by following my heart in the direction of what promised greater fulfillment, and by having faith. Many of my big life changes have been accompanied by wide-eyed "What the heck am I doing?" moments at 3 a.m. By the light of day, however, if my inner convictions were stronger than my fear and anxiety, I forged ahead.

A few years ago, I saw that the yoga center where I started was offering a new certification program. It looked great, but it was expensive. With a shaky hand, I picked up the phone, heard enough to convince me that this was the right thing for my career, and gave them my credit card number. Within months, the money that I was investing started coming back to me in unexpected ways.

In the end, I believe it's the things we don't try that haunt us more than our so-called mistakes and failures. As the poet Mary Oliver suggests, we have just one "wild and precious life" to live, and it's not a dress rehearsal. As I tell my students and clients, life is always ready to assist us, but we have to take that first, inertia-busting, empowering step.

Since that memorable dream, I've taken many more leaps of faith and trusted that I'd be transported with grace to my next adventure. And I have been.

~Kim Childs

24

Taking a New Direction

*Progress always involves risks. You can't steal second
base and keep your foot on first.*
~Frederick B. Wilcox

It was the third time in as many weeks that I had the same
dream.

*I stroll into a classroom and discover I need to take an algebra
exam. After sitting down, I realize I haven't attended a single class
and am definitely not prepared to take the test. My anxiety grows as I look
at the paper, clueless what to do next. All I know for sure is that failing the
exam means I won't graduate. I look around the room and notice everyone
else moving their pencils rapidly down the page. My stomach gets queasy, I
start to sweat, and then I wake up.*

In the comforting light of day, the whole dream seemed bizarre.
I'm not the type to neglect responsibilities, let alone ignore anything
related to an important goal. Though I know everyone has dreams, I
seldom remember mine. So why did I recall this one with such clarity?

It bothered me enough to finally discuss the dream with one of
my friends. She quickly assured me that all dreams had a meaning
and peppered me with questions.

"What's going on in your life? Has anything been on your mind?"

I pondered my answers. While we were far from wealthy, we were
comfortable. No one in the family was having any issues or health

problems. Finally I decided the only thing to do was simply let it go.

The next day at work, I weeded through a mountain of e-mails. One jumped out at me: My boss announced he intended to create a new position within our department and he needed a grant manager — someone to write and monitor all of our office grants. I considered the possibility. This could be a perfect fit for me. I enjoyed research, planning, and writing. In my view, such characteristics couldn't be more fitting for a grant writer. Without another thought I typed an enthusiastic response proclaiming my interest, but with the cursor poised over the "send" button, I hesitated. Something kept me from clicking it.

I'd been doing the same type of work for more than thirty years. I barely even needed to think about it. At this point in my life, why should I put myself in a position requiring entirely new knowledge and skills? If I hated the job, it wasn't likely I'd be able to go back to the old one. I slowly backspaced to delete every word I'd written. I started over and this time I wrote out a list of questions regarding the job.

I sent the e-mail and stared at the blank computer screen. I noticed my heart was pounding and my stomach fluttered. A fine sheen of moisture dampened my hairline. Something about how I felt seemed eerily familiar. My eyes widened when it came to me: This was the exact reaction I had to taking the exam in my dream!

I called my friend and told her what happened. Her voice rose with excitement.

"Don't you see? That's what your dream is telling you. You're too much of a worrier. Always afraid you won't measure up. I think you ought to go for it."

Easier said than done, I told myself at work the next day, yet as much as I tried I couldn't stop thinking about what she said. I did tend to assume that other people were more capable than I was. Such negative self-talk had often prevented me from stretching my wings in a new direction. I always feared the fall. I swallowed hard and shook my head at the notion. If I was prepared, why couldn't I be successful at an entirely new venture?

Before I could change my mind I inhaled deeply, squared my

shoulders, and marched straight to my boss's office to let him know I wanted to apply.

"I was hoping you would," he told me, and I felt as though I might float like a helium balloon to the ceiling. I silently congratulated myself on being so coolly confident, but the edge of my memory prickled as though receiving an unwelcome telegram. My dream. What if my dream turned into reality?

Right after work that day I drove to the bookstore for some instructive reading materials and found more online. I talked to a professional grant writer. I was determined to learn everything I could about grants, and the hours spent studying paid off. On the day of the interview, I didn't stammer or stutter a bit. I had an answer for every question. A week later I got the news: I had been appointed grant manager for our department.

Initiating a major career change definitely has thrown me some unexpected curves. Yet I don't regret the decision. Every day I arrive at my office with a bounce in my step, the way I did years earlier, once again believing I can conquer anything the world throws at me.

As for my classroom dream, it hasn't returned since the day I became the grant manager. Maybe my friend was right. My dream not only forced me to think about my life, it provoked me into taking action.

~Pat Wahler

25

The Curious Riddle of the Codpiece

If you put yourself in a position where you have to
stretch outside your comfort zone, then you are forced
to expand your consciousness.
~Les Brown

Codpiece. What an odd word. I didn't remember anything else from the dream. Just that one strange word: Codpiece.

I'd be lying if I told you I knew what it meant. If we were in casual conversation I might have fibbed and claimed I did. But on that morning about two years ago I was drawing a blank. All I knew was that it had entered my mind during the night, and that it was there for a reason.

As soon as I could I looked up the word on Wikipedia. The codpiece dated back to the fifteenth century, when some clever tailor invented a leather device to be worn as a flap over a man's genital area — an early athletic cup. Cod actually was the Middle English word for scrotum. The codpiece fell out of fashion in the sixteenth century, but made a modern-day comeback on the groins of 1980's heavy metal rockers.

As a history buff I found all of this fascinating. But it begged the more obvious question: What did a codpiece have to do with me, a woman years past my rock-star fan girl days?

My first answer was a big fat "I don't know."

Well, at least I would have something to talk about. Several months earlier, I had started attending a weekly dream circle. I had a hunch that learning how to understand my dreams would help me figure out why I was feeling so stuck and uneasy in my life. Sure, it would have been nice if I'd remembered the entire dream, which would have yielded more clues to this mystery. But this was typical for me. In preceding weeks I'd had so many petite dreams consisting of a single incident or a few disjointed thoughts that the leader of the dream circle dubbed me "the Queen of the Snippets."

It was a dubious honor, to be sure. I longed for the epic, mind-altering dreams others in the group were sharing, dreams that were long and meandering and filled to the brim with deep, profound symbology. My poor little snippets were no match for them.

Well, this one was the shortest yet — just one word. I could have simply dismissed it. Yet something within me told me I had to examine it.

I turned the question, "What does a codpiece mean to me?" into a game. I never really was a fan of heavy metal, so I dismissed that as a clue. I had no interest in living during the Renaissance, so I saw no connections there. The codpiece had to be a symbol, I concluded. It was something tough, something that was used as protection, to keep something precious safe. How did that relate to my life? What did I have that was hard on the outside and soft and important on the inside? If I could figure out what was behind the codpiece, I'd have been on my way to solving this curious riddle.

Then it hit me. It really was a very simple concept. But often it's the simple things that hold the deepest truths.

The codpiece represented the wall that separated me from the rest of the world.

The more I thought about it, the more it made sense. Little by little I had spent huge chunks of my life holding back, keeping my thoughts and ideas to myself. The labels "quiet" and "shy" were comfortable explanations that seemed to satisfy others, and when they kept their distances I grew comfortable with that too.

Over time I had unconsciously talked myself into believing that I was a boring, uninteresting, even shallow person. Was I really? No, that was fear talking. I was so afraid that anything I said would be met with ridicule or, even worse, be totally dismissed, that I said nothing. The result was that I was often ignored, passed over, and simply not included in things I might have enjoyed. No wonder I had this vague feeling of unease in my day-to-day life.

I was at a crossroad. I could dismiss the dream and continue living in fear. Or I could take action on the meaning of the dream. The codpiece protected something that men hold precious. That meant that if the codpiece was protecting me then I was something precious.

As if I needed further proof, two days later I had another one-word dream: almond. As I wrote that word in my dream journal I started to laugh. What was an almond, after all, but something with a hard shell that protected something good inside? I was making progress. The almond's shell is a lot thinner than a codpiece. That means it's possible to break through it.

This is where you might expect me to say that uncovering the meaning of the dream made me come out of my shell, and that resulted in newfound riches, friends, money, success and all that. But, hey, this is real life, not a fairy tale. No, the understanding was just that, an understanding. The real hard work started after that, the realization that I chose to live my life the way I did, and that it would take further choices on my part to change its trajectory.

Honestly, there was no rational reason to hide myself. But for me to un-hide I first had to come face to face with the ridiculous things that had been so embedded in the deep recesses of my mind I didn't even know they were there. These were self-limiting beliefs that were true only because I said they were true: things like I didn't matter, I wasn't important, I wasn't to be taken seriously, and even the thought that I was invisible.

Once I became consciously aware of those beliefs, I could see not only that they weren't true but that I had the power to replace them with more empowering thoughts: I am smart, I have a brain, I am creative, and I can make a difference to myself and others.

When I started looking at myself in a new light, I could see that I mattered. What I had to say and do was important. I started to believe in myself again.

I did see changes, little ones. They came in the moments when I did things like complain to a server that my food was delivered cold or when I asked the manicurist to redo my nail because it got smudged. These sound insignificant when I write them, but for me speaking up to strangers was truly new and different; in the past I would have suffered in silence and cursed myself for my reticence.

There were larger things, too. I furthered my interest in dream work and finished a program that certified me as a dream coach. I started a coaching business. I created a website. I even wrote a book.

Because of this dream, I found the courage to be comfortable with myself. Indeed, the very act of writing this would have been unthinkable if I were still living behind the codpiece.

~Debbie Spector Weisman

26

The Dream Team

We are continually shaped by the forces of coincidence.
~Paul Auster

"We'll need to remove the questionable tissue and take a biopsy," my doctor told me. "Someone on my staff will call you tomorrow to schedule the surgery."

Ugh. Not another problem. I had just nursed my brother to health after emergency heart surgery and now I was helping him sort through his medical forms and doctor bills. Thanks to that situation, I already felt emotionally tapped-out and now I'd have to start renegotiating the frustrating world of health insurance bureaucracy.

I walked through the medical center's parking lot toward my car. Wait. Did my doctor say "biopsy?"

That meant cancer.

Cancer. The word hit me like a boulder. Dazed, I sat down behind my car's steering wheel and caught my breath. Surely I couldn't have cancer, I rationalized. I felt well and strong, didn't smoke or drink, ate a sensible diet, and exercised daily. Certainly anyone with such a healthy lifestyle was protected against this diagnosis.

Or were they? I remembered what happened to Marguerite. She lived a good lifestyle, was young and strong. She wasn't protected, was she?

Marguerite, my mother's dear friend, had been like a second mother to me. The memories of her appeared in my mind now like a slide show: Marguerite and Mom sitting at the kitchen table chatting over tea and cookies; the tartan plaid skirt she gave me for my sixth birthday; playing in her breezy yard in the summer, giggling and drinking homemade iced tea with her daughter; the cool autumn afternoon we spent in her kitchen, just Marguerite and me, when she taught me to make her famous pumpkin pie. Then her cancer diagnosis: her brave fight, her decline, the funeral service where afterward her daughter and I clung to each other, sobbing. I found my body racked with sobs again. Marguerite was forty-seven years old when she passed away. I was forty-seven now.

That night, I tried in vain to sleep. I tossed and turned, counted sheep, even recited favorite lines from poems in an attempt to lull myself to sleep. When that didn't work I fluffed my pillows and kicked off my blanket. Dread and worry covered me in its place.

Just before my alarm clock was set to ring, though, I fell into a fitful sleep and began to dream: I was standing in my mother's kitchen where Marguerite and Mom sat at the table drinking tea and eating cookies. For what seemed like a long while, they just looked at me. Finally, my mother spoke. "Don't worry," she said, "Marguerite will help you." Then my alarm clock rang.

I'd like to say that I found peace as a result of my mother's encouraging remark, but throughout the day my confusion and dread grew as I continued to mull over my possible diagnosis. Later that afternoon though, as promised, I received the call from my doctor's office to schedule the surgery. The woman's voice on the other end of the line was calm and soothing as we selected a date. "Any questions or concerns?" she asked before we were to end the call.

"Well," I started, "I do have a few concerns." While I knew this kindly woman couldn't help me where my health issue was concerned, I could seek her expertise in navigating the business end of illness and all my worries about co-pays, prior approvals, and doctor's notes spilled out.

The soft-spoken woman on the other end replied quickly. "Don't worry," she said. "I can help you with those types of problems. Call me any time during office hours. My name is Marguerite."

Marguerite. Not Margo, or Margie, or even Margaret. I was silent for a moment as I took in the coincidence and finally, peace did come. To me, there was no denying that this moment was divinely directed and that the universe had sent me not one, but two women bearing the same name — one in heaven and one on earth — to help and encourage me. I felt as though all the bases were covered and went into my surgery with confidence in place of fear.

Does this story have a happy ending? You bet it does. The surgery was successful and the biopsy was negative. I was able to return to work in record time. In fact, my doctor commented that mine was one of the swiftest recoveries she had ever witnessed. But I knew it would be. Thanks to my heavenly dream team, the two Marguerites.

~Monica A. Andermann

27

Then There Was Light

*Knowing your own darkness is the best method for
dealing with the darknesses of other people.*
~Carl Jung

My thirty-year marriage was coming to an end. It had been a rocky road and it had taken its toll on my health, resulting in high blood pressure and diabetes. I had tried to leave numerous times but had been too afraid to cut the cord. My self-esteem was nonexistent. My husband had convinced me that I had no skills and wouldn't amount to anything without him. Finally, after one last altercation, I knew I had nothing to lose so I made the break!

I found myself alone for the first time in years, terrified and doubting that I could make it on my own. I was very anxious, especially at night. I couldn't sleep and I even found myself thinking about suicide. In the midst of the worst of my dark nights, I had the following dream:

I was driving my car on the freeway when I got a strong feeling that I was about to die. Everything around me was pitch-black. I held on to the steering wheel with all the strength I possessed. The only thing I knew to do was to continue driving. As I pushed down on the gas pedal, thinking at any moment I was going to die, I realized I couldn't stop the car for fear that the driver behind me would crash into me. I couldn't pull off the freeway and I couldn't change lanes in the total darkness. All I could do was keep going. My hands were shaking. Sweat was pouring down my face. So I began praying for help.

I kept praying and praying as I drove and stared straight ahead, willing myself to see something, anything! Suddenly, a tiny speck of gray appeared in the distance. I thought it was a mirage. I kept staring at it. It became the size of a dime. I kept praying and staring and driving. The gray speck grew to the size of a quarter. It kept growing… a little more… into the size of a half dollar. I still kept driving, praying for more light, and it grew a little more. Suddenly the darkness became a sheet of gray fog… but I could start to make out the other cars on the road. I began to think I would actually survive this.

I kept praying, but now instead of asking for help, it had become a prayer of thanks. I could now actually see the other cars on the road.

"I'm going to make it!" I heard myself exclaim.

When I woke up my pajamas were soaked with perspiration and my pillow drenched… with tears of joy! I was going to make it!

After that dream I felt like a heavy dark cloud had lifted and I had the clarity to reach out for someone to help me through this fragile time. I soon found a support group and a counselor for codependents. I'd always had visions of myself being a real estate agent, and my support group encouraged me to take courses to learn how to get my license.

The market was in the tank at the time I entered it, but I was feeling so good about my new life that I didn't know the difference. I just plowed ahead, and with my new upbeat attitude, I sold enough houses to earn the Rookie of the Year Award in my first year. I went on to win numerous awards, in fact. I worked "nine days a week" and made wonderful friends. I received tons of referrals from my satisfied clients, and bought and sold houses for my daughter and myself.

After ten years of successfully listing and selling real estate, I was approached by the owners of my company and was offered the position of Training Director. I held that position until my retirement this past year. I now golf as much as I can and lecture to as many women's groups as will invite me. My topic? You guessed it!

"Don't Be Afraid of the Dark… If You Keep Driving the Light Will Appear."

~Vicki Joseph

28

The Equinox

*There is such a special sweetness in being able
to participate in creation.*
~Pamela S. Nadav

"A baby?" I asked, untangling a pair of socks from my laundry bin.

His stare was steady. "Yes."

I felt the familiar tensing in my stomach. "I'm still not ready."

He sighed gently and then kissed my head before walking away. I could feel his disappointment.

My husband and I were in our thirties. I knew that time was of the essence, but I was afraid. The thought of diving into the unknown of parenthood and creating a family made me anxious. Maybe it was my mother's stories of delivering three babies in two years, and the ensuing chaos. It could also have been the painful miscarriages that had occurred to others close to me. I had so many fears: the pain of childbirth, the fear of a complicated pregnancy, and the overwhelming responsibility of parenthood. It all scared me.

"A child is born in his or her own time," my mother had told me. "You will feel the aching in your heart and know when the time is right."

And my heart did, in fact, ache. But I was afraid, too.

Then, one night, in a deep sleep, I had a miraculous dream:

An angel with majestic wings flew swiftly toward me, holding a ball of light in her hands. She whispered, "You will be given a child on the equinox."

She put the ball of light into my abdomen as she spoke and I immediately felt a warm sensation all over my body, calming me and instilling in me with a new courage.

I awoke and shook my husband. "What's an equinox?" He mumbled something about a moon and rolled over.

The next day I learned, of course, that the equinox is when day and night are of equal length. The next equinox was in three months — the spring equinox on March 20th. I told my husband I would like that to be the official start date of our "trying" period.

He gave me another smile, a goofy one this time.

Four months later I was in my doctor's office. He held the ovulation calculator in his hand, attempting to ascertain my baby's date of conception.

"Looks like…" He pushed his glasses toward his face.

"March 20," the doctor and I said in unison.

"The equinox," I explained, waving my hands about vigorously.

The doctor nodded. "You're not the first woman in my office who blamed the moon for this." He laughed out loud.

I put my hand on my belly and silently thanked that angel for her gentle prompting. I would be a mother at last.

~Michele Boom

Chapter 4

Dreams and Premonitions

Early Warnings

First Alert

And in today already walks tomorrow.
~Samuel Taylor Coleridge

Has a dream ever grabbed you by the shoulders and demanded to be remembered? I still recall the moment as vividly as when I first experienced it in May 1970.

In my dream I was driving a car, and when I put my foot on the brake it went right to the floor. The car turned over, but I got out unharmed.

I awoke with my heart beating rapidly, heavy beads of perspiration cascading down my face; even catching my breath was difficult. I looked around my bedroom for some trace of reality, something to tell me I was safely at home and not in an accident. I focused on the moving curtains and knew I was in bed. As a psychology professor teaching at a Washington, D.C. university, my first reaction to the dream was analytical. The dream had to be telling me to slow down in my academic activities before I crashed. I wrote down the dream and promptly forgot about it.

A week later I was driving on a busy street when I put my foot on the brake. The brake failed and my foot went right to the floor, just as it had in the dream. The emergency brake didn't work either. My intuitive voice came to my rescue and told me to make a quick right. I did, and the car came to a stop between two clothing stores — the only area of safety. My dream had alerted me to this possibility, though in real life I failed to get the brakes checked or make a connection between the dream message and the car crash. Little did I know at the time that I was being inducted into a strange new world — one where dreams really do come true.

I had another brake dream a week later, but it seemed implausible because I had a new Chevy Nova.

In this dream, I was driving down 15th Street, NW in Washington on my way to an 11 a.m. meeting. I put my foot on the brake pedal and it went right to the floor. I hear a pinging noise. A policeman came toward me and I noticed a No Parking sign. I asked the policeman if I could leave my car and go to my meeting. He agreed and off I went.

This time there was no rapid heartbeat on awakening, and I was amused at having another brake-failure dream. Once again, I wrote the dream in a notebook and forgot about it. Days later I was driving down 15th Street NW on my way to an 11 a.m. meeting. At some point, I applied the brake and, like before, my foot went right to the floor. This time I heard a ping. When I saw a policeman approaching, as well as the No Parking sign, I guided my car to the curb and realized real life was imitating the dream. How could this have happened? It turned out the brake cable had snapped in my brand-new car!

For weeks I was baffled and frightened that my dreams were coming true. There were no explanations about dreams predicting the future in my academic books.

I had another dream, in which I was frantically running to catch a connecting flight. In the dream, I missed my flight and lost my luggage. Though I dismissed this dream as a mere reflection of my fear of flying, I was in for quite a surprise the following day. The nightmare became reality when my plane was three hours late, I missed my connecting flight and my luggage was lost. The dream had warned me about the delayed flight and I ignored it.

I began to learn about nuance in these warning dreams. A dream about my big red handbag being stolen prompted me to take my small red bag to a fair. Not surprisingly that was stolen. When the dream showed a red bag, irrespective of size, I should have listened.

After ignoring many warnings about things that came true, I finally acknowledged these dreams as a great source of inside information. It took many years before I was introduced to the term "precognition" in the parapsychology literature to describe these dreams that came true.

Although these precognitive dreams provided warnings about bad things, there were also good dreams — positive previews of upcoming events. I was reminded about appointments I had forgotten, and foresaw an upcoming promotion, a new baby coming into the family and meeting my husband Jim.

Many years ago I asked my dreaming mind to help me locate a long-lost friend. This was before the Internet made such searches easy. I was trying to find Mike Malone, a well-known choreographer whom I hadn't seen for many years. Although he had lived in Washington, D.C., I had no idea where he had moved. I finally had an answer when I dreamt that I was talking to our mutual friend, choreographer, director and dancer Debbie Allen. I told her I was trying to find Mike, and Debbie said, "He's living on the West Side of New York." The next day I followed up and called information in New York City, which gave me a number for Mike Malone living on the West Side. Mike answered the phone and immediately recognized my voice. He said, "How did you find me? I just moved here yesterday." It was just another lesson for me that dreams can predict the future.

I learned the hard way that precognitive dreams can also prepare us for the untimely passing of friends and family. I had a precognitive dream preparing me for the untimely passing of my friend Victor. Sadly, I didn't heed the warning implicit in the dream and missed my chance to say goodbye to my dear friend. When the dream came, I had no idea that Victor would be going into the hospital two weeks later to have his heart medicine regulated. He unexpectedly succumbed right on the operating table.

My eyes are now wide open, and I am grateful for the inner compass that faithfully prepares me for upcoming events by sending me messages that prove dreams do come true.

~Marcia Emery

Technicolor Dreams

We cannot live only for ourselves. A thousand fibers
connect us with our fellow men.
~Herman Melville

It started as all Technicolor dreams do, brighter than real life, colors crisp and compelling, the scent of new grass growing and leaf buds blooming. The brisk warming scent of spring air was blowing in my face as I exited my car at the neighborhood Albertson's store and approached the entrance. As the automatic doors slid open, a friend and co-worker exited and we bumped into each other.

Vicki was crying. Huge sobs wracked her body. I grabbed her and asked, "Vicki, what's wrong?" She choked out, "Oh my God Susan, I can't believe he's gone. I just can't believe he's gone!"

I woke abruptly from the dream knowing full well that it was a premonition. My heart was racing and my thoughts and emotions were in turmoil. As I dressed for work that morning, I realized there was nothing I could do or say to warn Vicki that something bad was on the horizon. I only knew beyond a shadow of a doubt that at some point in the future she would depend on me to help her through a difficult time.

Still rattled by my experience, at break time that morning I was sitting with a close group of co-workers. I asked them for advice. We all came to the conclusion that there was really no way to predict who "he" was in the dream or when we would be called on to provide support to our friend, but we made a pact that day to be there for Vicki when we were needed. We exchanged home numbers to prepare for the predicted event.

Several months passed and my husband Lane came home from his night shift at the Boise Hewlett-Packard facility and told me that he had a new employee he was training. She was deaf, so it was difficult to communicate some of the technical concepts to her. He asked me, "Do you know anyone who has a beginning sign book that I could borrow so I can learn basic sign language?" The first person that popped into my head was Vicki, whose daughter was deaf. It was early in the morning, but I knew Vicki was an early riser. I called her at home, which I had never done before, to see if she had a sign book we could borrow.

The phone rang twice and Vicki picked up. She was crying. I asked immediately, "Vicki, what's wrong?" She replied, "Oh my God, Susan, I can't believe he's gone. I just can't believe he's gone!" The hair stood up on the back of my neck and my heart froze for a moment when I realized she had said those exact same words in my dream. Vicki went on to explain, "I don't know if I ever told you, but when I was younger, I had a son. I put him up for adoption. Last night he was driving home and was hit head-on and killed. I don't know how I am going to get back east for the funeral. With the medical expenses we've faced recently, we can't afford the plane ticket. What am I going to do?"

Calmly, I said, "Vicki, you stay right there. Let me call some friends and see what we can do to help." I immediately reached out to Brett, Betty and the rest of the support tree. To this day I don't know exactly how we pulled it off, but within four hours we had purchased Vicki a round-trip ticket. I called her and told her to get packed and get to the airport in time for the flight.

When Vicki returned from her trip and the funeral, she called me to thank us for helping. Then she said to me, "Susan, you never told me what prompted you to call me that morning." I explained Lane's need of a sign language guide for his new employee at HP. She said, "Oh my God! My daughter Deanna just started at Hewlett-Packard on the night shift. You don't suppose…?" It turned out that Lane's new employee was Vicki's daughter Deanna!

Lane was transferred to Loveland, Colorado and I was transitioning into a new career as a family search investigator when my co-workers decided to give me a going-away party at work. As we sat at the picnic table sharing cake and talking about moving plans, Vicki joined us. Brett looked at me, I looked back, and we both knew in that moment that we had to tell Vicki that she had received help in her darkest hour through exceptionally unusual means. As we recounted the entire event to her, from the premonition through the trip, she turned white, and then the tears started. I was never sure that she truly believed that a miracle happened when she needed it most.

Although twenty years have passed since this unusual event changed our lives, Vicki and I remain friends. I recently experienced another prompting that miraculously touched another family and shared that story with my friends, who have come to expect the unexpected when I listen to that small, still voice and act as directed.

When I wrote about the event on Facebook, Vicki commented on my post and mentioned her own story. I told her I had never shared her story before and asked if I could. If you are reading this today, you know that her answer was yes. We only hope that you are as touched as we both were by the events as they unfolded. Trust your small, still promptings and believe in your dreams.

~Susan E. Friel-Williams

Johnny's Flowers

Knowledge is the true organ of sight, not the eyes.
~Panchatantra

I attended my first funeral when I was about six years old. Our landlord's adult son, Johnny, whom I adored, passed from cancer. Although I had no concept of death at the time, I remember that, oddly, I wasn't surprised to hear the news.

I have a vivid memory of a crowded parlor packed tightly with people blocking my view. I was too short to see much, only catching a glimpse of a form lying very still in a casket whenever someone moved for a moment to allow me a glance. What struck me the most was the cloying smell of flowers that seemed to cling to everyone and everything surrounding me. It was then that I remembered smelling the same scent only a few weeks before, and then again on the eve of Johnny's death. Even at that young age, I was perplexed because it was winter and there were no flowers in our home.

I was both frightened and sad when I finally approached the coffin with my parents. Mama encouraged me to say goodbye, explaining that Johnny had gone to Heaven. I had heard about Heaven and knew it was a good place, so I waved at the still form.

"Bye bye Johnny. Say hi to Jesus," I whispered, sensing anything above a quiet murmur was unacceptable in the roomful of sobbing friends, neighbors and strangers.

As I grew, I often smelled Johnny's "funeral flowers." I called them that because, unlike regular bouquets, they had a distinct odor to my nostrils. They smelled like that funeral parlor long ago, so I associated the phantom redolence with Johnny's death. Even though the fragrance was always accompanied by an inner chill, I assumed it was his way of telling me he was thinking of me the way I learned angels do when they reach out from Heaven to say hello.

It wasn't until I was in my early thirties that I coincidentally realized there was a very odd, almost macabre, significance to the scent that had randomly haunted me since childhood.

I was visiting with my husband's aunts who lived upstairs from us. I began to sniff at the air without realizing that I was being obvious about it.

"Is something wrong?" one of the ladies asked me. I was immediately embarrassed, realizing she might be thinking I found her home stinky.

"Do you smell flowers?" I asked, knowing how she'd reply. No one ever did — including my own husband who was used to me inhaling deeply from time to time at the nonexistent odor.

"No, why? Do you?" she wondered, and I nodded. "Oh, wait — I used an air freshener earlier. Maybe that's it."

"Maybe," I agreed quickly, but knew that wasn't it. Like usual, goose bumps rose on my skin and, once again, I felt like that confused little girl in the room full of mourners.

I didn't give the incident much thought again until about three weeks later when I stood in my kitchen making dinner. The smell overwhelmed me again, even overwhelming the spicy aroma of the spaghetti sauce I was stirring.

Within a few minutes, I heard three distinct loud knocks on my ceiling — a code I'd long since established with the aunts as an emergency signal. Barely taking the time to turn off the stove, I rushed through the house and flew up the stairs.

"She's dead! I think my mother's dead," her daughter screamed as she yanked open the door.

"Call 911!" I shouted back as I ran down the hallway to her bedroom.

With the help of the dispatcher, who assured me paramedics were on their way, I tried to administer CPR, but knew instinctively that it was too late. We learned later that she had suffered a massive heart attack and died instantly.

The next day, still in shock, I remembered the flowers. Were they a premonition of her death?

A year later, my suspicions were confirmed. I was on a bus with a friend and we were discussing Christmas plans. That year we'd opted to stay home rather than make the customary hectic two-hour trip to my parents' house, deciding instead to spend several more relaxing days with them after the holiday instead.

As I mentioned my father, the familiar scent hit me, stronger than I'd ever experienced. I began to heave with nausea and had to get off the bus. My friend followed, asking what was wrong.

"My father is going to die," I gasped as she stared dubiously. "I need to get home and call him."

My tone was so powerfully urgent that she didn't even try to talk me out of it. We crossed the street, catching the next bus going in the opposite direction. When I got home, my phone was ringing. It was my mother. My father had been taken to the hospital by ambulance with severe chest pains. Though the doctors were concerned, they thought he'd be okay, but I knew with a strange certainty they were wrong. I told Mama I was coming immediately.

I stayed by his side in the hospital every night for two and a half weeks. The doctors still maintained he'd get better, but I disagreed. Two days before Christmas, I was forced to return home. I kissed my father goodbye. I knew in my heart I'd never see him alive again.

On Christmas Eve, right before midnight, the flower scent returned. An hour later I received the call. Papa had passed quietly in his sleep.

After that, I could no longer deny that I have a strange ability. Whenever I smell the mysterious flowers, I will hear of a death within three weeks. A second omen always comes during a twenty-four hour period before it happens. Sometimes I can predict who it would be, other times not, but inevitably, word that someone died will reach me. The odor can be extremely faint or overpowering depending how distant or close my relationship is to that person.

My family and close friends have become accustomed to what they refer to as my "creepy premonitions." Some are fascinated by it, others frightened, while others are convinced I am able to somehow stop the event from occurring. I can't. I only know it will happen and urge them to enjoy the little time they have left with their loved one when I can actually name the person who is going to die.

Over the years, I've done Internet searches on the subject. At first there was very little, but later there were more references to the phenomenon. Explanations vary — from the scent meaning angels are hovering near, or that Mother Mary is gracing me with her presence. There are even medical explanations that attribute this ability to the temporal lobe portion of the brain. Since I suffer from temporal lobe seizures, it seems plausible.

Psychics call it clairvoyance — accessing psychic knowledge through the physical sense of smell. I consider it a rare gift that has allowed me, and many close to me, to make peace with loved ones and friends and say goodbye to them before it is too late.

~Marya Morin

32

Banking on My Inner Voice

Our inner wisdom is persistent, but quiet. It will always whisper, but it will never stop knocking at your door.
~Vironika Tugaleva

It was August 1973. I had flown seventeen hours from Los Angeles for my first trip to Sweden. I checked into my hotel and asked how to exchange my U.S. dollars for Swedish krona. The friendly staff pointed out the bank next door. For some reason I changed my mind and decided to go later, after I dropped my things in my room and freshened up.

When I was ready to go to the bank, I again made a decision I did not understand. I chose to walk down all the stairs instead of taking the elevator from my high floor. When I finally entered the hotel lobby I could see something was terribly wrong. It turned out the bank was being robbed. I had almost walked into that bank at the worst possible time, just minutes before.

Because of security demands all the hotel guests were locked inside. Police negotiated throughout the standoff, in which four bank employees were held hostage in a stifling 11x11-foot vault. The employees started to identify with the robbers, and that was how the term "Stockholm Syndrome" was coined.

The ordeal lasted six days. My hotel was surrounded, so delivery trucks could not enter the roped-off zone. We hotel guests bonded with each other. The only food that was plentiful after a while was boiled white potatoes sprinkled with butter and parsley. To this day, that vision or taste takes me back to Sweden.

•••

And then it happened again!

It had taken me forever to refinance my house even though interest rates had fallen so much. I dreaded the paperwork. Finally I filled out the forms and went to the mortgage office. When we were finished, I was told to drive to the bank to finalize everything that very afternoon. I threw the thick packet of documents beside me on the front seat of my car and drove to the bank.

As I was pulling into the driveway I thought about people who were superstitious about banking on Fridays. I have never been superstitious yet that thought did cross my mind. I surprised myself by backing out of the driveway and driving to a nearby boutique instead.

I was barely in the door when there was an announcement over the loudspeaker: "Please stay in this store until further notice. The bank down the street is surrounded, with a robbery in progress. We are told hostages have been taken." All of us in the shop could hear the alarm and sirens.

It turned out that the robbers were not apprehended. Some of the hostages were hospitalized and one suffered a major breakdown. That could have been me.

•••

They say that things happen in threes. Believe it or not, it happened again!

A few years after the second bank robbery that I avoided, I was at Starbucks, hurrying toward the exit to get to my bank to order foreign currency for an upcoming trip. "Gail!" I heard. It was a former colleague I had not seen in years. I started to say I was in a hurry but then something changed my mind. We found a table and sat down to chat.

We were immersed in conversation when there was an announcement over the loudspeaker: "Stay inside until further notice. The bank in this parking lot has a robbery in progress." We could hear the alarm and sirens.

I have learned to listen to my inner thoughts and to trust my impulses. It has worked for me over the decades, again… and again… and again….

~Gail Small

Surviving Cancerland

*We have all a better guide in ourselves, if we would
attend to it, than any other person can be.*

~Jane Austen

O h no! It's happening again. I'm having the dream again: Tears fill my eyes as the dream shifts into a recurrent nightmare. I know what is coming.

A hooded, faceless Spirit-Guide dressed in a brown Franciscan monk's robe, complete with twisted rope belt and leather sandals, steps through the window that has become a doorway between realms. I have been taken there in three previous dreams over the past few months. "I know why you're here," I cry. "I did as you said and returned to my doctor without an appointment and asked for a different set of tests, but he would only give me another mammogram and a blood test. He said he could feel nothing where you put my hand in the last dream, and he told me to go home."

"Return to your doctor tomorrow and request exploratory surgery," says the voice behind the hood. "It will find your breast cancer."

"How can I get my doctor to perform exploratory surgery when he thinks I'm healthy? He says at age forty-four I'm too young for breast cancer; it doesn't run in my family, so I can't have it. If I do have cancer, and you want me to live, please help me," I plead.

The guide reaches into the sleeve of his robe and pulls out a tiny white feather. "Use this feather as a sword to verbally fence against your doctor's arguments, and you will get the surgery you need. Present your case as though you are a lawyer standing before an incredulous judge who does not like you." Then, he disappears.

What a Catch-22. Do I believe my learned doctor or my Spirit-Guide? And, how do I convince the one I do not believe that I am doing the right thing? Oh God! I'm so confused and frightened. All I have to fight with against a medical degree is an imaginary feather. Please help me, I silently pray during the hour and a half drive through snow and sleet to my doctor in Boston.

"Kathy, why are you back?" my doctor asks, after I follow him into his office.

"I know something is wrong and I want exploratory surgery on this area." I point to a spot at the eleven o'clock position on my breast. He looks aghast.

"I can't perform exploratory surgery on you just because you think something is wrong. All your tests have been healthy. It's against my policy and hospital policy. You have to think about complications like infection and anesthesia. Surgery is serious."

He's right. Surgery is serious, but so am I. Mentally, I point my tiny, white imaginary feather at him. "I know something is wrong, and you know me well enough to realize I'm not a hypochondriac. I'm not someone who relishes the idea of being sliced open and explored without reason. I don't know whom else to turn to. Please help me."

In the silence something miraculous happens.

"Okay. Let me see when I have an opening for surgery."

Did I hear him correctly? The feather worked. It cut right through the argument.

Two weeks later my doctor's voice drifts down to me in my floating anesthesia trance. "We got it all. Let's close her up." I claw my way up from the depths of inky nothingness toward a pinpoint of distant light, drag myself over the slippery side of the well of unconsciousness, turned my head and ask, "What is it?"

Pandemonium quickly follows the shocked silence. A voice behind my head asks, "Did she just speak?" as the blinding overhead light is blocked by pairs of eyes peering down at me. Eyes above masks surround me as everyone gathers to see the patient who awakened from anesthesia and spoke in the middle of surgery.

"It's what we thought it might be, Kathy — a fibrosis tumor. Nothing to worry about," my doctor stammers. "Give her more," are the last words I hear as pain engulfs me. I free myself from the sides of the well and slide back down into the blissful darkness of total nothingness.

"Pathology didn't like what they saw when they cut open the tumor," Dr. Wagner says in recovery while pulling the privacy curtain behind him and around us. That shocks me, and my grogginess and nausea are momentarily replaced by panic.

"Is it cancer?" I hold fast to the gurney, bracing myself for the answer I already know.

"Yes, I'm sorry. I'll get your husband and refer you to a specialist now."

Validation at last. My dreams were right and the tests were wrong. With my surgeon's words, the first shot of my ensuing battle has been fired, and it is not a warning shot across my bow. It is point blank into my breast. I glance down at the painful wound and weep. Thus begins my descent down the Rabbit Hole of Cancerland.

Dreams that drove me crazy also propelled me to action that may hopefully save my life. That must be the silver lining… if there is one to being diagnosed with cancer. I focus on that positive thought but cry louder. Through sobs, while cradled in my husband's arms, I speak to the guide in my head: "Thank you and please don't leave me now."

Over the next ten years of my numerous treatments and surgeries, my Spirit-Guides often return in prophetic dreams to help me survive two more cancers that include Stage 4 recurrence. Finding three cancers prophesied in dreams and validated by pathology reports is as lucky as winning the lottery three times in a row, though luck has little to do with it. Divine intervention does. The battles were eleven and sixteen years ago respectively. Today I'm still alive… and well.

My story proves that science goes only so far and then comes your own higher power in dreams, prayers and meditations. Your dreams and your nightmares may be a call to action, even a blessing in disguise. Let them guide you.

~Kathleen O'Keefe-Kanavos

In Midair

All a skeptic is is someone who hasn't had
an experience yet.
~Jason Hawes

"It's a small fast jet, it's a small fast jet!" The warning was loud and clear. I stood still as the voice warned of imminent danger. I looked toward the sky and checked my surroundings. As far as I could see there was only barren desert, with no jet in sight.

I could feel the hot sand under my feet and I suddenly felt the urge to run. I wove my way in and out of the dry vegetation, trying to avoid the rock formations jutting into my path, when I unexpectedly found myself sprawled out. I looked up and saw a small jet flying fast. I sat straight up to watch the jet, when it abruptly burst into flames!

"Oh my God," I shouted as I watched the jet plummet toward the desolate terrain. Instead of feeling the emotions of a bystander, I was now seeing everything through the eyes of the pilot. I floated toward earth as a new scene came into view. Below were numerous dark-haired men all dressed in forest green. I could feel their panic as I found myself on the desert floor running amongst them. Up ahead I spotted a small, frightened boy standing motionless amongst the chaos. I knew I had to get him to safety. I never slowed down as I swooped him up under one arm and continued running. Once I felt we were safe, I stopped and gently lowered the young boy to the ground. We spoke no words, yet seemed to communicate to each other that we were okay.

As I stood holding the boy's hand, one of the men dressed in green ran *into me, burning the palm of my free hand with a cigarette. I instinctively pulled my hand away, looking down at a perfectly scorched hole, as the dark-haired man dressed in forest green continued his frantic run.*

"Janie, wake up." I opened my eyes to see a concerned Michael holding me in his arms.

"It's just a bad dream, babe," he said sweetly. I sat up in bed and looked at my uninjured hand, realizing it was just a dream.

"Wow, that was a powerful dream." I closed my eyes and began to recount the dream. With each sentence I relived the vivid, realistic emotions I had experienced through the eyes of a pilot in distress.

"It was just a dream, babe," Michael repeated. "Go back to sleep."

"Sure, it was just a dream," I whispered, trying to convince myself.

The morning ritual at the King Abdul Aziz Airbase Hospital in the Radiology Department was always the same: coffee and a morning update. I shared my dream with the staff before I started my day as an ultrasound technologist.

Around 10 a.m. there was a knock on my door.

"They just brought in the pilot of an F-16 that crashed in the desert!" two staff members announced with disbelief.

"What?

"And the pilot is a Saudi prince!"

Could it be that I had actually foreseen a plane crash in a dream hours before it happened?

I quickly made my way to the workstation where our radiologist announced that I was forbidden to talk to the Saudi royal when he came in for X-rays. "You understand this man is royalty and you are forbidden to speak to him about this so-called dream?"

"Yes, Doctor," I lied.

Within minutes I had snuck into the back door of X-ray Room One, where I found a dark-haired man wearing a forest green jumpsuit. When the X-ray tech finished I fearfully approached the imposing figure, who thankfully didn't seem injured, and introduced myself.

"Hello sir, my name is Jane. I am the ultrasound tech here and I must tell you I had a dream about you and your fighter crashing in the desert last night." His eyebrows lifted.

"I'm so sorry to interrupt your exam, but I felt compelled to tell you."

I thought for sure the prince could hear my heart pounding as he contemplated my words. What had I been thinking? After what seemed like an eternity, in a deep, commanding, accented voice, the royal pilot announced, "I will send for you later." I thanked him and snuck out as quietly as I had snuck in. The last thing I imagined was that the prince would actually send for me.

Around 2 p.m. I found myself seated in what could only be described as Aladdin's cave. My eyes met with the imposing man regally seated upon his hospital bed when he commanded, "You will tell me about your dream."

I summoned up all my twenty-four-year-old courage and began recounting my dream. The fighter pilot validated my astonishingly accurate details. He told me he had a five-year-old son. He told me his only injury was to one of his hands. He told me the Saudi Air Force was doing maneuvers in the desert when his F-16 (a small fast jet) caught fire. He told me he safely ejected from the aircraft and landed without incident on the desert floor, where he was collected by multiple air force personnel all wearing the forest-green Saudi uniform.

As we drank tea from small, ornate gold cups the prince looked me straight in the eye and gave me this directive: "If you ever have another dream about me, you will call my commanding officer and you will ask for me and you will tell me about your dream."

"Yes sir," I responded.

"From now on I will call you the Dreamer," he stated, with his first smile.

For a moment I contemplated that future conversation: "Ah yes... Mr. Commanding Officer of the Saudi Air Force, this is The Dreamer. May I please speak to The Prince?"

I smiled, stood up and thanked the prince for seeing me. He looked at me with respect as we realized we had validated the power of the unknown, when our two extremely separate lives had intertwined with one giant leap and collided in midair!

~Jane A. Foley

35

Not My Child!

There is an instinct in a woman to love most her own child — and an instinct to make any child who needs her love, her own.
~Robert Brault, rbrault.blogspot.com

My friend Alice should have been sleeping. In fact, she had been sleeping, but her breathing had quickened until it came in gasps as though she was running. Suddenly she was awake, crying. Her dream had been so real, so vivid she stumbled out of bed and walked to the room beside the one she shared with her husband, Dan, just to check. Yes, all four children were there. It had been a dream.

But what a terrible one! Alice climbed back into bed, wide-awake now, and gripped with a heavy fear. Her mind replayed the dream: Their little family was walking over a footbridge crossing a busy city street. Dan was walking ten feet ahead of Alice with Evan by his side and little Joseph on his shoulders. Alice had the baby in her arm and Ellie by the hand. The baby slipped lower on her hip and, letting go of Ellie's hand for a second, Alice readjusted the baby. In that moment, a strange woman ran beside her, grabbed Ellie, and ran to a black getaway car that sat in a nearby alley. Ellie was gone!

The pain... the horror... the desperation... the futility of running after the car... it gripped Alice all over again until she felt tears raining onto her pillow.

"Please, God," she whispered. "Please lift this fear. It was only a dream."

Or was it? The days passed but the heaviness and guardedness Alice felt refused to lift. She told Dan about her dream and the nagging fears and together the two of them prayed over their children. They hadn't known that child trafficking was an issue in this Asian city until the dream alerted them and research confirmed that it was a major problem. "Oh, God," they prayed, "protect our children! Let this dream pass unfulfilled!"

Only when each child was thoroughly bathed in prayer did peace come. In fact, peace came so completely that Alice forgot about her dream until the day their family was restocking supplies in a large city miles away from the little outpost they lived in.

The city was crowded as usual and the footbridge they were crossing was clogged with people. Horns honked below them. Bicycle bells rang. Exhaust choked them. The children's tired feet were dragging, causing a little crowd to collect behind them on the narrow bridge.

"Let's stand to the side and let the people behind us go past," Dan suggested. "We're blocking the walkway."

The children, grateful for a brief rest, plastered themselves against the side of the bridge to let an equally grateful crowd pass them by. And then at the pace of the tired children, the little family made their way toward the bus stop. Dan, with Joseph on his shoulders, walked on ahead with Evan by his side. Alice followed them with the baby on her hip and Ellie holding her hand. Ellie's feet slowed and the distance between Dan and Alice widened.

Suddenly Alice felt uneasy. She glanced over her shoulder to see a lone woman still following them. It was the woman from her dream.

As if on cue, the baby slipped lower on Alice's hip. But Alice remembered the dream and there was no way she was going to readjust the baby now. Clamping her arm tightly across the baby's back in lieu of a readjustment, Alice picked up her pace, hurrying Ellie along. Ellie's small hand was clenched in her mother's iron grip. That woman wasn't going to get this child!

At the end of the footbridge was the alley from the dream. Alice stole a quick glance down the alley. Would it be there? It was. The black getaway car was there idling. Waiting.

Miracle of miracles, a rare taxi chanced past and was flagged by Dan, who had no idea of the drama unfolding behind him. As he opened the door of the taxi to lift the boys into it, Dan was startled as an ashen-faced Alice raced past him, leaped into the car, and pulled Ellie into it behind her.

The taxi doors slammed shut. Bus horns honked, the taxi horn responded in protest, and the little car carrying a family of six pulled away from the curb. The woman from the dream scowled. Her prey gone, she turned and disappeared into the crowd.

~Sara Nolt

Witness

Luck is where opportunity meets preparation.
~Denzel Washington

It was another beautiful day in Phoenix, Arizona. I had dawdled that afternoon and now I was stuck in rush-hour traffic. It was brutally hot, even with the air conditioner on. I just wanted to get home and have something cool to drink.

I was sitting at an intersection with traffic at a complete standstill. I saw a Chrysler convertible in the center lane facing me, waiting to make a left turn. I liked that particular model so it caught my attention. Normally I would have been looking at the horses in the field by the road. As I sat there looking at the car I heard myself say, "They're going to get hit." I watched.

There was a gap in the traffic and the Chrysler started to make a left turn. Just then a car illegally pulled onto the shoulder behind me and drove through the intersection! As she passed me I saw the driver, a girl, was looking at something inside her car. I watched as she slammed into the side of the convertible. When the debris stopped flying, she got out and made a call on her cellphone instead of checking on the other driver. From her body language, I didn't think she was calling the police. Nobody was checking on the driver of the convertible.

I pulled out of traffic, parked in the ditch and jogged up to the convertible. The windows were up. The driver, a middle-aged woman, was leaning against the door. She still had her seatbelt on and there was no blood. I opened the door slowly and asked if she was all right.

She told me she had hit her head on the window. She was dazed and confused and was trying to get out of the car. I stayed with her and talked to her to keep her calm. With that she seemed content to stay put until help arrived.

The police and paramedics arrived within minutes and soon had things under control. I left my contact information, returned to my car and left so there was at least one less vehicle in the way.

A couple of days later I received a call from an insurance adjuster wanting to hear my version of what had happened. I explained that the convertible did not whip out and try to make a fast dash across traffic, as the offending driver was claiming. The victim was making a slow and cautious turn, and could not possibly have seen the oncoming car, especially since it was speeding down the shoulder, where no one was even supposed to be driving.

"So you saw the actual impact?" he asked.

"Absolutely," I assured him. "I knew she was going to get hit so I made a point of paying attention."

He paused for a moment. "What do you mean, you knew she was going to get hit?"

"I don't know," I said, now realizing that comment made me sound like a nut. "I just had a feeling."

I was relieved when his next words were not dismissive or dripping with sarcasm. "You'd be surprised how often I hear that," he said.

~Beki Muchow

37

Too Busy to Listen

You learn something every day if you pay attention.
~Ray LeBlond

Raising four children and working part-time made for a hectic life. The last thing I had time for was analyzing my dreams. But one morning I woke up very disturbed by the video that had played in my head as I slept.

In my dream I was standing on the patio behind my house while a man dressed in a plain blue work shirt came walking through my back yard. The name patch on his shirt simply said "Utilities." He stopped about twenty feet away from me, turned his head to look me in the eye, and said, "You will not survive this." Then he walked out of sight.

The morning continued with all the usual fuss and confusion of children getting ready for school. The dream was pushed to the back of my mind until later that day when I shared it with a co-worker. She suggested I check my house for any safety issues. I suggested I stop drinking caffeinated soda before going to bed.

Six weeks later the school year ended and summer was in full swing; my dream was forgotten in a haze of planning vacations and barbecues. Then one day, while I was weeding a flowerbed, a truck pulled up in the front of the house and a lady from the gas company jumped out. She began walking down the street stopping at each house.

I assumed the lady was reading the meters, but when she entered our yard I saw that she had an unusual handheld tool that I had not seen before. I commented on the beautiful weather and asked what the tool was for. She explained that she was checking for leaks in the gas lines and offered to show me how it worked. I walked with her to the meter while she explained. She told me that to get a reaction from the tool there needed to be an unsafe amount of gas in the air. I thanked her and turned to go back to my flowerbed when I heard a beeping sound.

The rest of the day was spent watching a front-end loader dig up my front yard! My gas was shut off, and after several hours I was told that the leak was definitely on my side of the meter. I needed to have it repaired before the gas could be turned back on. I had four kids, three dogs, two cats and one husband with no hot water. I ate a lot of chocolate that week!

Three days went by before a repairman showed up, only to tell me that it would be another two days before the heavy equipment could get there to begin digging. Finally, with the yard dug up, the basement busted open and my bag of chocolate almost empty I wandered out to the side of the house to offer the repairman a glass of tea. He showed me our very scary leak.

Apparently, the pipe that connected the gas line to our furnace had numerous holes in it. The repairman held up a foot-long section of pipe that looked like it had been shot up by a machine gun. He explained that over time the pipe had deteriorated and leaked gas both into and outside the house. He told me that we were the luckiest people on earth. He said the next time I saw a news report about a house blowing up I should thank my lucky stars that it was not my house. He went on to explain that in his more than twenty years of working on gas lines he had never seen a more damaged pipe.

We got lucky for two reasons: There is a block wall in the basement that stopped the fumes from reaching the water heater, and the house was well over one hundred years old and not very well insulated, so we had good venting by accident.

The following day at work I explained everything to my co-worker. She thought about it for a moment and said in an ominous voice, "The dream."

Thinking back I realize that there were signs that something was wrong. The slight smell of gas I would encounter when getting home from work — a smell I usually forgot about shortly after ushering the dogs outside and running out to check the mail. Not to mention the heating bills that seemed to get higher and higher every year. And finally, the dream. That dream was trying to tell me something that I must have known subconsciously.

I promise to slow down and listen next time.

~K.S. Bair

Tuned In

*Making the decision to have a child is momentous. It is
to decide forever to have your heart go walking around
outside your body.*
~Elizabeth Stone

I gave birth to my only child when I was five months pregnant. He weighed one pound, seven ounces, and wasn't expected to live more than seventy-two hours. Those first three days were filled with uncertainty, tears, and lots of prayers. But he made it through his first month, with the help of multiple blood transfusions, and it was on to his second month.

Very early one morning I had a dream that I was driving through parking lots around old buildings looking for my baby. I kept saying, "I have to find him, he can't breathe." As I circled the lots, I became more panicked, until finally, I was inside an abandoned school building. I ran though corridors and up staircases looking for him until I opened the door to a classroom that contained one antique student desk. I looked around the room, and there it was: the incubator that housed my baby boy. I felt relief, and yelled to no one in particular that I had found him. He was breathing again, but I noticed that it was extremely cold in the classroom.

I woke up and immediately called the hospital. Instead of hearing the usual morning report about how much he "ate" through his feeding tube and how much he weighed, the nurse was flustered and shared that my son was in distress. She said that the doctor decided to remove the ventilator to see if he could breathe on his own. He took one breath and his lung ripped. He was too underdeveloped to attempt breathing independently. A breathing tube was surgically inserted into the lung, and he was given a significant amount of morphine to ease his pain. The nurse told me that I needed to get there as soon as possible.

I arrived at the hospital to find my son terribly weak but no longer in respiratory distress. I approached his incubator both relieved and thankful. I checked his oxygen levels and all other numbers on the multiple monitors to which he remained connected, and noticed straightaway that his temperature was significantly lower than usual. Upon closer inspection, I found that the opening to the rear chamber of the incubator had been left ajar. I stuck my hand inside, and it was frigid, just as in my dream.

I was sure that I experienced a premonition in my dream that morning, but I couldn't understand the reference to the parking lot and the old school building. Why did I find him in a school and why was I driving through parking lots?

Eventually, I read a history of the hospital and discovered that in the nineteenth century, before operating as a medical facility, the building was used as an orphanage and maternity home. In the early 1900's, it added a nursing school and its transition to a full-fledged hospital began. In the 1950's, the medical center moved to its current location and the former facility was torn down. Today, a parking structure stands in that original location. Needless to say, I have a full understanding and appreciation of that dream and I know I'll never forget it.

When all was said and done, my beautiful son stayed in the Neonatal Intensive Care Unit four months and he got better and better. I was able to take him home when he tipped the scales at four pounds, one ounce. In that month, he became a proud recipient of the NICU's "Little Piggy Award!" Now in his twenties and a father himself, I am proud to say that he beat the odds. He has strong lungs and no deficits... and I'm still paying close attention to the meanings and messages of my dreams.

~D.L. Teamor

Dreams and Premonitions

The Next Generation

Dreaming Rose

Family is not an important thing. It's everything.
~Michael J. Fox

The baby appeared to be about eighteen months old. Her eyes caught me first: large, dark, slightly almond shaped, and gazing at me with an unblinking, imploring look. I noticed that she had stringy dark hair and was wearing nothing but a saggy cloth diaper.

As I wondered who this sad, beautiful child was, her skinny arms reached up to me, appealing wordlessly for me to pick her up. I had never seen her before but something about her looked strangely familiar.

Before I could figure out who she was, I woke up.

The next night, the sad little girl appeared in my dreams again. This time she reached up to me right away, whimpering, a desperate look on her face. Heart aching, I crouched down to pick her up.

Once again I awoke too soon. I knew what I had to do. Startling my husband out of his own slumber, I cried, "There's a baby out there that needs me!"

Mark moaned and rubbed his eyes. "Who needs you? Are you talking in your sleep?"

"Wake up! You need to hear this," I told him, and described how the same baby girl had come to me two nights in a row needing my help. Mark sat up straighter. I had his full attention now. We took dreams seriously in our family; conceiving our first child had also been presaged by a dream about having a baby three nights in a row.

Who was this particular child, and where in the world could I find her? She looked somewhat Asian, and we weren't, so I knew we weren't having another baby. No — this child was already alive. There seemed to be only one possibility: We were fated to adopt this little girl, and divine forces were getting the ball rolling by introducing us in the dreamtime. Our task now was to find her. The enormous hurdles of legal requirements, paperwork, and other red tape were the furthest things from my mind.

For the next few weeks I researched as obsessively as one could in those pre-Internet days. I lived in one of the most international communities in the States. I knew adoptive parents, international lawyers, and people who had worked abroad with refugees. I asked everyone who knew anything about overseas adoption — for I was convinced this baby was not American — where a baby who fit my dream-child's description might be living.

With a few leads in hand, I suddenly remembered that my younger brother, Jay, had just returned after a long stint with the Navy in Southeast Asia. Perhaps he had seen firsthand where there were at-risk or orphaned children. Having not spoken to him in years, I found Jay's number and called him out of the blue. After a quick greeting to welcome him back home, I jumped right in to describe my quest and asked if he could point me in the right direction. After a long pause, Jay cleared his throat and said, "Funny you should ask…"

And then he gave me the surprising news that he had married an eighteen-year-old woman in the Philippines who stayed behind with their baby while he looked for a job and house in Texas after his discharge. When they went to the airport a few months later to join him in their new home, however, they were detained by government officials who asked for a large sum of cash to allow baby Rose, whose paperwork or passport was apparently not in order, to be taken out of the country. Because Lily, my sister-in-law, didn't have the money, they refused to let the baby go, so Lily left their daughter with her sister, who had driven them to the airport.

She didn't know what else to do. She thought her husband could fix things, only he couldn't do anything about it because he didn't have money for flights and legal costs either. He was already too much in debt with the only lender he knew — our father, who had been adamantly opposed to Jay's marriage — to ask for further help. He had been trying to save, but was making very slow progress with his meager income. By this time, his daughter had been in the Philippines for six months, his wife was beside herself with anxiety and feelings of powerlessness, and my brother wanted to make things right but just didn't know where to turn.

Hearing Jay's story was shocking on so many levels I could barely breathe. Then it struck me: My dream-baby was his! Regardless of the circumstances that led to her abandonment, little Rose needed help, and help she would get.

"Jay, are you saying that all it will take to get your baby back is money? That's it?"

"That's it. Lily could fly back to get Rose tomorrow if we had the plane fare and paperwork fees."

"How much are we talking about, exactly?" I asked, expecting to hear a number so high that it would put into perspective his fears about asking to borrow such a sum. Indeed, Jay named a not-insignificant sum. As luck would have it, I had exactly half of what he needed in a savings account I had opened for emergencies six months earlier — the same week my niece had been detained.

Events moved quickly after that. I raised the rest of the money needed from other family members. My sister-in-law got a flight within days and headed to the Philippines to retrieve her baby, with a planned layover in my city on her way home. Two weeks later, I stood waiting at the airport to meet both Lily and Rose for the first time.

I worried about being able to pick Lily out of the crowd of young women emerging into the terminal, having never seen her picture. My fears melted away when I recognized Rose, my dream-baby, in the arms of a lovely young woman. "Lily!" I called, rushing in their direction before waiting for an answer. Rose held her arms out to me, just as she had in my dreams, and Lily offered her up to me.

Snuggling my niece felt so familiar, though I was startled by how light she was. She was very small for her age, frail, and painfully thin.

The past six months had apparently not been kind to this innocent child. I hugged her tighter, sending a heartfelt prayer of thanks to all of divinity for sending those dreams and saving our sweet girl in time.

Rose, Lily, and my family spent a wonderful week getting to know each other. My daughters doted on the baby, sharing their toys and serving her the tastiest treats from their own plates. We shopped for baby clothes, necessities, and toys. By the end, just in time to fly to her new home, Rose finally smiled for the first time.

Never again did I dream of my lost baby. She had been found, bringing all of us — her family — together in the process.

~Gale Roanoake

Baby in a Matchbox

Sometimes the heart sees what is invisible to the eye.
~H. Jackson Browne, Jr.

She was five and a half months old when a teenaged Chinese nanny put her in my arms in the Hangzhou Overseas Chinese Hotel. For two months I'd been staring at her picture, a grainy black and white photo of a girl on her back, her toothpick arms ending in tiny fists. Now she looked up at me, swaddled in three layers of ragged wool sweaters and a green and yellow knit cap. Under the layers she was thin, sweaty and hungry.

Two hours later, at a round table in a Hangzhou restaurant, six families were holding, stroking, and comforting six brand-new black-haired baby daughters amid the clanking of plates and the sizzling smells of garlic and fish. Jin Mei sat in my lap and began to suck on a bottle I held for her, and I started to cry.

But I loved her even before that. She was born in May of 1995. Nine months before that, in September of 1994, I had an intense dream:

A tiny baby girl, the size of a fingernail, is being kept in a miniature pink plastic doll inside a one-inch-square matchbox. The parents don't want to keep her and have given her to my Aunt Mary. I tell her it is important to keep babies next to your skin, and she answers that she did that with her children. I am worried about how vulnerable and crushable this baby-in-a-matchbox is, so I take on the job of carrying her against my skin. I wish they would give me the child to raise, that I could have her for my own.

I was forty-one years old when I had this dream. I wasn't married and had no plans to adopt. I was living with a busy man who did not understand the extent of my hunger for a child. A few months later, when I finally broke down in despair, the hero inside my partner woke up. Suddenly the lights, which had been red for so long, were all green.

Swept along in the speedy early days of Chinese international adoptions, we got married in April, filed our sheaf of application papers in May, and by Halloween we were parents. It didn't seem fast to me. It seemed wonderful, holy, as if some slow-growing cactus had suddenly blossomed and brought forth an orange.

The exact timing of the dream only dawned on me later as I combed through my journals and collated all my big dreams. I'd had it around the time she was the size of a fingernail. I became in some mysterious fashion pregnant with her, though she was thousands of miles away and in some other woman's body. The dream was right about the matchbox: she was a tiny match, ready to kindle a fire and be a light for us.

That moment in the restaurant when she took her first hard suck from the bottle I held was the spark of our new life, the one where I got to feed her. She was thin, but gained a pound a week for six weeks after we got home, until she caught up. In eighteen years of living together I never got over the sweetness of cooking for her — fried rice, latkes, lasagna — because she eats so happily.

Now she's a thousand miles away, a stressed-out college student. She works three jobs, is ashamed to get an A-minus, teaches swing dance, and rides the city bus for four hours to practice at a ballroom studio. She doesn't have a boyfriend, worries about money, and slams out fine essays overnight.

She doesn't call much, and her younger sister Zhen Zhen watches me fret and miss her. She told me, "Mom, I won't abandon you," and has applied only to colleges within driving distance. I'm glad she'll be closer. I'm not cut out for the empty nest thing.

It was a life's work to find these girls and nurture them. The trail led through infertility surgeries, a teeth-gritting ectopic pregnancy that cost me my only fallopian tube, and two divorces. I was forty-two when Jin Mei was put in my arms in Hangzhou and forty-five when

Zhen Zhen's nanny handed her over, screaming, in Changsha.

The other day on the phone, Jin Mei's voice was flat with distress. I started to suggest that she drop one of her projects, but caught myself. "I'm just trying to keep you from hitting the wall," I said. "But I guess it's your wall to hit."

"Yeah," she said. "Just be there to peel me off after I hit it."

My mother peeled me off the wall when I came home broke and shaken from a year of rough travel in Europe at the exact age Jin Mei is now — turning twenty. I had fifty cents left in my pocket when I landed in Boston. My parents sent me a plane ticket home to Oregon. I hope my daughter never feels as lonely and in need of rescue as I felt then. Of course I don't want her to hit the wall, any more than I want her to live outside my sphere of everyday cuddling. I'm heartsick that she is far away, but if I look sideways and breathe deeply, she isn't.

Ever since she started to suck on that bottle in the Hangzhou restaurant, loving her has meant taking care of her. That's the job I took on. But now that she is a thousand miles away, I get to step back into the dream I had before she was born and let it carry me as I once carried her. The miracle of how that dream turned out — that she landed in my arms a year later in her too-many sweaters and knit cap — tells me our connection continues whether she is in China or Colorado. We belong to each other.

~Tina Tau

41

What Grammy Knew

*He who has gone, so we but cherish his memory, abides
with us, more potent, nay, more present
than the living man.*
~Antoine de Saint-Exupéry

One of the most important women in my life was my grandmother. She was already seventy-two when I was born. Her only daughter had died when she was one year old, and her other kids — my dad and uncle — were boys. Grammy was very excited when my sister and I were adopted, because now she had granddaughters.

My mama had her hands full with a two-year-old boy and two newborn baby girls, so Grammy helped out for a while. She told my mama she could take care of my sister when she was with us, but I was hers. Maybe that's why we always had a special bond. Even though we weren't biologically related, everybody always said I inherited my grandmother's personality. I have a picture of us when I was very young. We had been watching a parade, and I was passed out in her lap. It's my favorite picture of us.

Grammy died suddenly during my senior year of high school, just one month before her March 18th birthday. She would have been ninety-one. Every weekend for months after that we made the two-and-a-half-hour drive to clean out her house.

It was a sad time. We had just spent Christmas with Grammy in that house. Now it was cold and every room held nothing but dusty belongings and memories. I remembered eating breakfast at that kitchen table; sitting on the heat register upstairs to get warm on a frosty morning; trying to play her electric organ while she sat at her desk across the room. I missed her.

Many years passed, and then, in June of 2013, just before my twenty-seventh birthday, I had the first dream. At that point, I was experiencing a lot of stress in my career and I wasn't feeling well. In my dream, Grammy was sitting on my bed, smiling, and telling me something very important. I couldn't figure out what she was trying to tell me, but I woke up feeling calm and reassured.

Almost three months later, my fiancé handed me a pregnancy test. I couldn't believe he suspected I was pregnant, because when I was sixteen, I'd been diagnosed with Factor V, a blood clotting disorder. It can be very hard for women with Factor V to become pregnant, so I'd been devastated.

But the test was positive! That week, I took six more tests. All positive. A blood test and an ultrasound confirmed it. I was going to have a baby. Was that what Grammy had been telling me in my dream?

In the following weeks, the dreams kept coming. In one, we were in her front yard and everything was in bloom. She was telling me to take care of myself because she had something very special for me.

As I got further into my pregnancy, I continued to dream of Grammy. I was usually at her house, drinking lemonade and listening to her stories. She told me I would have a girl and that she would be everything I expected, and more. She talked about when I was a baby, and told me what a cutie I was.

Finally, as my due date approached, I started having a very puzzling recurring dream. For a couple of weeks, I kept finding myself in Grammy's house, back in the same room where I used to try to play the organ. The dream was so real and vivid that I could feel the warmth of the sun coming through the windows onto my face. Grammy sat at her desk, the way she used to. She didn't speak to me at all — just tapped some small object on her desk and smiled at me, as if she was trying to tell me something about it. Maybe this was the special surprise she'd said she had for me.

I took my maternity leave March 1, 2014. I'd already been diagnosed with gestational diabetes, and a week later I was also diagnosed with preeclampsia. My doctor scheduled me to be induced the next Monday. I was already sleep-deprived because of the pregnancy, but now I had new worries to keep me awake at night.

That weekend, my fears even invaded my dreams. I was sitting on my bed crying and Grammy came and sat down next to me. She held my hand, hugged me and wiped my tears. She said everything was fine and that she would be with me the whole time.

Early Monday morning — March 17th — my fiancé and I went to the hospital, expecting we would be having a St. Patrick's Day baby. It was the longest and most painful day of my life. My mama and sister came to give me support and encouragement, but midnight came and went with no baby. Finally, I told them to go home and get some sleep.

No sooner had they made it home and into bed, about 3 a.m., than the doctor decided I needed an emergency C-section. They made it back just in time to see me being wheeled into the operating room.

About 7 a.m., we were blessed with a beautiful baby girl. Everything Grammy had told me was true.

As we were waiting to be moved from the birthing suite to a private room, my mama said, "Well, you didn't get your St. Patrick's Day baby, but do you know what today is?"

It was March 18th — what would have been Grammy's 100th birthday.

Mama said, "It's like it was planned this way."

Was this what Grammy knew all along — what she'd been telling me? As my daughter celebrates her first birthday, I can't help but feel that Grammy is watching over us and enjoying her great-granddaughter.

But all I can do is imagine it, because after I went to the hospital to be induced, my dreams of Grammy stopped. I haven't had one since.

~Elena Mankie

42

The Journey to Grace

*I do not at all understand the mystery of grace — only
that it meets us where we are but does not leave
us where it found us.*

~Anne Lamott

I had gone on this retreat wanting to improve my business skills, and came out of it having experienced a personal and rather unexpected premonition with a clarity that startled me. It happened during a visualization exercise, when I closed my eyes and traveled to some point in the future:

I sat in my office at home in my rocking chair. A young woman came to the door and lingered there a few moments, smiling and talking. She wore a long white dress and no shoes, and she was radiant. She had very dark skin, short hair, a round beaming face, and huge beautiful dark eyes. She said "Hi, Mama" and somehow I knew she was my daughter.

"How was the retreat?" my husband Robert asked the day after I arrived home.

I burst into tears. "We are going to adopt a little girl from Africa!" I sobbed, realizing I sounded like a nut case. We already had two sons and a hectic and frequently stressful household. Robert usually took everything in stride, but this time he looked at me in shock, nearly choking on his coffee.

"What?"

I told him all about my premonition, but said, "We don't need to do this right now."

I decided I would call our adopted daughter Grace. The 'G' stood for Gillian, after my mum, fulfilling a Jewish tradition to take the first letter from a special family member's name. The name Grace represented beauty, calm, peace, and a regal elegance to me. I loved the name.

I started researching adoption. Over the next few weeks, the Democratic Republic of the Congo kept appearing on my web searches and e-mails. Whenever the DRC popped up in my inbox, I would think, "I hope it won't be there. It's too scary. I don't want to go there." This is a country at war almost perpetually since 1998 — a place where the weapons of warfare are rape and sexual violence against women and girls. I felt a connection to the country, but at the same time a great fear of having to go there to adopt a child.

I threw myself into my research. Within the adoption community, so many caring people reached out to help. We spoke to many families who had adopted children from the DRC. As I gathered information and connected with them, the picture improved dramatically. When we finally settled on adopting from the Congo, it felt right for us both.

Six months after we started the adoption process, I was in London on a business trip. It had been a fantastic day. After wrapping up a workshop I was running, I headed back to my hotel. I was happily exhausted and getting ready for bed when I called Robert at home in California to check on him and the kids and say goodnight.

"Did you receive the e-mail?" Robert said.

"What e-mail?"

"There's an e-mail in your inbox from our adoption agency. You must have seen it by now."

I scanned through my e-mail quickly. "No, nothing."

"Well, check in your deleted folder or your junk folder."

"I still don't see it."

"Well," he says, "You have to see this e-mail because it's about a little girl up for adoption. It wasn't specifically sent to us as an option because she is four, maybe five, and we asked for a two-year-old, but I think you should see this e-mail. I'll forward it to you."

The e-mail pinged into my inbox:

Subject: Need a home for a waiting child.

Message: Please pass the word. This girl is at our orphanage and is about five years old. There is very little background on this child. I am sorry we had to shave her hair. There were lice when this group of children came in. She is 41 inches tall, so that is 50% for age four, but since most of the children are malnourished, we added a year to be on the safe side.

Attached was a photo of a little girl with huge eyes and a little half smile. Her eyes were huge, like two deep pools of hope. She was holding a placard in front of her, which I didn't register initially, because I was completely immersed in her eyes, as if she were looking right into me and saying, "Mama, here I am. I'm waiting for you."

My eyes flooded with tears of joy, relief, calm, peace, and excitement all at the same time.

"There's our girl," I whispered. I was in love, instantly and undeniably. It was exactly like the moments when I gave birth to my sons, when I held them in my arms — I could have walked across the earth and back for them. I had read somewhere this could happen when you adopt, that you see that first picture and you somehow know. To tell you the truth, I thought the story was a bit of adoption folklore. How could it possibly happen with a photo? But it happened that day to me and I knew, somehow, that she was the one.

I sat on the bed in my hotel room, still dressed up in business attire and make-up, on the phone with Robert, tears streaming down my face. I could hear Robert talking away on the phone. His words became coherent again and he was saying something about the placard and wasn't it so cool?

"What's cool?" I said, finally conscious.

"I said look at her name placard," Robert repeated.

I looked. "Her actual real name is Grace?"

If ever there was a moment in my life where time stood still and my heart thumped inside my chest, this was it. I may have actually heard angels singing! It was such a confirmation. I didn't need one, but there it was. This was our Grace.

~Dr. Sam Collins

43

I'll Be Back

Dreams are today's answers to tomorrow's questions.
~Edgar Cayce

People often laugh when I say that each of my children came to me in a dream before I even knew I was pregnant. I strongly believe this gift came to me because of the incredible experience I had with my first child — a child I nearly had as a teenager.

I was living a fairly irresponsible life when my two friends and I ended up at the women's clinic. All three of us were pregnant. The weary OB/GYN suggested we each meet with a counselor to decide what to do.

I didn't meet with the counselor, nor did I feel the polar reactions of my two best friends — one terrified, the other elated. Instead, I went home to an empty, dirty apartment in shock. I knew how my boyfriend would react. I would be completely alone, my family half a world away.

I moved through the next several hours in a fog, attempting to deny the truth. Finally, I accepted my painful reality.

Then suddenly, I was in paralyzing pain and it was clear I was having a miscarriage. I felt so guilty. Had I wished this to happen? Late that night, after hours of agony combined with relief, I had a vivid dream.

I can still recall the smell of the meadow in which I sat. Surrounded by bluebells, snapdragons, and myriad wildflowers, a young curly-haired toddler stood on our red-and-white-checked picnic blanket facing me. An overwhelming warmth and joy enveloped my heart as she spoke. "It's all right, Mom. Now's not the right time. My name's Krystal Kaye, and I will be back." Hot, wet tears streamed down my face as a gentle breeze blew through my hair. I became aware of my boyfriend sitting with his back to me on the blanket. Krystal Kaye stepped closer, whispering, "It's okay," as she hugged me fiercely.

My crying woke us both, and the story of my dream poured forth between tears. My boyfriend's response temporarily shattered my sense of newfound comfort. "That's stupid; you're just upset about miscarrying. Besides, I'd never name a girl Krystal."

A year and a half later I was pregnant again and felt sure Krystal planned to keep her promise. Even though our ultrasound tech told my fiancé that we were having a boy, I held tight to my belief. One day, a couple of months before our "son" was due to arrive, I casually asked what girl's name we should use in case the tech was wrong. The news played quietly in the background, and the reporter's name lazily scrolled across the screen: Crystal.

"Well, that's a pretty name," he casually replied. "Though I think it should be Crystal with a K. Wait, that's perfect. If we have a girl, how do you feel about Krystal Kaye?" I held my breath tight, determined not to spoil this moment by bringing up the dream. "Of course, you know that's really unlikely, right? The ultrasound tech said we're having a boy. I can't wait to meet Jasper."

Two months later, we proudly held Krystal Kaye in our arms. My baby girl kept her promise, and the picture I drew of her from my dream sits proudly next to the identical real-life photo of her picnicking in a meadow. Our family was always meant to be.

~Kirsten Nelson

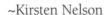

44

The Fertility Specialist

*Mother love is the fuel that enables a normal human
being to do the impossible.*
~Marion C. Garretty

My mother was a special woman. It's hard to put into words, but somehow we all believed she possessed a rare gift, like she always knew a bit more than she let on. Her premonitions were always spot-on. Deep down I knew I had inherited this ability, but I spoke of it infrequently or only when one of my predictions was proved accurate.

I was living in California in the 1990's, married with a five-year-old daughter. We had tried unsuccessfully for the past four years to have another child. I called my mom and she asked the usual question: "So, when are you having another child?"

I was one of nine, so having an only child to her was inconceivable. I explained to her that I had made an appointment with a fertility specialist. She responded as expected: "You don't need a fertility specialist. You just don't pray enough." I assured her that I prayed, but unfortunately I needed more than prayers at this point. My thirty-second birthday was around the corner and I really wanted answers.

A few days later, my beloved mom, who was barely seventy and in good health, unexpectedly died in her sleep. I went back to New Jersey for the funeral. It was surreal walking through the door and seeing her petite body in a casket; and then something even more surreal happened. I was halfway to her when I felt a force hitting me in the gut. It was like an air gun had hit me. I felt my body pushed back. I continued to make my way to her, but now with a smile. I knelt before her and shook my head. "I know what you just did. I know what just happened there. You never cease to amaze me, Helen."

The following day, which was my thirty-third birthday, my mom was laid to rest. I returned home to California exhausted and drained. I missed my little Lauren and needed to be home. I lugged my suitcase out of the car and began walking up the path to the front steps. The first thing I noticed was a box on my front porch. I put down my suitcase and with trembling hands I opened it. The first thing I saw was her handwriting on the outside of the birthday card. Inside the box was a beautiful white statue of a mom holding a baby boy. Today it remains in a hutch in my living room.

Logan was born on August 13, 1996, exactly nine months to the day my mother was laid to rest.

~Mary Ellen Flaherty Langbein

45

Knowing

Happiness, I do not know where to turn to discover
you on earth, in the air or the sky; yet I know you exist
and are no futile dream.
~Rosalia de Castro

I kiss my son goodnight again. He is fast asleep now, arms around his Ugly Doll, stuffed animals gathered all around him. I touch his thick brown hair that gets wavy if it isn't kept short. I kiss his eyelids that cover brown eyes so dark the pupils are almost indistinguishable. I kiss his nose, its shape beginning to emerge as the cartilage and bone come into formation defining his proud Maya heritage.

He is my youngest. Is my precious son aware he is where he is meant to be? I know it, and it humbles me.

My son came to me in dreams, little wispy yearnings growing more insistent until I could no longer ignore them. It came to a head one year in November when my husband and I were in Chicago, taking a weekend break from our son and daughters. I had had an emotional week, crying over just about anything. I felt full and raw, emotional as if I were pregnant. While waiting for our table at a restaurant, amidst the Latin music, margaritas, and bar conversations, I blurted out to Mark that I wanted to adopt another baby.

The conversation was emotionally wrenching and full of surprises for both of us. I hadn't planned this exchange. I answered my husband's questions, not knowing where the answers originated. I felt as though

I was being guided to answer, and all of the answers just popped into my head without any forethought.

Mark, taken aback, asked me, "Where do you think this baby is?"

I heard myself say, "In Guatemala."

"Why?" he asked.

Shaking my head, I said, "I don't know. I just feel that the baby is there."

He paused, really looking at me, "And what do you think this baby is?"

"A boy." I smiled at him through my tears.

"A boy?"

"Yes." I had his full attention now.

Silence from my husband, and then, "Has he been born?"

Wow. This one threw me, but the answer came with certainty. "He has or will be soon."

That surprised him. Me, too. I felt my child's soul doing everything it could to get my attention. And I was sharing all of it with Mark.

My husband didn't say no; it would have been hard to. I had unintentionally ambushed him there in the restaurant with hysterical tears. He said he would think about it and that I should just leave him alone with it for a while. I was more than willing to give him the time. I felt very hopeful.

Two weeks passed. Holden, our oldest, came into my upstairs bath to tell me, "Dad said to tell you yes."

I walked out into the hallway where Mark stood. He was crying.

"Is this about the baby?"

Nodding, Mark drew me into his arms. Holding me tightly, he said, "I don't know what's going on. I went into Holden's room saying I needed to talk to him about something important, something that affected our family. He asked if it was about his baby brother. I don't understand this, but somehow Holden is connected to all of this. You need to start the paperwork."

Here's the thing—neither Mark nor I had been talking to our son or daughters about the possibility of another child.

Paperwork was completed very quickly; it was our third international adoption. We began The Wait. We were familiar with the process, so we settled in for what we thought would be months of waiting for a referral. But just two weeks after submitting the paperwork to our agency I received a phone call.

It was our agency director. "Are you dossier-ready?"

"Yes."

She knew we were, so I found the question alarming.

Starting to panic, I asked, "Has some of our paperwork been lost?" Paperwork did get lost from time to time. There was so much of it for each adoption. The FBI had lost our fingerprints within the first week and we had to be re-printed.

She answered, "No. It's complete. Would you be ready to act on a referral if one came?" she asked.

"Absolutely! Something soon, you think?" I asked.

"I might have something soon." she answered.

We said goodbye and my husband called. I began to tell him about the phone call when he cut me off saying, "Hold on, I have someone on the other line."

He was gone just like that. Then he was back on, conferencing me with the agency director. She asked me if I was parked and I assured her that I was. She had our referral and had e-mailed a picture of the baby to our home computer. Mark and I told her that we wanted the baby. We didn't need to see the photo to know. She insisted that we go home and look at the file she had e-mailed to us. She wouldn't accept our answer until we had read the file and seen the baby's picture.

Mark and I met at home. The computer was on and, true to his word Mark had not opened the file. We wanted to see the baby for the first time together.

We opened the file. The information was all there, along with the picture. There he was, a beautiful baby boy, less than a month old. Of course we wanted him. There was never any doubt.

He was born in Guatemala. He was born on November 6, during the week that I was so full and raw, on my mother-in-law's birthday.

Our son finally came home when he was eleven months old. He attached to me like Velcro. The bonding with his siblings was profound and immediate. He had, and still does have, a wonderfully strong personality full of passion and constant energy.

I close the door on my sleeping son. I heard you, my sweet boy. I was listening.

~Judy M. Miller

Dreams in Triplicate

Brothers and sisters are as close as hands and feet.
~Vietnamese Proverb

My sister and I were always close when we were kids, but when we grew up she married and moved halfway across the country with her husband. So, one June afternoon when my sister called to say that she and her husband were coming for a visit, everyone was very excited—they hadn't been home for a visit since Thanksgiving. Mom planned a get-together for all my aunts and uncles. Dad went to the store to get the supplies to barbecue his special recipe ribs on the grill.

I was glad that my sister was coming home too, but I was anxious to see her for my own reasons. Over the past couple of weeks, I had been having bizarre dreams. My sister had always been interested in dreams and dream analysis. A few years earlier she had taken a "dream workshop" at the local community center. In the past she had even analyzed some of my dreams for me—when I dreamed about falling it probably meant there was some aspect my life that I felt was out of control. Or when I dreamed that I kept getting lost while on my way to a familiar destination, it probably meant that I was confused about something in my future.

But this time I wasn't dreaming about falling or being lost somewhere. This time I was dreaming about "threes." It was very strange.

One night I dreamed about *The Three Musketeers*.

Another night it was the three little kittens who lost their mittens.

I dreamed about reading *The Lord of the Rings* — a trilogy.

I had a dream about a genie — who granted me three wishes.

Then I dreamed about *The Three Stooges* — Larry, Moe and Curly.

It was months before Christmas, but one night I had a dream about The Three Magi!

There was a dream about *The Three Little Pigs*.

Even our neighbors' old dog Jake, who had three legs, made an appearance in a dream.

I was looking forward to discussing my dreams with my sister.

So, on the morning I went to the airport to pick up my sister and her husband, I skipped the part where I asked about their health, jobs or even their flight, and I jumped right to the discussion about my dreams.

"What kind of weird dreams?" asked my sister as we stood waiting in the baggage claim area.

I told her about it all — Musketeers, Stooges, little pigs, even the three-legged dog.

"That is weird, but it actually makes sense," said my sister, smiling at me.

"Makes sense?" I replied. "How? Why? Am I going crazy? What's wrong with me?"

"Nothing's wrong with you," my sister told me. "I think you've just been dreaming about us."

"What do my dreams have to do with you?"

"I've been so excited about seeing you! We're coming home to tell everyone... I'm pregnant... with triplets!"

Now, I don't know if I was really dreaming about my sister's big news or not, but I do know that the night after my sister told me what was going on, the dreams about threes disappeared immediately.

And in February of the next year, I became an uncle — times three!

~David Hull

A Mother Knows

The soul has been given its own ears to hear things that the mind does not understand.
~Rumi

The appointment was on a Tuesday morning, while our three-year-old daughter, Stella, was in school. When we walked into the waiting room, we were the youngest couple there by at least three decades. Actually, we were the only couple. All of the other patients were older men, presumably taking care of some kind of private-part malfunctions.

The doctor said he would be happy to perform the surgery. Just a quick nip, and then my husband and I would never have to worry about birth control again. We would become voluntarily infertile. The urologist unkindly joked that our first child must have been a monster. Why else would a happily married couple decide to end their childbearing potential with only one heir?

For starters, my first pregnancy was a nightmare. I was sick for six months, and when I finally started to feel a tiny bit like a human again, I got gestational diabetes. Then I endured forty-eight hours of labor only to end up with an emergency C-section. I swore, as so many other new moms do, that I would never, ever, go through that agony again. And I meant it. Or so I thought. But driving home from that appointment, I realized through a tearful epiphany that I did not want my husband to have the procedure. I did not want to be the one to decide whether or not we had another child. It just felt like too big of a thing. I'm not a religious person, and I'm certainly not one who easily gives up decision-making rights of any kind, but this time I wanted God to be the one to decide if our family was complete.

And so, we started to "not not try." At first it felt pretty casual, like, "sure, another baby would be nice, if it's in the cards." But, soon, it was all I could think about. I suddenly wanted this second baby more than my next breath. I became completely consumed with all things baby. The few people that I told were more than happy to tell me "I told you so," and as much as I hated being another statistic, I couldn't deny my feelings. Call it biology, or a mother's uncanny willingness to suffer for love, but something was pushing me toward another pregnancy.

And then it happened. I was lying in bed one September night, and a voice came to me. It wasn't my voice, and to this day, I can't quite explain how it sounded, except to say that it was calm, and I wasn't scared. The voice said that I would have a son, and that his name would be Gabriel. It said that Gabriel would be conceived in the spring and that I should be patient. It also said that Gabriel wanted to be born in a new house, one where he could have his own room. And then, as quickly as the voice appeared, it left.

I lay there, considering my options. Being a psychologist, I wondered whether I might be having a psychotic break. But the voice didn't tell me to hurt myself or anyone else. I also thought that I could have just made up the voice. But it didn't sound like me. Like I said, it was very calm, and my thoughts tend to run just a wee bit on the neurotic side. So, I decided to tell my husband about it, which meant that I was committing to this notion. I just hoped it didn't sound like I was the one who needed to be committed.

My husband didn't doubt my experience for a minute. He immediately became elated, not only with the news, but also with the way that it came through. He, like me, had many questions, and we both hoped that the voice would come back, so that we could clarify a few things, like when exactly in the spring, and how would the pregnancy be, and how were we supposed to afford this new house with enough bedrooms for each of us?

The next several months were filled with giant ups and downs. Even though the voice told me that I would be pregnant in the spring, every month that I got my period, or worse, was late, only to take a negative pregnancy test, was torture. My faith was absolutely being tested. At thirty-nine, I wasn't even sure that I had any eggs left. And if online articles were any indication, I might even have secondary infertility, a condition that affects nearly three million women in the United States alone. (Actually, in those months, I researched every possible fertility and pregnancy problem that one could develop. Did I mention that I'm a bit of a hypochondriac?) But there were good days too, like the day that I found out that Gabriel was the name of the angel that told Mary that she was pregnant. That had to mean something!

But still, the doubt was painful, like a knife to my heart every time that I questioned my own experience. My inner critic can be relentless, tearing to shreds any sense that I might be special or worthwhile. I remembered having doubts about my first pregnancy too. Mostly about whether I was right in my feeling that Stella would be a girl. I knew it in my heart, even before I conceived, but everyone, including my doctor, told me not to get my hopes up in case I was wrong. But no one understood that it wasn't a wish, it was a knowing. I had promised myself, after my daughter was revealed to be a girl, that I wouldn't doubt my inner truths again. But promises are like cookies, easy to make and hard to keep.

Until finally, spring arrived, and with it the news that I was pregnant! Calculations showed that we had likely conceived on February 16th, our daughter's fourth birthday. Six months after we conceived, we moved into a new house, one with a bedroom apiece. And three months after that, Gabriel Zachary Medina was born.

~Hayley Bauman

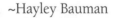

48

Welcome Home, Marti Joy

Trust yourself. You know more than you think you do.
~Benjamin Spock

In January of 1980 I drove past a baby store and noticed a big "Sale" sign out front. I wasn't pregnant, or even able to carry a baby to term, but something struck me. Something told me that this was the perfect sale at the perfect time. I parked my car and walked in like any expectant mother. I didn't know how, but soon I was going to have a daughter. When I left the store I had purchased a crib, dresser, high chair and dressing table. They were all in yellow and white, but I was really thinking pink. I explained to the saleswoman that we were on an adoption list and right at the top, so they agreed to hold everything for three months.

Around the same time, my uncle's wife sent me her two sons' gently used and unused baby boy clothes. It was all very nice of her, but I went out to counter all that blue stuff with pink. A baby girl's wardrobe soon took shape. I also couldn't resist pink and yellow crib sheets and crib bumpers. Around the same time I went past a children's specialty shop and ordered a pink, lace-trimmed pillow with the name MARTI JOY appliquéd on it. I clearly was not in my right mind, but neither was my husband. Maybe he was just humoring me, or maybe he too was caught up in my craziness. Soon after, Jeff decided to wallpaper the bedroom. He forgot to match the patterns — all different dizzying combinations of pinks, oranges, and yellows. In his defense, he is a little color blind.

A month before, we had visited Jeff's parents in San Diego. On a day trip to Tijuana I bought a huge piñata. It was the same combination of dizzying colors as the wallpaper, but in the form of a peacock. Who could have known then that it would soon be hung over a crib?

March came, but no baby. However, the furniture was all delivered, and I still couldn't shake the feeling that our daughter was out there, somewhere, being carried just for us.

We were adopting our foster child Josh at that time. He was a blond-haired, blue-eyed, dimpled six-year-old — a little devil who had everyone wrapped around his finger, including my mother, who doted on him. She was a self-declared "girl person," though, and also a wonderful artist. She had gone to The Museum College of Art on a full-paid scholarship. There was a juried art show every year in New Hope, Pennsylvania, and for the first time, that year, she not only entered but also was accepted. Her piece was entitled "Judy's Girl." It was a painting of a little girl with beautiful, curly red hair sitting on a stool counting her ten little toes. She had an offer of more than $100 for it — a lot of money then — but she refused to sell. She felt this indeed was my girl. That painting hangs in my hallway today.

When May arrived, so did some friends from Israel with their eighteen-month-old daughter. The crib was there, and the high chair, both unused. I told my friend Karen that she should use them for her daughter; maybe Haddas using them would be good luck. It was! The day they were flying back to Israel was May 21st, and that ended up being the day that changed our whole world.

Jeff had left the house early to go rafting with his Special Ed class; he was a teacher then, but striving for more. Later that day, in fact, he would learn that he was accepted into the University of Pennsylvania, where he would earn a Ph.D. in Biostatistics. But that morning I was getting ready for work as a Field Office Supervisor for the 1980 Census. My friend Ruth, who worked as a delivery nurse, called us at seven to deliver startling news. She had helped a woman deliver a baby girl and we could have her. The woman only wanted two things: to be anonymous and to know that the baby would be raised Jewish. These were the days before cellphones, so Jeff was oblivious of all that was happening while he was rolling down the Delaware River. He was the last to find out.

I was fortunate that my boss was a retired social worker; she guided me through the legalities. The Census Bureau was a microcosm of real life. We had had illnesses, deaths, and marriages in our group, and now finally a birth! The collective excitement was palpable. My mother was working for the Census as well, in a different part of the building. I rarely saw her so elated. On May 21st she was high as a kite. I think it was because my girlfriend said my daughter was the picture of my mother, red hair with hazel gray eyes when she was born.

Coincidentally, this all happened on the holiday of Shavuot, the day we commemorate receiving the Ten Commandments as a gift from God. He gave us an amazing gift that day, too.

Our Marti Joy was named for my Grandpop Martin who raised me, and for my great aunt Goldie whose husband, my uncle Benny, was always my favorite. My Grandmom (Grandmom Eva to Marti and Josh) said something very wise. She told me that "sometimes the vessel that carries a baby is not who God intended as the keeper of the child's soul." This baby girl was always meant to be ours.

The premonitions had all been right on the mark. Two days later, the little girl with curly red hair and steel-gray eyes the color of my Grandpop's was put into my arms while her Daddy, Grandmom, and Pop cried with joy. The entire neighborhood was outside my parents' house for Marti's arrival. She had three great-grandmothers and her big brother Josh waiting for her in the house. My parents had a crib set up in the living room, and the outfit we sent to the hospital, a pink and white dress with a little red ribbon to keep away the evil eye, matched the crib's sheets perfectly. Marti slept through the party, but the big cake on the table said it all: "Welcome Home Marti Joy!"

Six months and one day after Marti arrived, we went before Judge Mimms to get the adoption formalized. When they got word of it, the foster agency agreed to fast-track Josh's adoption, too. In 1981 we went once more before the same judge, all together as a family. Judge Mimms said it was a highlight of her career.

~Judy Davidson

Dreams and Premonitions

Waking Up to a New Life Path

My Vision of Heaven

The purpose of life is a life of purpose.
~Robert Byrne

It was the ninth day after my thyroid surgery and I was feeling rotten. My neck was red, sore and swollen, so I decided to go to bed early to get some sleep. As I lay down on our bed I felt something pop on my neck. I put my hand on my T-shirt and felt something wet.

"Susan, something's wrong. My T-shirt's all wet."

As my wife turned on the bedroom light she realized my whole shirt was covered in blood and that my neck had literally "exploded" at the incision.

"We've got to get to the hospital right away; you're bleeding all over the place."

Within four minutes we were in the car racing to the hospital. After triage at the nurse's station we faced a long wait to get medical attention. Finally, seventeen hours later, I had surgery to repair my neck. As I was waking up from that operation, a doctor came into the room and shook my hand. "I'm your cardiologist."

"I think you've made a mistake. I've never had heart problems."

"Well, you do now. Your heart rate is way up at 190 and we need to bring it down."

I had difficulty concentrating because my mind was still fuzzy from the surgery.

"What can you do?"

"We have to shock your heart in the next forty-eight hours."

"Oh." I paused. "Do you mean tomorrow?"

"Yes. Here's what we'll do…" We talked some more and then he left.

The next evening I was rolled into a small anteroom next to a regular operating room. I was hooked up to an IV and heart monitors but no painkillers.

"The anesthesiologist will be at least another half hour. Are you okay here alone?" the nurse asked.

"I'm not going anywhere." I smiled weakly as I was left alone.

For some reason I looked at the clock on the wall above my feet; it read 7:05 p.m. I closed my eyes for a little rest and then it happened.

I found myself standing in a very bright place on a long narrow ridge. It was about a foot high and it extended as far as I could see in either direction. Right in front of me was a huge curtain or veil that was thin and transparent. It extended way off to either side and I couldn't see the top.

I immediately became aware of music. It was the most beautiful music I had ever heard but I didn't recognize any of it. Just on the other side of the veil I saw a beautiful garden. The colors were dazzlingly bright and clear — yellows, reds and greens. And every single flower and bush was perfect. Although everything was bright, strangely there were no shadows.

Straight ahead of me was a large white gate, which was opened wide and filled with people. They were all young, probably in their early twenties, and in perfect shape.

Everyone I saw was smiling as they milled around in front of me. They were all looking my way and motioning for me to join them. They didn't talk, but somehow I knew what they wanted me to do. As I stood on that ridge I wanted to join them. My heart ached to join them. All I had to do was walk ahead through the veil and I would be free. I would be with them forever. But something held me back.

As I watched this scene in front of me I realized that I had no pain at all and no incisions from my surgeries. In fact, I felt great — as if I were floating. The music and the beauty of the scene in front of me were all consuming, and every worry and concern in my life had disappeared.

I knew without anyone telling me that I was looking straight into heaven. It was just on the other side of that veil, and I could walk into it. It was so perfect and so beautiful. I wanted all of it. I longed to step into it and leave all my pain behind. But I didn't take that step.

The next thing I knew someone had put his hand on my shoulder. I looked up and saw the time on the clock was 7:39 p.m. More than half an hour had passed. I was back in the hospital and the pain from all the medical procedures hit me like a brick.

Someone touched my shoulder again. I turned to see the anesthesiologist. He introduced himself and said, "I'm going to put you under so they can reset your heart. Are you ready for the injection?"

I nodded weakly, and the next thing I remember is waking up with a normal heartbeat. However, my visit to heaven stayed with me. It shook me to the core. For three weeks I couldn't tell anyone about what I had experienced — not even my wife. Partly I was afraid no one would believe me and partly I was struggling to accept what I had experienced. However, as I began to share what I had seen, people did believe me and I began to accept it all myself.

Ever since that visit to heaven my fear of death has evaporated completely. I know that when my life here is over I will be in the paradise I saw firsthand. In the meantime, I am determined to make a difference in what I do for others.

Four months after my surgery I went to Nigeria as part of a team to work with widows and orphans. There was one particular orphanage we visited where every boy had experienced violence and torture. We distributed clothes, toothbrushes and toiletries to everybody. One seven-year-old boy whose back was covered with multiple stab wounds came over to thank us with tears in his eyes. He had never been given a new set of clothes before.

Almost two years later I was ushered into the maternity ward of our local hospital. The walls were all bright colors and I could smell the baby soap. As I rounded the corner I saw my daughter in bed holding a little bundle wrapped in blue. I came to the far side of her bed and saw my grandson for the first time.

"Let me present Ethan," my daughter Kristen said. "Do you want to hold him?"

I needed no convincing. As I held Ethan I ran my finger along his cheek. It was soft and pink and perfect. His eyes fluttered open and he looked straight at me with his clear blue eyes.

I watched his little chest rise and fall as he breathed. I saw his eyes focus on me, then the new world around him, and then back to me. I melted as I held him and I felt exhilarated as never before. At that moment I knew one reason I had not crossed through that veil. He was in my arms.

~Rob Harshman

50

The Mentor

If you want to be happy, be.
~Leo Tolstoy

I had been teaching high school for nearly two years. The job was stressful: I planned lessons, I helped students, I graded papers, and I sponsored extracurricular activities. And I was never happy. I was always tired, feeling empty and unfulfilled. Worse, my co-workers seemed to love their jobs — or at least, they found fulfillment in teaching. My inability to share their joy left me feeling nauseated and guilty on top of everything else. I felt sick most nights and I was sleep-deprived.

That was what I was thinking about when I met my grandfather. It was the middle of the night, and I was lying on the hallway floor — close to the bathroom door, just in case — wrapped in a comforter. I had been fighting hot and cold flashes and had been shivering as I dozed into a strangely still sleep.

And then I saw him — my grandfather — in a dream.

It was a shadowed world, and when I entered I had the impression that I was being allowed in against the rules. It was calm in a way I have never experienced before. In the darkness, a single spotlight shone down upon the world, affording me a view of the only thing I was allowed to see: my grandfather, who had died twenty-five years earlier, a year before I was born.

All I knew of my grandfather was what I had learned from my mother. He was her paragon: a caring, dedicated teacher, a talented linguist, and a loving father. He was my mother's guide and mentor, her inspiration as a teacher and a parent. I had seen a picture of him once, and I recognized his silhouette. He stood just far enough in the spotlight for me to recognize him, but no further.

When my grandfather saw me, he held up his hands the way a police officer directing traffic might do. He was directing other shadowed figures, and they all stopped at his gesture. When he turned to me, he still wouldn't let me see his entire face.

"Why in the world are you so worried?" he asked me. "Why are you doing this to yourself?" His tone of voice was caring but matter-of-fact. He didn't question how I had come to him; he merely accepted the fact that if I was there, it meant that I needed help.

"I think I've chosen the wrong career," I said. "I chose to be a teacher because my mother loved it so much. But I don't think I have her passion. I'm always tired after work, and I feel like something's missing."

He simply watched me. He knew I wasn't finished speaking before I did.

"The problem is, I've always wanted to be a writer — ever since I could first hold a pencil. It's what's in my blood, and I feel that being a teacher I'm betraying that dream. I feel like I've already given up on it." I was shocked at my words. I hadn't even realized my dream of being a writer was an issue.

I could just see him smile through the shadows. It was the same expression a parent might have when explaining away a toddler's irrational fear of the bogeyman. Once again, his voice was soothing and rational.

"I don't understand what the problem is," he said, and the way he said it immediately calmed me. "Your teaching ability is intuitive. Lesson ideas come easily to you. The desire to help others is in your blood. You're making such a big deal out of it, but it's all in your mind. Go to school each day, teach your students, and then go home and write. It's as simple as that. If you want to be a writer, then write. Spending your days at school has nothing to do with it. Write, and your dream will happen. The only one stopping you is you."

It was such sound, simple advice; I had made the problem so complicated that I hadn't been able to see the answer. Of course being a teacher didn't mean giving up on writing! I just needed someone else to tell me.

I wasn't given a chance to thank him or to say goodbye. Instead, I woke up wrapped in that comforter feeling better than I had in a long time. Serenity flowed through me as I climbed into bed and slept straight through to morning. After school the next day I began work on the first short story I had written since college.

All of my publication credits — from articles to short stories, novels to performed plays — have come since that encounter with my grandfather. I even dedicated my first novel to him. Since the dream, my students asked me how I could be so much calmer than many other teachers. And, of course, family members noticed the change, too.

My mother questioned the motivation behind my renewed calm and subsequent success in writing. "What happened to you?" she asked. "What changed?"

When I described the dream to her, tears welled in her eyes. Her loving father had spent his life mentoring her, and she took comfort in the fact that even from the great beyond, he was still working his magic. Whenever I feel the threat of stress, I just remember that dream: my grandfather's smile and the most important lesson I've learned in life. Change is possible in all things; it just needs to come from within.

~Val Muller

51

Dreams Even Change the Lives of Corporate Execs

We cannot become what we want to be by remaining what we are.
~Max De Pree

I was a fifty-one-year-old corporate vice president directing the global telecommunications strategy of one of the largest corporations in the financial industry. Because of the size of the company, my staff and I were making major technological changes not only in the way that our corporate networks operated but stimulating major changes in the telecommunications industry as a whole. I was enjoying the outright fun of working with my team, watching our creative efforts result in huge cost reductions and performance improvements, and having our information technology recognized by the board of directors to be an invaluable corporate asset. I was at the peak of my career... but it was all about to end.

The company had a change of upper management from the chairman on down, which involved restructuring and outsourcing that affected every division, even the technology sector that included my division. The first to go was the senior executive above me, who was replaced by someone charged with figuring out how to outsource much of information technology. I remember that sinking feeling when

I was told that my job, if I chose to stay, would be to accomplish the downsizing and outsourcing of most of my own organization. I was dumbfounded that there was no understanding of the value of what we had achieved and could continue to achieve for the company. None of that mattered — the marching orders had been given.

As devastating as all this was it did not even cross my mind to walk out the door. I feared that I would find nothing equivalent at my age and would lose a rather significant retirement package. Instead I pursued other executive positions in the company. Many were uncertain and those that seemed open to me, although still in technology, did not satisfy my true career interests. I remember sitting in the office, devastated by the thought that my cherished telecommunications career was over, but at this point I feared losing financial stability more than a career change. I was so stuck in this frame of mind that when a Park Avenue search firm came after me, indicating that a major firm in the New York area was interested in me, I did not even consider it, but instead gave them the name of my boss, who had been let go. Then I had the dream that changed all that.

In this dream, I am a passenger in a boat adrift in a dark black ice cave, trying all night to find a "position" in the windows that would "show me a way out" of my predicament. It was a picture-perfect metaphor of the emotional situation I was in. At one point a booming authoritative voice behind me says, "You CAN walk out that door." I look around and see no one. Again the voice booms, "You CAN walk out that door." I begin to argue with the voice that I do not understand because I see no open door. The more I argue the more the voice insists, when suddenly an open door appears at the front of the boat. I still do not understand what it all means, but I reluctantly walk out the door. When I do the boat emerges from the dark ice cave into a calm stream in a beautiful sunlit setting of colorful flowers and green trees. The air is filled with beautiful music and when the boat lands at a rock on the shore it rings like a bell resonating deep into my soul.

I woke a changed person. That morning on my way to work I could not imagine how I had gotten so caught up in my fear of change and doubt in my own potential that I was ready to trap myself in the "dark tunnel of ice" that my existing situation represented. Halfway to work the song "Calling All Angels" (performed by Jane Siberry and k.d. lang) came on the radio. It contained the phrases "calling all angels, walk me through this one" and "we're trying, we're hoping… 'cause we're not sure how this goes." I began to sing along, but in my new state of mind I began to sing the song like it was a fervent prayer. Something inside me had shifted at a deeper level.

I got to my office and sat down ready to meet the pile of challenges on my desk, but to my amazement less than ten minutes later the phone rang. It was the search firm. They said, "The company we represent does not want your boss; they are specifically looking for you, and we will be there in the morning to interview you." It turns out that the company was IBM, which offered me the equivalent corporate executive position managing IBM's global telecommunications strategy. It was a huge opportunity — and this time, after completing my existing obligations, I "walked out that door" without hesitation.

It turned out to be all that my dream had promised and more. Lou Gerstner had taken over as chairman to manage a turnaround when IBM was at a very low point. I not only experienced the joys of working with this dynamic senior management team and doing my part in the turnaround, but the effort was so successful that my financial gains allowed me to retire early. It more than made up for that retirement package that I had been so afraid of losing. Had it not been for that dream none of this would have happened!

~Bob Hoss

52

Somebody's Daughter

You may choose to look the other way but you can
never say again that you did not know.
~William Wilberforce

I woke up with my heart pounding. The screaming in my ears was my own. As my eyes adjusted to the 3 a.m. darkness, it dawned on me that it was just a dream. No, it was a nightmare.

In my nightmare, my daughter, who was studying in Australia at the time, was abducted and sold into slavery. I remember every agonizing detail of the dream, from the faded floral pattern of the peeling wallpaper in the stairwell where they grabbed her to the dread in her eyes, the terror in my heart, and my panic that it would take me twenty-four hours to reach Australia, way too long to start the search for her.

With my husband still lightly snoring, I grabbed my phone and texted my daughter to make sure she was okay. While I waited for her reply, I started to search for flights to Australia — as if I were Liam Neeson in the movie *Taken*. Unlike Liam Neeson however, I had no idea what I'd do when I got there.

Finally the ping of her text. "I'm fine, Mom. What's up?"

I sank into the pillows with relief and prayed. "Thank God it wasn't my daughter" was immediately replaced by the awareness that it had actually happened to somebody else's daughter.

Somebody's daughter had been abducted and sold into slavery that night. Somebody's daughter ran away and was sucked into the web of human trafficking. Somebody's daughter was brainwashed to think there was no hope, no way out. Somebody's daughter was being used for profit and the salacious enjoyment of men in a dark and evil underworld. Somebody's daughter was silently crying out for justice.

That night, across the world and in my own state of New Jersey, people of all ages, colors, and genders were being held against their will, their passports confiscated by unscrupulous "employers," and forced to work as nannies, maids, and bonded laborers with no hope or chance for freedom.

It's a tragic fact that there is more slavery in the world today than there was during the Civil War, in fact more than at any time in history. There are an estimated thirty million people caught in human trafficking — modern day slavery — whether it is the sex trade or forced labor or child prostitution. It's the fastest growing and second largest criminal activity in the world.

Shortly after my nightmare, I saw a post on a friend's Facebook page about purchasing items made by survivors of human trafficking. I left a comment that I was interested in this issue. Then another Facebook friend, one with no connection whatsoever to the one who created the post, left a comment saying, "If you do something, let me know."

I stared at her comment for several minutes. I wondered if this would be one more time when I would want to do something, yet actually do nothing. Maybe it was time to actually *do* something.

So I reached out to Tanya, who created the original post. We'd only met once, but still we were friends, at least in the Facebook sense of the word. I knew I needed to do something even though I had absolutely no idea what it was.

Over her kitchen table, Tanya and I shared our thoughts and some information about the subject and the few organizations we were familiar with. We were just two suburban moms, outraged over this colossal issue, wanting to answer the question, "How can we make a difference from here?"

We committed to pray about it, and we agreed to meet again to watch a movie that we could possibly show to others.

I knew so little about an issue that was so big. I wondered what we could accomplish. After all, there were just two of us. That phrase "just two of us" reminded me of a Bible story where the prophet Elisha and his servant were facing an army of evildoers. The servant feared that there were just two of them, but the prophet answered, "Do not be afraid. Those who are with us are more than those who are with them." (2 Kings 6:16) I realized that even though there are thirty million caught in slavery, there are more than seven billion people in the world. And most of those people would be opposed to slavery. If they knew about it.

Edmund Burke, who famously said, "The only thing necessary for evil to triumph is for good men to do nothing" also said, "Nobody makes a greater mistake than he who did nothing because he could only do a little."

Around this time, I saw a photo of a cardboard sign that read, "I always wondered why somebody didn't do something about that. Then I realized. I am somebody."

That quote and picture galvanized my decision to at least "do a little."

In the days that followed, I casually mentioned my new endeavor to selected friends and family. With each discussion, my boldness and excitement grew because each person in one way or another said almost the same thing: "I was looking for a way to get involved in this, but didn't know what to do." Just like me!

In less than two months, our group grew from two to twenty-two! Within this diverse group, we had people of different ages and from all walks of life. Some had experience and wanted to be involved with the legislative and government side of the problem. Others were more interested in compassionate care for the survivors. And others were somewhere in between. We even had two members who were moving to Cambodia, which is a source, transit, and destination country for human trafficking.

We created a mission statement, a website, and a plan of action. Justice Network was born. Less than four months after that kitchen table conference, we hosted the movie showing of *Trade of Innocents* with over 100 people in attendance and an information fair featuring representatives from eight local and global organizations. And that was just the beginning.

Justice Network was formed to raise awareness of the issue and support for organizations locally and globally that are already on the front lines fighting this heinous evil. JN exists to educate, equip, and empower friends and neighbors to become abolitionists, providing education about the facts and ways to fight the issue and directing support to those organizations rescuing victims.

We are part of the New Jersey Coalition Against Human Trafficking, participating in and contributing creatively to their activities, particularly events leading up to the Super Bowl. Large sporting events are an attraction to human traffickers, and the Super Bowl is the number one such event annually. With the Super Bowl coming to New Jersey just six months after Tanya and I met in her kitchen, we never believed that we'd be taking such an active part in raising awareness in our communities.

Through both secular and religious organizations, change is taking place. Traffickers are going to jail. Victims are rescued and redeemed. People are changing the world. I'm a real housewife of New Jersey out to change my corner of the world and do what I can to positively impact the lives of those in peril. And it all started with a nightmare.

~Susan Allen Panzica

Playing with Fire

A foolish heart will call on you to toss your dreams
away, then turn around and blame you for the way
you went astray.
~Grateful Dead, "Foolish Heart"

You never forget a dream like that. Especially when it is telling that you are going to die. My mother being a Pentecostal Christian meant I'd heard about dreams and their meanings — every dream had a deep, other-dimensional significance to Mom. But this one was easy — I didn't need Mom's interpretation. And besides, I didn't want to add more weight to the burden on her from my rebellious living. She worried about me enough as it was.

I was twenty and already a full-time drug user. It was mostly light stuff during the week — pot, pills, and booze — and worse on the weekends: LSD, cocaine. The plan had been to take a year off after high school and save money before going to community college. That year had turned into two.

I'd faced death at least two times by the time I started having the dream. The first time my friends and I were held up at gunpoint in a fast food restaurant parking lot for hitting on the gunman's girlfriend inside the restaurant while he waited for her in the car. After he put the gun down, my friends and I jumped in my silver Thunderbird and made a speedy getaway.

The man with the gun, a thug named Casper, followed us in his growling Mustang. A high-speed chase ensued on highway 78 by Stone Mountain, as I swerved in and out of heavy Friday night traffic like a racecar driver. For the first time since I'd had my license, I was hoping the police would show up. But they didn't.

We miraculously escaped — and I never heard from Casper again.

Not too long afterward, I was standing two feet behind the tailgate of a lifted truck when the driver decided to back out as fast as he could. Even though I was inebriated and not an Olympic hurdler, I jumped four feet in the air and toppled safely into the bed of the maniac's truck.

A few nights later I had the dream.

In the dream I have a bird's eye view of someone running as fast as he can. Even though his back is turned I know I'm looking at myself. I'm not running on a track or in the woods. I'm on the moon — in a dry and rocky crater. I'm casually dressed; no oxygen suit is necessary. The atmosphere is dark and lonely. The only color is an intermittent orange-reddish glow. While I'm running for my life, glowing fireballs the size of compact cars — broken pieces of fiery comets — are crashing all around… except in front of me. I have to zigzag left and right to avoid being hit. That's what I'm doing the entire dream: dodging fire.

And then I woke up.

I knew that if I didn't change I was going to die. I'd never been more convinced that something as transcendent and ambiguous as a dream could become reality. I needed to change my life, and the way to do it was by going back to my faith roots. Walking away from my faith years earlier was the reason I was playing with fire in the first place, I concluded.

I paid a visit to the church where I grew up. I hadn't been there in four years. I was glad to see my old friends, and they seemed glad to see me. I told the ones who played music I'd been playing guitar and was looking for guys to play with. I gave them my number and asked them to call me whenever they got together and played. This was a gutsy move, putting myself out there like that. At home I fought to get and stay sober, to stay out of trouble. I was looking into signing up for college courses. I stayed home more.

Changing the course of my life would not be easy. I needed to separate from the people who helped perpetuate my destructive lifestyle. I not only smoked marijuana at least three times a day, but I was depressed when I wasn't high.

One Saturday night I was at a house party when I heard the shouts of "Police!" By then I'd fled so many underage parties that I didn't need to think twice. I dropped my beer and ran out the back door, straight into the dark woods.

It took me about an hour to get to my car, which was at a friend's house. In the car the Grateful Dead were blaring through the speakers. My throat was dry, my mind hazy, my clothes dingy and reeking of smoke, and my soul, weary.

I decided I had attended my last party. From that night on I would do whatever I could to get straight. One member of the Grateful Dead, Brent Mydland, had died of a drug overdose, and another, lead singer and band leader Jerry Garcia, had died of a heart attack while in rehab after years of drug abuse. I wasn't going their way. I would succeed.

By my twenty-first birthday I was well on my way to complete sobriety and a new kind of life. I had begun hanging out with people whose idea of fun didn't revolve around drugs and booze. I'd been playing music more, and I was signed up for classes in January.

Then, one of my old friends unexpectedly dropped by with a six-pack of beer and a birthday joint. I greeted him kindly but told him I wouldn't partake. He realized this time I was for real. I wouldn't see him again for twelve years.

I never had the Dodging Fire dream again. I have been healed of my depression and my social ineptness. I have remained sober and drug-free for a decade and a half. Most importantly, I'm living a life of purpose. I have healthy relationships with friends and family. I work and play. I write, and occasionally, I still play music. I'm "the bestest uncle" to two wonderful nieces. I have lead small groups at my church.

And this is just the beginning.

The dream was right. In front of me, there is nothing hindering me.

~Paul Dragu

54

At the Same Table

We are never so lost our angels cannot find us.
~Stephanie Powers

The year 2007 had been horrible and I couldn't wait for it to end. In May, my mother lost her battle with cancer, and then two months later my twenty-three-year-old niece Melissa was killed in a car accident. I flew up north to stay with my sister, and two days before Melissa's funeral I received a call from my doctor about a suspicious chest X-ray result from my last exam. With Mom gone and Lena in a fog after losing her youngest child, I kept my fears to myself.

When I returned home about ten days later I learned I'd been laid off from my job when my company eliminated my entire department. I cleared out my desk, returned to my apartment, and sat with my hands over my face. I was afraid of what would happen next. I didn't even want to go outside.

My doctor ordered an MRI of my chest, which was clear, and just to be sure, a bronchoscopy. The findings were benign and I started to relax. But a few days after the procedure, I developed an inflammatory reaction called uveitis in my left eye. The treatment was six weeks of steroidal and dilating eye drops. Now I couldn't go outside even if I wanted to; the Florida sun was too bright.

I am not by nature a religious person. I do believe in a higher power, but I don't necessarily feel we have access to this power. That's why I didn't turn to prayer in those days when I sat in the house with the lights out and my sunglasses on. I just complained on the phone to my friends about how awful things were and how fearful I was of everything.

My inflamed iris would burn as I lay in bed trying to sleep. I had a series of cold packs I'd cycle through every night, kept in an ice bucket beside my bed. I'd wake up when one pack had gotten warm and reach for the next one in the bucket. I'd place it on my eye and try to get back to sleep.

On one particular night in the beginning of December, I woke at 2:04 a.m., but not because the ice pack had warmed. I woke because I had one of the most vivid dreams I can remember.

Throughout my life, I'd gone for long periods of time without having any dreams that made an impression. Then suddenly I'd have one that jarred me awake and had me running for the voice recorder to capture it. This was one of those dreams. It was so significant that snippets of it come back to me even to this day.

The first thing I saw was a sterile, white room with a long, white table. The door opened and three figures walked in. The first looked like the stereotypical image of Jesus, with a white robe and a beard, just like in a painting we had in an upstairs hallway when I was a kid. The other two were my mother and my niece. They all sat at the table—Jesus at one end, Melissa at the other, and Mom in the middle.

Melissa had her usual young adult swagger. "Okay," she said, plopping her hands on the table as she got settled. My mom was exactly how I remembered her, with her reading glasses and a legal pad, prepared to take notes. They both wore blue and white, their favorite colors. Mom had a deep tan, like she'd just come off the golf course. Melissa wore a zipped up tracksuit with a silver zipper hanging by her chin. They looked the way I remembered them, with the same gestures, the same physical attributes.

Melissa ran the meeting in the blunt manner she was known for. "Listen. You have been totally freaking out. You have to realize, this is just life. Stuff like this happens; it's not that big a deal."

"The doctor said uveitis is chronic," I said. "People get it again and again throughout their whole life."

"Did the doctor say you were going to get it again and again throughout

Waking Up to a New Life Path | 199

your whole life?"

"Well no, but what if —"

My mother took off her reading glasses. "Anneke, you always do this, thinking 'what if.'"

"But I read that this happens —"

Melissa put up her hand. "Stop! You're doing it again."

So it continued, everyone interrupting each other, like all the conversations in my family. I relayed my long list of woes and fears. Melissa and Mom countered each of them and traded quips, while Jesus sat at the end of the table with a bemused expression.

Occasional random comments would send one of us into a laughing fit, just like we used to do at long holiday dinners. And like always, Mom eventually called an end to the fun, looking at her watch. "Okay, it's getting late. We need to get going."

They all stood and began to fade from view.

"But wait —" I said.

Melissa laughed. "Don't worry, we'll see you again."

As they all filed out of the room, Mom turned back to wave just before my eyes opened.

What I came to realize through that dream was that my fears had not really been about me. My fears had been about them. All along, part of me had been subconsciously worrying, "Where are they? Are they all right?" But now I knew. They were okay. Melissa was still herself, telling it like it is, sharing her infectious laugh. Mom was still golfing and making lists. They hadn't changed at all. Everything was exactly the same.

The next morning I noticed the burning sensation in my eye had calmed, and I began to see a way out of my fears. Mom and Melissa were safe in their new world. And if they were okay, then I was okay, and when the time came for me to leave this earth, they'd be waiting for me, maybe sitting at the same table.

~Anneke Towne

My Priceless Dream

Life is what we make it, always has been,
always will be.
~Grandma Moses

My life had become a nightmare. I had just lost both my parents to suicide, and within six months I lost almost all the money I had inherited from them, in the stock market during the tech collapse. I lost the remainder investing in a private company that collapsed after 9/11.

Shortly thereafter my home was in foreclosure and I found myself in an abusive relationship. I became severely depressed as I felt I had lost everything. I decided I was going to end my life.

But then I had a dream that would change my life forever:

I was running down a dark alley, and I remember feeling like I was going the wrong way, so I turned and starting heading in a different direction. No sooner had I turned to go than I saw out of the corner of my eye a homeless person and a dog tied to the rear bumper of a car. I sensed that the driver had no idea the person and the dog were tied to the car. I saw the brake lights go on as the car was starting. I panicked! I had to get the driver's attention before the car backed up!

All of a sudden a red delicious apple appeared in my right hand and I threw it as hard as I could to get the driver's attention! As soon as I released the apple, the car morphed into an ambulance, backed up and ran over the dog!

I sat straight up in bed, literally gasping. Being an avid animal lover, I was horrified by what I had just seen. I soon realized it was just a dream, but there was something about it that was haunting. I couldn't go back to sleep. I knew on every level of my being that something was trying to get my attention.

The next day — journal in hand — I went for a walk, determined to discover the message in my dream. I remember asking for clarity and insight. What was the meaning? It felt very profound, but absolutely nothing came to me, despite my best efforts.

And then, two days later, I received the most amazing clarity. The entire script and its meaning poured through me. Here's what I received:

Running down a dark alley symbolized being in a situation I didn't trust.

Turning around and going the other direction represented a new direction in my life.

Cars symbolize our emotional body, but I was not in the driver's seat.

The homeless person tied to the rear bumper of the car represented my greatest fear — being homeless, with my home in foreclosure.

The dog tied to the car represented me being tied to and invested in something or someone other than myself.

The car morphing into an ambulance symbolized being rescued.

The message I received loud and clear was that I was waiting around to be rescued and it was killing me! It was time to invest in myself! Amazing!

Shortly after my dream, I chose to surrender and let go. I opened up to my best friend and shared with her that I had been considering suicide. Choosing to be transparent with her was one of the most profound gifts of my life.

My life began to open up in amazing ways. Sponsors and ambassadors of well-being began to stream into my life.

I have since written a book called *Priceless Principles* and created a coaching and consulting organization to help other people remember the power that resides within them.

I am so grateful that I was listening, and that my nightmare has led me to live my dream.

~Laura Fredrickson

56

Mom Comes to Play

The day I decided that my life was magical, there
was magic all around me.
~Author Unknown

As a child and teen, I was fascinated with dreams—I even made a presentation to my high school English class about dream symbols—but I didn't pay serious attention to dreams until after my mother's unexpected death at age sixty-nine. I say "unexpected," but somehow I knew it was coming. At the very moment I got the news, I was staring at a book, *Life After Death*, by Deepak Chopra. It was on my desk at work.

When my mother passed, it reawakened my childhood hobby from twenty years earlier. I started journaling my dreams and began to read more books about death, such as Sylvia Browne's *Visits from the Afterlife*.

Like most thirty-five-year-old women, my life was still ridiculously busy. There was no time for spiritual quests. A week after my mother died we closed on a bigger house in the suburbs, and barely three months after we moved in I became pregnant with our second child. It was a lot of change at once, and there wasn't much time to grieve her loss.

One night, about a month after we moved into our new house, I found myself roaming around in a stupor, unable to find anything. This house felt too big! I began to sob uncontrollably.

Then it hit me: My mother was really gone, and I was moving on without her. I couldn't bear the thought. She would never get to see my new house, never know that I was having another baby. I would have no memories with my mom in this house, the one where I would raise my children.

I felt guilty. How could I enjoy all this without her? My mother was dead; I shouldn't be allowed to be happy. I didn't think I deserved this nice house, this family, or this life.

I curled up on the rocking chair in the corner of our huge bedroom, sobbing and wailing, the sound muffled only by my husband blow-drying my three-year-old daughter's hair after her bath.

That same night my mother came to me in an incredible dream that changed everything.

She was at the foot of my bed. She ripped the covers off, grabbed my hands and pulled me right out. I giggled, "Mom! What are you doing?" I was so happy to see her.

She led me to the big open space in our bedroom and started dancing around with me in a circle. She was so joyful and playful!

Then my sister, my daughter and my husband were all there too, holding hands and dancing in a circle, all of us laughing and happy.

Next, the scene moved to the closet in my daughter's room, where my mother and I talked for a long time. She looked very young and pretty, like in her teens. Her voice was high-pitched, as if it came from somewhere else. I asked her if she liked being on the other side, and she said she did. It seemed like we talked for an hour in there. I felt so incredibly happy to see her and to be able to ask her all those questions.

The last thing I remember was being back in my bed. She deliberately put my hand into my husband's hand—and then I woke up.

I felt such a deep sense of peace after the dream; it was like nothing I'd ever felt before. I immediately woke my husband to tell him about my extraordinary experience.

It was as if my mother came to tell me to enjoy all these wonderful things in my life. She was still with me. She was fine. She wanted me to give my love to my husband and children now. The dream lifted the spell of depression I didn't even know I was under.

Little did I know that my mother was also showing me all the wonderful moments to come in our large master bedroom, all the many times that I'd be dancing with my children in a circle, filling that big empty space with laughter, play, and joy, appreciating its size.

It's been six years since her passing, and Mom doesn't visit me in my dreams very often now. But I know that if I ever truly need her, she will be there for me.

All I need to do is focus my thoughts and the energy that I put out into the universe — even my tears — and I have direct access to her.

~Sharon Pastore

57

Diving In

Don't wait for your ship to come in — swim out to it.
~Author Unknown

I lay flat in my bed because kneeling beside it was too painful. I clasped my hands in prayer. I had been experiencing extreme pain as well as vertigo and migraines from brain swelling for a solid two months, with no medical explanation. I was thirty-seven years old and doing everything right. I ate the right foods, exercised, got massages, saw chiropractors, talked to therapists, did spiritual work, and meditated. Yet some undefined force was taking over my body. The doctors were leaning toward a diagnosis of multiple sclerosis and had told me to take it easy. I had been taking it easy for two months and I was now incredibly sick and tired of being sick and tired.

So I prayed. I begged: "Please God, angels, ancestors, and any benevolent beings willing to help. Give me a dream; show me a sign; tell me what I can do to heal."

Somewhere in the midst of my prayer I fell asleep.

The next thing I knew, I found myself sitting in an emergency room hallway. My mother was with me. I asked her how long we had been there. "Two days" she said.

"What?" I cried.

I needed to get her some help, so I tried to stand, but my legs wouldn't move. My joints were frozen, and when I looked down I saw that my arms and legs were beginning to atrophy. We were clearly not in the ER for her.

Waking Up to a New Life Path | 207

We were there for me!

I was suddenly flushed with fear about this inability to move my body. With everything I had in me, I worked myself into a standing position and made my way to the nurse's station. I asked the nurse for help but she said the doctors were busy and there were too many people to see. I found the strength to throw my hand down on the desk and said, "I demand to be seen!"

She glanced at me for a second with a disapproving look and then returned to ignoring me. Suddenly the door behind the nurse's station flew open and a woman came out. She was the first person there to look directly at me and she asked, "Are you here for the foster kid audition?"

"Um… I have no idea what that means," I said. "But sure! Okay."

I did have an interest in foster kids and upon hearing the laughter from inside the room I felt compelled to sit and wait for the doctor in there rather than out in the hall. Inside the room, kids were on stage telling stories and everyone was sitting on the floor, chairs, or tables. It was bright and colorful and full of energy, sunlight, and life. I made my way to the middle of the room and sat down. A young girl recognized me and came to sit next to me. It seemed that we knew each other fairly well. I asked her if she was auditioning and she said, "Oh yeah. I'll do something for sure!"

"Me too," I said instinctively and we laughed at some invisible secret between us. Then she asked me if I would take her swimming. She told me that the last time I took her swimming was the first time she wasn't afraid of the water. I was astounded. Something so simple had made such a profound difference for her. I could see it in her face. No more fear. Only excitement.

"Of course I'll take you swimming!" I said. "Let's go now!" Her face lit up and I could feel mine doing the same.

When we got to the pool I was still in a lot of pain and very stiff. I felt a lurch of fear that I would not be able to swim in my condition but the girl was heading in first and holding out her hand to me. I knew I couldn't turn back. As I eased my way into the water, the pain dissolved entirely and the stiffness disappeared. Then I closed my eyes and floated in a perfect moment of sun-lit happiness.

I woke from that dream and thought about what it meant. I had been dreaming for the last month about opening up foster homes across the country. In the daylight, I loved contemplating that possibility. It felt like a wonderful vision, but also impossible in my current physical condition. However this dream was different. It was as if I had been given a prescription for how to heal myself. I needed to work directly with foster kids. My healing would come when I got into the emotional waters and built relationships directly with the kids.

I started doing research, listening to my gut, and following the daytime clues for how to work with foster kids. I continued to actively self-care my physical body as I reached out to various groups and organizations that worked with foster kids. One organization resonated the most with me: CASA (Court Appointed Special Advocates). CASAs are trained through the courts to advocate and "be the voice" for a foster child for the length of the time that his or her case is open in dependency court. One child. One foot in the water. I applied.

Then I put a second foot in and was interviewed. A third foot and I was accepted. During this process I joined another group that helps foster kids and we did a Thanksgiving dinner for fifty kids. Next we did a Christmas resource fair for about seventy-five. I was not only able to attend, but I felt great — strong and happy!

After two months of training I was sworn in by a judge as a CASA and I got my first case: a girl who had been through more in her young life than anyone should have to go through in multiple lifetimes. I sobbed in my car after I read her file and I was overcome by the fear that I could not do this, that I was not strong enough. I wanted to run away, go back to the hallway and wait for the doctor to see me, forget all this craziness about working with foster kids, and get the heck out of the pool. But then the dream washed over me in reverse. I saw the girl, waiting alone in a big pool for someone who would never come. There was terror in her eyes and despair. Then I saw my own body returning to its crippled form. That did it. I was in, moving forward, to heal both of us.

~Jenny Karns

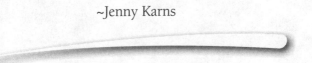

Chapter 7

Dreams and Premonitions

Life Savers

58

I Could Have Died on the Side of the Road

The invisible intelligence that flows through everything
in a purposeful fashion is also flowing through you.
~Wayne Dyer

I had just finished having a really fun girls' night out with my friend Debbi. We hadn't seen each other in ages and spent hours chatting without paying much attention to anyone but ourselves. We suddenly became aware that it was after 10 p.m. and the wait staff had started putting chairs on top of tables. They were closing up for the night. We giggled and admitted it was probably time to head home.

As we stepped outside to go to our respective cars, we discovered a raging thunderstorm. Debbi and I quickly hugged each other goodbye, wished each other a safe drive home, and raced to our cars trying to avoid getting drenched.

I was about twenty minutes into my one-hour drive when the rain started to come down even heavier, which seemed pretty impossible because I was already having trouble seeing the road. Although I had my windshield wipers on the highest speed they still didn't seem to be working fast enough. I knew this was not the best night to be on the highway driving and I started to get scared.

I'm not usually a nervous driver, but I could feel my heart starting to beat fast in my chest. Although the speed limit was fifty-five, I was driving only thirty-five and even at that low speed I could barely see the lines on the expressway to know where my lane was located. In fact, I couldn't really see the road at all. The rain was crashing so hard on my windshield that the sound was deafening. There was a car in front of me that I considered following but then I decided that the driver probably couldn't see any better than I could, so what was the point?

I passed under an overpass and saw a few cars waiting out the rain under the bridge. I decided that I would do the same thing and stop under the next bridge.

As I passed under the next bridge I started to pull over, but right before I started to move over a lane, I heard a voice in my head shout so loudly I wondered if I was going crazy. "No, don't stop; keep driving! A single woman on a night like this should not be pulling over on the side of the road." That was the moment I felt the hair on the back of my neck rise straight up and I felt chills and goose bumps throughout my entire body. I was suddenly terrified. Something else was terribly wrong besides the bad storm and my limited visibility.

I was only at Exit 52 and I had twenty more exits to go until I reached my home exit, 32. "Still too far away," I cried to myself. The only thing I could think to do was to pray. Not being at all religious I found myself repeating over and over again, "Please let me get home safe and in one piece." All of a sudden I saw a white light from out of nowhere come down over my car and encircle it. I imagined I was driving in a circle of white light, and thought, "Wow, it looks like the light is protecting me."

And then still driving, but slightly less freaked out, I called my husband. "Honey, I'm driving home, it's raining really hard and I'm kind of nervous. Can you stay on the phone and talk to me until I get home?"

Without further incident and with my husband talking me through the rest of the drive, I finally made it home safe and sound. Before going to bed, I recounted the details of the drive to Chris, and shared the strange voice in my head that had warned me not to pull over under the bridge at exit 52 on highway 495 and the evil feeling and goose bumps I felt as I was considering stopping.

The next morning, as Chris and I were getting dressed for work, we saw the local news on the television. We were speechless when the reporter said, "Last night at 11 p.m., a man with a rifle was standing under the overpass at exit 52 on highway 495 shooting randomly into oncoming traffic. The man has been identified and taken into custody."

I learned that night that my inner voice provides powerful messages I am meant to hear, ones that might even save my life.

~Wendy Capland

59

Angela's Warning

*We are not put on earth for ourselves, but are placed
here for each other. If you are there always for others,
then in time of need, someone will be there for you.*

~Author Unknown

I was born and raised in Montreal. In 1999, when I was thirteen, we moved from Quebec to Kansas. My first year in Kansas was terrible. With my French-Canadian accent and different sense of style, I stuck out like a sore thumb and I had a difficult time making friends.

Then I met Angela, who had recently transferred also. We quickly bonded. Tragically, by the time I left Kansas in 2005, I had lost eight friends to suicide, the second one being Angela. She had called me the night that she ended her own life and I remained on the phone with her, trying to reason with her and keep her mind busy. Angela's mind couldn't be changed and she proceeded with her plan. I was wracked with guilt. Not only had I failed her, I failed her whole family. She called me for help, but I couldn't stop her.

After Angela's death in 2002, Kansas became a dark place. Day after day, my mind was tortured, and night after night she visited me in my dreams. I decided to move to Florida. The cleansing nature of the beach, the sound of the gulls and waves crashing on shore, the smell of the salt in the air and the warmth of the constant sunshine on my skin, all made life seem so much brighter.

I began working at a convenience store where I quickly made

friends and began healing. An instrumental part was a wonderful person named Anthony. Handsome, intelligent, witty and funny, he was the remedy I needed. The ghostly visits from Angela subsided. Anthony and I became really close, telling each other that men were jerks for breaking our hearts, spending our time at the beach or drinking wine, fantasizing about what our futures held.

In 2010, Anthony moved to South Carolina with his partner and although he was far away, our bond remained strong. After a rough breakup, he decided to come back to Florida and everyone was ecstatic to have him back, even if he would be living forty-five minutes out of town. It was definitely better than him being in another state. Because I was working Monday to Friday, he would come and stay with me on weekends. We were typically in high spirits, spending our Saturday mornings at the beach taking in some sun and spending our evenings with a little bit of rum or a bottle of Sangria.

Then I had a horrible nightmare.

Angela and I were seated at a wooden table across from each other. The room was dark and Angela looked anxious. This dream had a different feeling than the others; it felt real. I could feel the grain of the wood under my fingers; I could smell the scent of her favorite perfume.

"I'm so sorry, Angela," I said.

"He's not me," she replied.

Her words made no sense to me. "Who isn't you?" I asked.

"He's not me. He needs you this time," she said cryptically.

Once again, I tried to make sense of her words. "Who's he?" I pressed.

"He won't be mad. It's an emergency. This is my chance. It's not your fault, Jewels," she said as she stood up from the table. Her anxious look melted away as she gave me a warm smile.

I woke up crying. My fiancé was sleeping next to me and Anthony was upstairs. Everything seemed to be okay, but it took me three days to get over that nightmare.

A few months later, I had just arrived home from work and was beginning to settle in for the evening. My betrothed was working an overnight shift and Anthony had sent me a message earlier in the day through social media, telling me that he had left his phone at a friend's house. I turned on my laptop and began messaging him, looking to catch up on the day's events. I got the sense there was something wrong. After some probing, he admitted that he had been feeling pretty depressed. He was missing his ex and was having a hard time finding work. As a result, he felt that he was a burden on everyone he loved. He began talking about suicide.

Immediately, Angela's warning came to mind and everything became clear. She was warning me about Anthony. My heart began to race as I typed out a message letting him know that I was going to change to the mobile messenger and that I was on my way to his home. That was when I got the worst message I could ever imagine: "It's not worth it." I grabbed my purse and ran out the door. I jumped into my car and made the hardest decision I have ever had to make. Anthony lived forty-five minutes away and I knew that even if I went 100 miles an hour, I might not get there in time. I dialed 911.

"911, what is your emergency?"

"It's my friend. He's — he's going to try to kill himself," my voice cracked as I spoke the words.

"Is he with you ma'am?" the operator asked.

"No, he's alone at his house. He lives with his father and his father is working the night shift. I can't get there in time," I cried, hot tears streaming down my cheeks.

"What is his address, ma'am?" she continued calmly.

"I don't know his address, I just know the name of the apartment complex and how to get there." I gave her directions to his apartment and a description of his car so they would know they were in the right area. After collecting the information, the operator told me that she would give my information and phone number to the responding officers. She did her best to reassure me before allowing me to return my full concentration to my driving.

I sped down the highway, cutting a forty-five minute drive to twenty. As I was pulling off onto his exit, the responding officers called me. "We have arrived at the apartment complex and we have identified your friend's car. Can you direct us to his apartment?" I guided the officers from the phone as well as I could.

I arrived at the apartment complex five minutes later. I spotted the police cruiser parked next to Anthony's car and I saw an officer coming out of his apartment. She said, "We got here right on time. Anthony had the keys to his car in his hand. He was going to intentionally crash into the cement divider. He opened the door as we were about to knock. Do you want to see him?" I started crying again, but these were tears of joy.

I ran into the apartment and wrapped my arms around Anthony and wept. "Don't be mad at me, Ant. I had to call them," I cried, hoping that he wouldn't hate me for his involuntary stay overnight in a hospital.

"Thank you Julie. You saved my life," was all he managed to say. We cried in each other's arms until the officers told us that they had to take him.

Angela's warning was the last time I ever had a dream about her, and to this day I'm not sure if she was just a figment of my subconscious picking up on subtle signs or if it was a ghostly visit from a lost soul trying to find peace. Either way, the message was received and Angela, whether in memory or spirit, helped save Anthony from the same fate. It was a lesson to me that we should never disregard our dreams. Just ask Anthony.

~Julie Mac Lellan

60

Saving Reece

Follow your intuition, listening to your dreams, your inner voice to guide you.
~Katori Hall

I heard my daughter shout, "Uncle Reece is dead. Uncle Reece is dead." Then I woke up. It was 6 a.m. and my alarm clock was playing some random song. I couldn't figure out why I would dream such a thing. I went to work and the dream slipped away.

The following morning, it happened again. My daughter yelled, "Uncle Reece is dead. Uncle Reece is dead!" I woke up in a panic, not needing an alarm clock because this time I could "see" my brother lying in a black void with red on his chest. I assumed the red was blood. This didn't feel like a dream; it felt very real.

I felt an urgent need to call my brother. Would he think I was crazy? If anything happened to him and I hadn't warned him, I could never forgive myself. I dialed his number.

Reece was at work when I called. I composed myself and told him there was something I needed to tell him. I choked up when I described what I saw. I knew he was on a baseball team after work so I suggested he be aware of his surroundings. His job was head of the produce department at a supermarket. A good guy at heart, my brother liked to catch shoplifters. He should have been either a stuntman or a police officer. He had a few close calls when he stopped people stealing from his store. I told him to be careful if someone came in to rob the store. Knowing him well, I told him not to be a hero and to think of his wife and three daughters before he did anything rash.

I worried all day about Reece. I finally called him in the evening. He didn't seem to want to talk. When I asked him if anything had happened during the day, he hesitated and then finally told me the story: Reece heard a commotion at the front of the store. He quickly started in the direction of the noise but then remembered my phone call. He cautiously continued until he could see the checkout counters, where he saw a man with something shiny in his hand. The man was shouting at a terrified clerk to open the cash register. My brother ran to the dock area at the back of the store and saw a car waiting. He was careful to stay out of sight. The robber ran to the car and they took off. Witnesses confirmed the shiny object was a gun.

Reece was in shock that my dream had predicted this. Years later, his daughters told me that Reece's initial inclination had been to try to take the gun from the robber. But he remembered my admonition — don't be a hero — and he stayed safe. His family told me that my dream saved his life.

~Cheryl Elise

Saved

Follow the light of your intuition, and keep away
from the darkness of convention.
~Michael Bassey Johnson

I almost didn't go to work that Saturday morning because of Hootie, our fifteen-year-old Terrier mix. I told myself I was being silly; there was no cause for concern. Hootie was old, but he was in good health and showed no signs of separation anxiety. He and our Doxie mix, Roxanne, had the run of the house, plus a dog door to the back yard.

Besides, my husband Lee and I were home with them most of the week, and only left them on weekends when we sold our artwork at an artisans' market in San Francisco, a half-hour away. They were always fine when we returned home around seven in the evening, overjoyed to see us and demanding their dinner.

Still, I worried about Hootie that Saturday and felt an urgent need throughout the day to get home early. "We need to be home by four o'clock," I told Lee. "I have no idea why, but it's important."

Lee and I packed up our displays early and arrived home shortly before four. Roxie greeted us at the door, leaping and twirling and barking with joy. Petting her, I looked around for Hootie, my worry intensifying as I hurried down the hall to find him.

He stood in the doorway to our bedroom, strangely quiet. "Hootie," I said, in a questioning voice, as he gave a subdued little greeting and took only a few unsteady steps toward me, before suddenly stopping, turning sharply to the left, and keeling over onto the floor.

Reaching down, I lifted his little body and placed him gently on the bed. His eyes were wide open and to my horror he threw his head back and cried out as though in great pain. Yelling loudly for Lee, I bent to soothe Hootie, who cried out again. I thought he was going to die right there in front of me.

By the time Lee rushed into the room, with a frightened-looking Roxanne at his heels, Hootie had gone silent and lay still on the bed. "Get the Rescue Remedy," Lee said, bending over the bed. Fighting panic I backed from the room. "Come on, son," I heard my husband murmur. "Breathe."

Returning with the calming homeopathic medicine, I saw Lee take a deep breath and blow air into Hootie's mouth, filling his lungs, again and again. Several breaths later, Hootie stirred, moved his head.

"Yes! He's got a heartbeat again," Lee said, just as our little old dog opened his eyes and looked up at us. Limp with relief, we squeezed Rescue Remedy into his mouth and gave him low-dose aspirin. By evening he was his usual bouncy self, gobbling his dinner like he hadn't eaten in weeks and demanding a Greenie for dessert.

Exhausted by the strange turn of events, we all piled in bed at nine-thirty, with Hootie curled between us and Roxanne's little head resting on his hip. Thanks to my premonition and Lee's quick action, Hootie had survived his heart attack. I couldn't stop petting him, running my hands over his furry little body, realizing how close we'd come to our final parting.

~Lynn Sunday

62

Safe Travels

Out of this nettle, danger, we pluck this flower, safety.
~William Shakespeare

I know that when we are on vacation in the USA, many people are surprised to learn that my husband does all the driving and I don't even have a license. In Scotland, this is not so unusual for women in their sixties, but if I were to confess I don't drive because of warnings in my dreams, eyebrows would be raised on both sides of the Atlantic.

It started when I was in my teens and had a very vivid dream about being in a red open-top convertible driving down a hill near St. Cyrus. A big truck was in front of us as we turned a corner and we drove straight into it. I was then looking down on the wrecked car and thinking how devastated my mum was going to be when they broke the news to her. I woke up with a start, and even though I was too young to drive at the time, the dream seemed very real.

When I first began my driving lessons, I had one lesson, and then my friend took ill and I rashly offered to take her place on the local hockey team. Now, hockey and I were never very compatible, and this was proved when I tripped over the ball and dislocated my knee! Naturally, this put an end to my driving lessons.

Undeterred, in due course I picked up on the lessons again. This time, as I was helping my aunt up some steps, she lost her balance and sent me flying down them. Three months of an elbow in plaster made my mum say, "Every time you take driving lessons, you seem to be unlucky."

I dismissed all that as coincidence, but then the dreams started. By then, in my early twenties, I had the same dream a number of times in different forms. The first time I was driving a milk float — a small van that delivers milk to people's homes. It suddenly went out of control, and I was going down a hill and around corners and couldn't stop it until it threw me out onto a grassy mound. The next time it was a forklift truck, which kept ramming into things in a warehouse. Because I don't like milk and think forklift trucks just look dangerous, I was surprised at these dreams.

I did attempt more driving lessons and got as far as taking my test, but that was the biggest disaster of all! When I failed, the examiner gave me a long serious look and said, "I am not usually this blunt, but I honestly feel you should re-think trying to get a license. You seem like an intelligent young woman, but your coordination and judgment are totally unsuitable for driving." Now, Scots are not renowned for their subtlety, but this was blunt indeed and I was upset by that comment.

On the other hand, it was followed by a series of dreams where I was driving all kinds of vehicles and they all ran out of control or crashed. Finally, it got through to me that the dreams were warnings, so I gave up on driving. I explained all this to my husband when he offered to give me driving lessons.

After we were married about three years we were visiting a friend up the coast for a barbecue. We had intended to get a taxi home, but their neighbor had not been drinking and offered to drive Eric and me home. I happily followed the two men around to the neighbors' to get in the car. I stopped dead when I saw the red open-top sports car parked in the drive. At first even Eric thought I was silly for refusing the lift, putting it down to too much wine. When he saw the fear in my eyes, though, he just shrugged and said, "Okay. Look, Joyce has a thing about red sports cars. We'll get a taxi. There are others who would be glad to take a lift."

We went back into the house, and because we were getting a taxi decided to stay a little longer. A couple we didn't know took our lift instead. I can never put into words how we felt when within an hour another neighbor came through and told us, "Mark has had a very bad crash with his sports car. It's awful!"

We all just stared at her until finally someone asked what happened.

"Apparently a truck had jackknifed across the road, and they went straight into it. Mark's quite badly injured, but it's not life threatening," she told us.

"What about his passengers?" I asked.

She shook her head, "Neither of them survived. It's awful."

Eric came over and put an arm round me as he asked, "Where did this happen?"

"Going down the hill at St. Cyrus," the lady said.

I still find it difficult to take in that my early dream had been a warning so far in advance. I had always assumed that I was driving, but thinking back, that was just my assumption. There is no doubt in my mind that this dream saved our lives, and that all the others about vehicles going out of control when I was driving them were further warnings. Am I happy to let Eric do all the driving? Of course I am. Do I believe that dreams give us warnings? You bet I do!

~Joyce Stark

63

Finding Sarah

*Talking to your best friend is sometimes all
the therapy you need.*
~Author Unknown

It was a Saturday morning and I was just finishing up the breakfast dishes. I had been listening to music, but my thoughts were not on the music. I had a feeling of doom hanging over me, and my friend Sarah kept popping into my mind. It had been a year since I had talked to her.

Sarah married Ben right out of high school and I married Rick at the tender age of seventeen. Ben and Rick became friends while working at a small manufacturing company. The four of us were inseparable. You would find us together almost every weekend — fishing, camping or hiking. When the weather turned cold you would find us together at one house or another playing pinochle or having a barbecue.

Sarah and I had our first children within a few months of each other. I started driving a newspaper route, which allowed me to take my child with me to work. Sarah liked the idea so much she applied and soon had her own paper route. While working for the same company we were able to see each other every day. We would often meet for lunch and let the kids play with each other before we had to be at work.

When my marriage took a nosedive and I caught my husband cheating on me, Sarah was my rock. I could call her night or day. She helped me through a very difficult divorce. Sarah encouraged me to start dating again and she was my biggest cheerleader when I found my husband Terry.

Soon after we married, Terry was offered a better job out of state. It was hard for Sarah and me to maintain our relationship; we kept in touch through phone calls and letters.

After four years of being out of state, my husband found a new job just forty-five minutes away from our family and friends. It was great to reconnect with Sarah, but we were so busy raising families we could only find time to get together once in a while. Even so, Sarah and I found our kind of friendship wasn't hindered by time or distance. I think she will always be a part of me.

On that Saturday morning I had a strong feeling I needed to track Sarah down. Something told me she was in trouble.

I finally reached her by phone, and from the moment I heard Sarah speaking in a monotone I knew she was, indeed, in trouble. Even after I identified myself there was little lift in Sarah's voice.

I decided the only approach was an honest approach. I told her that I woke up with her on my mind and how throughout the morning I had a feeling she was in trouble.

Sarah started crying as she explained that she was getting ready to take an overdose of pills. She said she couldn't stand the pain any longer. I made her promise she wouldn't do anything until I got there. I prayed with her before I got off the phone.

The forty-five minute drive seemed like an eternity to me. I pulled up in front of Sarah's house and as soon as she saw me she flew down the stairs and into my arms. The next few hours were precious, scary and productive. Through a lot of prayer and searching we realized part of the problem was the medication she was on. I stayed with her until we both were sure she was thinking for herself and not letting the medication do the thinking for her.

I didn't leave her until I watched her dump the pills down the toilet. In the weeks that followed Sarah confirmed that the medication that was meant to help her sleep and to help with some of her depression

had contributed to more depression, almost to the point of suicide.
I thank God for the premonition that warned me about my friend!

~Lavina Norlin Litke

64

The Afterlife Movie that Saved My Life

It is said that the present is pregnant with the future.
~Voltaire

I dreamt of a silly little dog decked out with fake antlers for a Christmas show. The dog ran out on the road and was killed. Later he was magically revived by a bizarre character.

When I woke from this dream, my feelings were neutral. I had been a detached observer. The dream experience had been almost like watching a movie. I had no particular associations with the dream, and barely had time to write it down in my journal before rushing to the airport to catch a plane.

I was bound for Denver that day, but missed my connection and was put on a different flight. When the in-flight movie came on, I looked up at the screen and saw a silly little dog decked out in fake antlers for a Christmas photo shoot. Later in the movie, the dog ran out on the road and was killed. He was magically revived by a bizarre character — a low-flying angel portrayed by John Travolta in the movie *Michael*. I realized I had previewed the movie in my dream the night before.

This seemed to be a straightforward example of dream precognition. I had no way of knowing what movie they were going to show on the flight to Denver. I wasn't even scheduled to be on that particular plane. If I had even heard of the movie *Michael* at that time I did not know anything about it. A hardheaded skeptic might say that the correlation between my dream and the waking incident was coincidence. I can agree with that statement, as long as we drop the notion that coincidence is *merely* coincidence, as Jung and many others have rightly urged us to do. When coincidences of this kind happen again and again, we begin to realize that something very interesting is going on.

If it is possible to dream a coming event as trivial as the in-flight movie on the wrong plane, isn't it likely that we dream about more important things that lie in our future? From what I have observed and experienced, the answer is clear. We do it all the time.

Dreams of the future not only show us things that will happen, they also show us probable futures, things that may or may not happen depending on whether we are able to clarify the dream information and apply it to avoid possible events we don't want or manifest happy events that we do. Learning to discern and act upon early warning dreams can even save your life. On September 13, 1996, I recorded this dream:

I am driving up the hill on Route 2 toward my home in Troy. As I approach a fork in the road the sky becomes very strange. It fills with a purple and yellow bruise. Is this a twister? The traffic has become crazy. There is a blind spot to my right where something is blocking the road.

The scene ends abruptly. Now I am being propelled effortlessly, painlessly, through masses of air. I know I am leaving this world and feel a pang of regret for people I will miss.

I enter a world without color. It's a bit like being in a 1950s black-and-white movie. I find myself on an open, grassy hillside with a group of people of varying ages. They are looking for guidance. They want to go to the house at the top of the hill, and I agree this would be good. I tell them we can go there by power of thought. We join hands, and then we are there.

I enjoy exploring the house on the hill. There is so much to explore—libraries, art, music collections. Other visitors keep arriving at the house. Some seem to be unaware that they are dead. I somehow know that it is part of my responsibility to educate them, and I start trying to make them aware that they do not have physical bodies anymore.

At this point the color returns. Everything is bathed in a wonderful light.

I am excited to meet new people, and begin to embark on new adventures with new companions. Then I remember that I left a body behind in a bed in my house on Route 2 in Troy, New York — and that if I want to keep it going, I had better get back to it and record the details of the scene in which everything stopped under that strange sky.

So I traveled back from the *bardo* zone with the house on the hill and recorded my dream. I tried to locate, as exactly as possible, the place where the action stopped when I was driving on that road going up the hill.

Active dreamers learn to recognize certain markers in their personal styles of dreaming. Death in dreams is often symbolic, sometimes indicating moving on from an old way of life or a dead relationship. But dreams also provide warnings of a possible physical death. For me, being thrown unintentionally into what felt like after-death transition states in a dream was a clear marker that there was a risk of physical death.

Three days after that dream I was driving up the hill on Route 2 in Troy. The sky was stormy and strange. Just before a fork in the road, my view was blocked by a big delivery truck that was parked.

The scene fit the dream almost exactly. I would normally have pulled out and passed the truck, but my recollection of the dream led me to slow my car almost to a stop. Because I paused, I missed a head-on collision with an eighteen-wheeler that came barreling down the hill at sixty miles per hour, twice the speed limit.

Dreams can be movie previews. They can be brilliant full-dress movie productions. And they can even give us picture shows of the possible future that can help us survive and thrive.

~Robert Moss

65

Into the Panther's Cage

Nothing in life is to be feared. It is only
to be understood.
~Marie Curie

I was soaking up some summer sun in my garden when I got the call from my son: "Mom, Dad's had a seizure. He's in hospital." With that call, I knew my life would be forever changed. My world started to crumble. I could imagine my life without him, as we'd been divorced for several years, but I couldn't imagine him no longer in the world. Nor could I imagine our sons without their father.

Then, on August 22, 2013, my deceased ex-husband visited me in a dream:

"I drew this picture of a seal for you," he says before taking my hand for a walk along the beach. I look down to see I am wearing his worn leather hiking boots, the ones with the thick soles and red shoelaces wound around my ankles a couple of times. Next we're driving inside a big store like Target, looking for the exit.

I woke up feeling anxious and not liking the meaning of this dream at all. I knew the seal represented our pact of always being connected through our kids. Did walking in his shoes mean I had a deadly health issue like he had? Did those long red shoelaces symbolize our souls forever entwined? What did the future have in store for me? Would I need to shop around for solutions? Would I soon be facing my own exit?

I tried to brush my concerns aside but I was scared. This was not a normal dream.

Soon after this dream, an excruciating migraine came over me that landed me in Urgent Care. The doctor reassured me that my blood work looked good and I had nothing to worry about. I was sent home with pain pills, told to drink lots of fluids, rest and return in a week for a follow-up.

A few days later, still recovering from the migraine, I dreamt that I was at a big party with my favorite music playing. Everyone was talking how courageous I had been!

Now I was really concerned. My dream made me believe I had something seriously wrong with me.

My doctor listened intently as I told him about the recent dreams and what my intuition was telling me. Fortunately, he agreed that there might be something to my dreams and referred me to a neurologist for an MRI to rule out anything serious.

I went in for the MRI. As I was getting ready to leave the technician stopped me. "Deborah, we've found something we're concerned about. I need to take you to the Emergency Room."

Two days later, on November 2, 2013, the day my ex would have turned sixty, the apricot-sized tumor was completely removed. I had a glioblastoma multiforme, the most common and deadliest kind of brain tumor! I was stunned by the confirmation that my dreams were right and that the visit from my deceased ex-husband saved my life. I was in awe that this happened, and I felt flooded with love and the belief that regardless of the circumstances of our imperfect human relationships, love is what prevails.

To help me recover, before going to sleep the next night I asked for a dream to help me continue along my healing journey. That night, I had the following dream:

I'm hiking along a parched riverbed. A black panther silently slinks up behind me. A man appears and orders her into the cave that has appeared in the hillside. Bars drop and cage her in. "Guard this dry riverbed," the man growls before disappearing. I'm distraught that I can't release the panther. I'm terrified to realize the only way to free her is to get into the cage with her. I slip easily through the bars and snuggle up to her luxurious silky chest, feeling it gently rise with each warm, calm breath. I'm amazed at how peaceful, yet powerful, it feels to be in sync with her. Suddenly, with a whisper of air, the bars disappear, and the black panther and I descend the dusty trail that becomes an abundant jungle.

I awoke from this dream feeling elated, realizing that stepping into the panther's cage was what I had just experienced by facing and embracing my worst fear, cancer.

It's been two years since my surgery, and, though I'm told glioblastoma is incurable, so far I've beaten the odds for survival. Every time I envision my black panther walking beside me, I feel fearless, powerful, free and invincible. I've even turned the story of my black panther dream into performance art, and I feel ecstatic as I empower others, through my story, to pay attention to their dreams and find the courage to face their own fears and become empowered and free in the process.

~Deborah Dutilh

The Still, Small Voice

*When we feel love and kindness toward others, it not
only makes others feel loved and cared for, but it helps
us also to develop inner happiness and peace.*
~The 14th Dalai Lama

It was the deepest, darkest part of winter and we were living out in the country near Clarksville, Tennessee, surrounded by pastures and forests. Our closest neighbors were a farmer and his wife. For the sake of privacy, we'll call them Bob and Mary Smith.

The Smiths did everything together: She would go out with him to the fields to cut hay for their cattle; he would help her with dinner and dishes in the evening; and every night she would turn on his favorite music so he would hear it when he came home after feeding the livestock. His favorite music was classical, especially piano. She herself was quite accomplished at playing the piano and would often play for him after dinner as he sat by the fireplace, pipe in hand, listening and dozing off. They were one of the most contented couples I'd ever met.

Then, disaster struck. One evening, Bob came home as usual. He told me later that right away he knew something was wrong. When he approached the house, he noticed there were no visible lights and he heard no music coming through the walls. He opened the door fearfully.

There on the floor lay Mary. The coroners said she had died of a heart attack hours earlier, thus the dark house. They said it was a blessing—she hadn't suffered and she had died instantly.

It wasn't a blessing to Bob; it was his life's greatest tragedy. He told me before the funeral that he'd fought in World War II and had seen death many times, but his wife's death made him feel as though his heart had been cut out of his body. How I felt for him then!

A week later, the flurry of visitors — friends and family — had come and gone from Bob's house. Sympathizers surrounded him before and immediately after the funeral, but I could see that he moved like an automaton. When he sat in his chair in the living room he'd shared with Mary, I noticed his eyes darting around the room, in disbelief that his beloved wasn't there. Over and over I noticed him glancing over at the piano, and tears would run down his cheeks at the sight of the empty bench.

I was home making supper for my family. Bob had said he wanted to be alone now and we were trying to give him some time to grieve. But a feeling kept nagging at me. It stayed through dinner, gnawing at me. Even the lively conversation with my husband and two children, then four and six, didn't lessen the feeling or subdue the inner voice that kept saying, "There's something you should do."

At the kitchen sink, once the kids were watching *Sesame Street*, I finally gave in to the voice in my heart. I spoke aloud — after all, I was alone in the kitchen and there was no one to tell me I was crazy — and said, "Okay, what am I supposed to do?"

Clear as day, in my heart more than in my head, I heard it: "Make a plate to go." Without any doubts, I prepared a plate of what we'd had for dinner: pan-seared catfish, salad and couscous with French bread. Then I paused to "listen."

I asked, "Now what?" Again, I had the inner thought: "Take it to Bob. He needs someone."

I looked outside. It was a moonless night, pitch black and so cold the owls weren't even calling as they hunted. There were five inches of snow mixed with ice on the ground, and the most light I had was an anemic flashlight.

Feeling more than a bit foolish, I put the plate in a fabric grocery bag and called out to my daughter Sarah to see if she wanted to walk with me the quarter-mile to Bob's house. To her, it was an adventure; to me, it was someone to walk with me for company, as I was questioning the inner voice with every passing minute.

Leaving my four-year-old son Gus with my husband Eric, I helped Sarah get into her snowsuit and boots and we headed out. The dim streetlights made the icy snow glint a pale blue, and our booted feet crunching through the crusty ice was the only sound we could hear as we trudged through the ice and snow to Bob's house.

As we approached, we both noticed it was totally dark; no lights shone through the windows, and I couldn't tell if Bob's car was in the garage. "Mommy," Sarah said, her voice loud in the clear, cold air, "I don't think Mr. Smith is home." Her voice wavered a little. "I'm kind of scared."

"It'll be okay," I said to her, squeezing her tiny mittened hand. "We'll just ring his doorbell and if he doesn't answer we'll leave this food hanging on the knob where he can find it when he gets home." I hoped I sounded more confident than I felt.

Stepping up to the dark stoop of the house, I rang the doorbell. I listened for the sound of footsteps or Bob calling out, "Who is it?" But there was nothing.

"Mommy, nobody's home," Sarah echoed again. "Let's just go back home."

Just then the light came on over the stoop and the door opened slowly. In the overhead light, Bob looked like someone in the throes of inner torment. He stepped aside and waved us in without a word. The front room, a combination of dining room, living room and kitchen, was totally dark. I flicked on the nearest switch and shut the front door. Bob said to me, "It's a bit late. Why'd you come see me tonight?" His usually gruff voice was low, as though it was difficult for him to get the words out.

"I brought you dinner," I said, and pulled the plate out of the bag. "It's still warm, and I have a feeling you haven't eaten."

Bob nodded and waved us over to the dinner table. I went to the kitchen area and found utensils and a napkin and brought them to him. When he sat down, we did as well. For a time, Sarah and I kept him company as he ate his dinner. He listened to her talk about school and the latest finger art she was doing in class. I remarked on the ice and snow, which had come unusually early in the season. Finally, Bob finished, wiped his chin with the napkin and said to me, "I'm glad you came, I have to say. I've been sitting here in the dark since coming in from the field, and this is the first time there's been no one here when I got home. I've had so much family around, it didn't really hit me that she's gone. Not until tonight."

With a nod to me, letting me know Bob was putting something into words that Sarah wouldn't understand, he added, "I've been thinking about…" and he just let the words hang there in the air like forgotten laundry on the line. But I knew what he meant, and reached over and squeezed his hand.

"We're here for you, Mr. Smith," I said gently. "Don't ever do that; there are too many people who care about you."

"I was thinking that it was all over, with Mary gone," he continued. Then he looked straight into my eyes. "I'm glad you came when you did."

We chatted a bit longer, until Sarah's eyelids began to droop and I knew it was time for us to go. Bob offered to drive us the quarter-mile home, but I didn't want him risking an accident in the ice and snow on the road. When we left, he gave us each a big hug. He still, of course, had the look of one ravaged by grief, but somehow he had a glimmer of hope in his eyes.

After promising Sarah that he'd give her and Gus a ride on the tractor next time he was out in the fields, Bob let us go. He said one more thing to me before I left: "You might've saved my life."

I responded with something like, "You would have done the same for me," but as we trudged back home, crunching through the icy snow, Sarah remarked on what had happened.

"Mommy, we did a good thing, didn't we?" she asked.

"Yes, Sarah, we did," I said to her.

Since that time, Bob has expanded his farm and a niece has come to live with him. He regularly gives the children tractor rides, as he promised. He and I never discussed that night again.

~T. Jensen Lacey

67

Eyes Wide Open

Not everything we experience can be
explained by logic or science.
~Linda Westphal

As I waited for my car to come screeching down the parking garage ramps, after a long day of college, I had no sense of danger. There was probably a misty haze over the Cincinnati skyline, but I just wanted to go home. After two years of photography school, my days had become routine. I handed a crisp five-dollar bill to the garage attendant, said "see you tomorrow," climbed into my compact white Toyota, turned left, and merged onto I-71 northbound.

I maneuvered through the heavy traffic. I preferred the center lane. The fast lane had the concrete median, which made me feel a bit claustrophobic, and the lane to my right was a mishmash of merging.

It was quiet and comfortable. The only sound was cool spring air seeping into the window as my cigarette smoke escaped.

I felt the rain before I saw it: a light mist on my left arm. Not enough to close the window. As I rounded a sharper curve, and caught the silhouette of the General Electric building, the rain began to fall harder. Enough to focus my eyes, put my cigarette out, and close the window.

I maintained my second lane position under the darkening mist of dusk. The traffic moved in harmony as we wound under a large overpass. The sound of the rain stopped for one protracted second, maybe two, and in that silence I heard a voice: "Joanne, someone is going to hit you. Put your seatbelt on."

I had never heard "a voice" before, but I simply obeyed and buckled in. I rounded the next bend and heard, "He's going to hit your door."

I had both hands on the wheel now, at ten and two. I leaned forward squinting through the raindrops and quivering slightly at the prospect. I never took my eyes off the road.

"You're going to be okay."

There it was again.

The traffic climbed uphill, and then, as the road flattened, my peripheral vision seemed stuck on a 55 MPH sign near the next exit. My car was parallel with that sign when I caught a flash of red on my left side.

I said aloud, "Here we go."

Everything slowed down and became a blur. The red flash smashed into my door. My hands dug into the steering wheel, and my eyes stayed straight ahead. I saw lines of colorful rain, sprays of water, and bursts of steam rising around me, and I heard: "You're okay, just hold on."

I held on. I held on as I spun to the right. I held on as that spin gathered momentum into one, two, three complete circles. I kept my eyes open as the spinning changed to a forward momentum, and in a sea of boxy blurred colors I saw the concrete median up ahead.

"You're going over the median but you'll be okay," the voice said.

I watched and consciously anticipated the impact of that gray wall. My front right bumper crashed into the wall and the sheer force and speed hurtled me up and over the barrier. For a moment I felt like a teeter-totter balancing on top of the wall. I closed my eyes. There were obscure noises: tires throwing off water, metal grinding, glass breaking. I was falling, there was another crash and I was sliding, screeching to the end of a terrifying roller coaster ride. I opened my eyes.

I realized, as my eyes focused on a wet surface, that my car was on its side and my head was pressed against cool, shattered, glass just inches from the asphalt. I never felt panic or fear. The voice was gone.

I unsnapped my seatbelt, forgetting that gravity would slide me closer to the jagged window and cold cement. I took a deep breath, rested one foot on the gearshift, and reached up to push open the passenger side door. It swung high and wide into the wind. I crouched on the car's frame, facing the speeding traffic, and jumped.

My feet landed securely in the emergency lane. I unfolded my tucked torso, tested my legs, and began to walk away from my car.

"Oh my God, are you okay?" a voice shouted behind me.

A bearded, six-foot tall man in khaki overalls was charging toward me.

I shrugged. "Yeah," I said.

His wet arms wrapped around my shoulders in a quick embrace.

"I almost killed you," he said. "If my brakes hadn't worked..." He shook his head and held me at arm's length.

I looked around him and saw a white box truck with its bumper mangled. He wasn't the only one; several cars were stopped along the northbound median. For a second I wondered what shield kept them all away from me.

"Where's the driver?" voices shouted in unison, disrupting my thoughts.

I suddenly realized the air was filled with the sound of sirens. Two fire departments were on-site, an ambulance was parking, and uniforms were moving through the steam in a graceful dance.

"Here," I said, raising my hand like a child.

A man in white looked at me and looked at my car in disbelief. Then I was surrounded, shuffled about, and events fell back into a blur. I saw a massive hole in my gas tank, I stepped on broken glass, and when I pointed to my cameras in my car I was swiftly redirected to the ambulance.

I refused treatment and followed directions to the back of a police car. I sat quietly as we pulled off the exit at the 55 miles per hour sign.

"I've never seen anyone so calm after such a bad accident," the officer said.

"I'm okay," was all I could say.

Hours later my parents took me to get my belongings. My Tercel was a heap, a skeleton with doors hanging off like broken arms. There was a sunken pit on one side, half of a front end, and the roof was more black than white.

There was nothing to reclaim. My equipment had been retrieved, paperwork had been filed, and I was left staring at an embarrassing pile of spilled cigarette butts.

I turned to go, and in the halo of a single floodlight, I saw tears fall from my mother's eyes.

The car was replaced, I had no scars, not even a scratch, and my story was often met with quiet reserve.

I have learned not to question fate; but I do believe that premonitions are miracles that find a way into the silent spaces. We just need to listen.

~Joanne Moore

Chapter
8

Dreams and Premonitions

True Love

Arranged Marriage

What's meant to be will always find a way.
~Trisha Yearwood

Breathing in the hot dry air of Botswana, I puffed on. I was out for my daily jog on the dusty roads, praying in my mind as I listened to the children shout *Lekgoa*, which was the local word for white lady. In this part of the world, seeing a white person was rare. People always stopped and stared.

After being a missionary for almost a year, I was used to it. I was here to minister to the people, but I thought I could never become one of them. Their life was too different from mine on so many levels! I still struggled to understand Setswana, their language. People used a community standpipe for water and had no indoor plumbing. Electricity was a luxury. I grew up so differently — going to our family's country club in South Georgia, spending summers vacationing in Europe.

Suddenly, as I trekked along, a distinct thought came to me: "You will marry Percy Thaba." That was weird. The thought came again stronger and clearer: "You will marry Percy Thaba." I had never even met Percy. He was the big brother to one of the youth in the local church I worked with. He was away at college.

"You will marry Percy Thaba!" Was this God speaking to me? Didn't He understand that an American like me wouldn't be compatible with a man from Botswana? What would we have in common? Could we ever understand each other? We were raised in such different cultures! How would we raise our children?

What would people say? I was here to reach out to the people, not marry one of them! That would be a distraction to my mission! My parents would never approve. What color would our kids be? And their hair… I didn't know how to take care of that! Reason after reason came to mind as I argued with the "voice" that was so clearly repeating over and over that I would marry Percy Thaba.

Physically exhausted from running under the hot African sun, I returned home. As I stretched my legs, I surrendered. I realized that the majority of my reasons for not wanting to marry an African man were because I worried about what people would think. Ultimately, I trusted God. I whispered, "God, if this is you speaking, prove it to me today!"

I showered and went to the Saturday youth group I led weekly at Francistown Baptist Church. After a few minutes, a taxi drove up and a young man got out. All the youth shouted, "Percy! You are home from university!"

My stomach dropped. My mouth grew dry. This was Percy? Today? I had been there more than ten months and had never met him. What were the odds that I would meet him today? I took a deep breath and calmly asked one of the youths, "Is that Percy Thaba?"

Excitedly, he responded, "Oh yeah! You have never met Percy? He is so cool!" It was too much to handle. I fled to the outhouse to gather my thoughts. Normally, I avoided that hot, smelly mud brick building, with its small hole dug into the ground, but today my heart was racing so fast that I barely noticed the awful stench!

I composed myself, walked out and almost bumped into Percy. He smiled and thrust out his hand confidently: "You must be Ashley! I have heard you are doing great work here in this church. It is nice to meet you. Actually, your supervisor called me and asked if I could help you while I am off university."

I mumbled something about needing to gather the youth and get started. I was too shocked to speak. He was supposed to partner with me?

After youth group, he casually sauntered over: "Wanna come by my house tonight so you can catch me up with what you are doing with the youth? I want to figure out where I can pitch in." I agreed. It was time to get to know my future husband.

Before heading over to his house, I called my friend and told her everything. "So," she said. "Did you walk up to him and say 'Hey, I had a vision today that I was going to marry you?'"

I gasped. "No! I don't even want to marry him!"

By the time I headed to bed that night, after spending three hours talking about our goals for the youth program, I had changed my mind. Would a guy so holy ever look at a girl like me? This guy was amazing! I had never met such a smart, kind, considerate, and godly young man.

Being the good Southern girl I was, I kept quiet about my developing feelings. I waited for him to make the first move. After two weeks of working side by side in ministry, I got a shock. Percy pulled me aside one day, asking if we could talk about something important. My heart raced. He took a deep breath and began to share his heart. "Ashley, when I became a Christian at age fifteen, I looked around my country. I saw the extremely high HIV rate and how easily people fall into temptation here. I made a vow to God that I would not even date a woman until she was the one I would marry. In order to do that, I must avoid any tempting situation. My feelings for you over the past two weeks have grown into more than friendship. Therefore, I am going to talk to your boss and ask her to find you a new partner."

"Wait!" I blurted out, desperate not to lose him. "I had a vision! God told me I would marry you!"

He responded, "But you are an American! It would never work!"

I laughed and said, "I know! I told God but He didn't seem to care!"

Three years later, I married Percy Thaba. We celebrated our tenth wedding anniversary this year. I still think he is the most amazing man on earth. I thank God every day for the clear premonition that Percy was the man for me. It made me look past my fears about color and make the best decision of my life!

~Ashley Thaba

True Love | 249

69

Surprise! You're Getting Married

Love isn't something you find. Love is
something that finds you.
~Loretta Young

My mother kept asking me why I didn't find some nice young man and settle down. At age twenty-two I hardly felt that was a priority. But, because she married at age seventeen, I guess that a twenty-two-year-old daughter who didn't date seemed rather odd to her.

I was happy in my career as an administrative assistant and was considering ways to get a promotion. I wasn't even sure that I wanted to get married. Finally, my mother asked one too many times. I replied rather forcefully, "I don't have to go out and beat the bushes for a husband. When the time is right, he's going to come right up and knock on my door." Mom must have finally gotten my message, because she quit bugging me about it.

Three months later, I had the strangest experience. I woke up one day and found myself saying, "Prepare, for within six months you'll be married." I was mulling this over when I started having thoughts about a specific man, a man I had never met who I seemed to have conjured up, complete with random facts about him. I was so taken aback by this that for several days I could hardly concentrate on my job.

A month after that I called a high school friend, Theresa, whom I kept in touch with, and asked if I could come over and tell her about my premonition or whatever it was. She and I always loved talking about weird things that happened to us, but this time I was sure she would think I was delusional.

I told Theresa everything, starting with the mysterious six-month timetable. "I kept having all these facts bombarding my mind. He has deep blue eyes and a smile that could melt your heart. He loves the outdoors, hunting, fishing, hiking, camping, anything outdoors. He has something to do with Colorado." This didn't sound at all like a man I would marry, because I was definitely not the outdoors type. "He's athletic and loves all kinds of sports." Again, that's not me! I don't have an athletic muscle in my body. "He loves reading and has lots of books. He wants a wife who can cook, sew, keep house, loves kids, and is a strong Christian." That was more like me. I continued, "He's quite a bit older than me, but doesn't look it. And, he drives a little blue sports car." Then, I sat and waited for her to burst out laughing.

I wasn't prepared at all for what Theresa said. "I know that man! He's exactly like that and he goes to my church! He's hunting in Colorado right now. And he just bought a little blue sports car!" She had a shocked look on her face.

"You're kidding!" I exclaimed.

"No, and he desperately wants a Christian wife who wants to raise a family, loves cooking and sewing, and would enjoy his library with him. And," she said, "I think that he said he's in his thirties. He sure doesn't look it."

At this point, I was staring at her, not knowing what to say. "Okay, you're serious, aren't you?"

"You've got to come to church and meet him as soon as he comes back." So, we planned our assault on poor, unsuspecting Lyle.

A few weeks later, I went to church with her and her family. Even though she had not described how he looked, I spotted him in a church of about one hundred people. I just felt like I should be sitting next to that man. When I met him face to face, his smile melted my heart. Of course, Theresa agreed to keep my secret.

A few weeks later, Lyle called and asked me for a date. When he came to our front door and knocked, I told my mother, "That will be my husband." Since I had not told her about my premonition, she just laughed at me.

Although I didn't tell Lyle about my experience until months later, he said that he felt like he had known me all his life. I felt the same. He asked me to marry him. Five months after my strange experience, and five weeks after our first date, we were married. I always wanted wedding bells to ring on my wedding day, but the church didn't have bells. So, I asked God to fill the trees with birds and have them all singing. Lyle thought that was funny and not likely to happen because it was February. But we had a beautiful spring-like day for our wedding and the trees were filled with birds singing joyously, which had everybody talking. God gave us his wedding bells.

On our honeymoon, Lyle told me how his friends had tried to fix him up over the years, but it never worked out. As he told me about a co-worker who tried to get her cousin to go on a date with him six years earlier, I realized that co-worker was my cousin and I was the girl who wouldn't go out with Lyle on a blind date!

Then he told me that he once knew a waitress who had taken in a single woman as a roommate. He invited her to bring her roommate and attend a concert with him. She tried, but her roommate didn't want to go, so she brought another friend. We were dumbfounded when we realized that I was that roommate.

Lyle told me about another set-up that hadn't worked out. He was expected for dinner at a friend's house, when a single woman dropped in on them unexpectedly, just an hour before he was scheduled. They invited her to stay for dinner, but she decided not to, because she didn't want to be considered a blind date. I was that woman!

Three times over the course of six years I nearly met Lyle. I guess I needed a more direct push to finally meet him. We enjoyed thirty-three years of marriage, and had two children and eight grandchildren. My soul mate and best friend died of cancer on Easter Sunday at home, with our daughter and me by his side. I greatly look forward to meeting him again and being by his side forever.

~Rebecca Gurnsey

70

Meant to Be

*Loving someone and having them love you back is the
most precious thing in the world.*
~Nicholas Sparks, The Rescue

When they began, the dreams were puzzling. I thought they couldn't possibly be premonitions or visions.

It's not that I'd forgotten the man. How could I, despite the fact we'd been lost to one another for nearly twenty years? I'd met the foreign physician when we were young, and we seemed like soul mates. I was a divorced mom, but he was married with three children and upfront about family loyalty, no matter how attracted to each other we felt.

I married again, divorced again. Eric remained the gold standard of men, but what good could come of contact with a married man who lived on the other side of the world? I forged ahead with my life, making one long-held dream come true by buying a houseboat and living there part-time.

Then I dreamed that Eric and his wife (whom I had never met) were standing in my kitchen. She was somehow giving him to me, wordlessly urging me to take him. I awoke and wondered what could be happening in his life to cause my dream. I knew kitchens are symbolic of nurturance, but this dream left me stumped.

About five months later, this unforgettable man popped up again in a dream. We were scrambling up separate sides of a mountain that happened to have Swiss cheese–like holes in it. Every once in a while, as we climbed toward the peak, we could peer through at each other. Again, the dream left me curious.

A few months later, with both dreams sharp in my memory, I typed Eric's name into the new search engine at work. There he was, listed among the employees at the same Swedish hospital he'd been with for years. My heart beating fast, I e-mailed him. Wouldn't it be wonderful to correspond with my old friend, even though romance was impossible? After all, this was a man I didn't dare dream of finding again — and yet he kept appearing!

Eric replied promptly, saying he'd been searching for me for six months. His wife had died years before, he'd had a subsequent relationship and broken up, and he'd reduced his work responsibilities.

The e-mails zipped back and forth across the Atlantic Ocean. He phoned early one morning from a medical conference just a few states from my home. I promptly bought a plane ticket and surprised him at his hotel.

That magical night, when we finally fell asleep in each other's arms, I dreamt a third dream about us. In it, Eric and I had just married, clasped hands and made the jump off a steep cliff — happily but amazingly surviving our leap. Yet again, I was perplexed. After all, my two marriages had failed. How could I possibly survive another leap into love?

Now you're probably way ahead of me here. After visiting one another in both our countries, I took early retirement and moved to Sweden. We married in both countries — the happiest leap I ever took. We are each close to the other's three children and savor grandparent duties on opposite sides of the globe.

And sometimes, when I awaken from one dream or another, I look over at his pillow and grin with gratitude. After all these years, we are still holding hands.

~Jann M. Mitchell

71

Dream Date

Love makes your soul crawl out from its hiding place.
~Zora Neale Hurston

The wedding ceremony took place on a sunny August day, charming everyone in attendance. Blossoms filled each corner of the garden at the historic inn and a soft breeze rustled the leaves as we all waited for the bride to appear.

And then, she was there, moving with grace down the length of the aisle, a picture of simple beauty and style. Her dress and the estate grounds reflected a modest elegance in a silent nod to this, her second marriage.

I wiped away a stray tear. This wasn't her first time to recite the vows, but I was certain it would be her last.

She reached the podium and turned to gaze at her groom, his face beaming with an infectious joy.

I smiled as I watched this young man, once such a mystery, now as familiar as if he were my own God-chosen son. And in a way, he was.

• • •

It all started around a year earlier in the middle of the night. Was it too much pizza, or had I watched one too many romantic comedies? Or was it something more that caused my subconscious visitation?

The dream had felt so real.

I stared at the man, his tall, stocky frame filling the crowded kitchen's threshold. He looked about five or ten years younger than I, with curly salt and pepper hair topping a sensitive, intelligent face. Brown eyes shone behind wire-rimmed glasses, his grin exuding confidence.

Watching him from across the room, I felt an impulse to speak with the stranger. Somehow I sensed his kindness and knew he'd protect those he loved. In an instant, my thoughts flew to my twenty-something daughter. My single daughter.

I glanced away to scan the space, hoping to spot her long blond hair or hear her laughter nearby. I couldn't see her anywhere. A moment later the people overflowing the area vanished. When my gaze returned to the doorway where the figure had stood waiting, it was empty.

I jolted awake, the glow of the bedside clock my only witness in the midnight quiet. Darkness shrouded the bedroom, and the street lamp outside my window sent a solitary ribbon of light across my comforter.

What was that all about? The gentleman's visage burned into my mind like a brand, forever committed to memory, whether welcome or not. But why? What was so special about this dream figure? Questions riddled my rest until morning.

As sunlight brightened the sky, I headed downstairs to set some coffee to brewing. Sounds coming from my daughter's room alerted me she was awake. The door squeaked open and she joined me in the kitchen.

"Morning."

"Hi, honey. Did you sleep well?"

"Yes, fine." She poured some of the brew into our cups and passed one to me. I had waited a long time for "fine" to become the norm for her.

Our daughter had left an abusive marriage and accompanied my husband and me in a cross-state move. Three years had passed and for the most part the scars had healed. There were no more nightmares or flat, unemotional responses. No crippling self-esteem issues. Even her pets seemed secure sharing their lives in our home.

I sipped the coffee and gazed at my child, her blond hair flowing down her back in a silky stream, her dark brown eyes reflecting warmth from within. My heartstrings tugged a notch tighter. "Do you work tonight?"

"No. I'm getting together with one of my friends."

I glanced out the window. A blue jay perched in our old walnut tree, preening, its azure feathers catching the light like a blue flame. A few fleeting moments later it took flight and was gone. My throat tightened.

I refused to ask whether or not she had a date — I knew the answer. The men she'd met since her divorce had left her hurt and wary and she'd all but stopped pursuing romantic relationships. A couple of months earlier, she'd joined the online dating community, choosing a service that focused on our faith and offered a free trial period. Nothing lasting had developed from that venture. Over time, both her interest and participation waned.

I was worried. Would she never experience the blessings I'd found in marriage — laughter and tears born of time-tested love?

"Let's go upstairs and check out the dating site together."

"Mom." She rolled her eyes as well as any teenager.

"Come on. It'll be fun." Crossing the dining room, I turned my head to see if she would follow.

"Oh, all right."

Minutes later, we snuggled together in our pajamas in front of the computer. She scanned a few profiles, not settling on any one.

She opened another and there he was, the man from my dream! His smiling face seemed much younger and his hair darker than the fellow in my vision, but he was unmistakably, undeniably the individual who'd stood in my kitchen's entry, as if waiting for something... or someone.

I gasped. "That's him."

"Who?"

"That's the man I dreamt about." My heart skipped a beat. "I think he's the one."

"The one what? What are you talking about?" Her gaze remained on his photo.

And I knew. "The one you're going to marry."

Disbelief shadowed my daughter's expression, but she listened as

I relayed my nighttime vision to her. "So you think I should meet this guy?" I could hear the excitement in her voice as her focus returned to the picture.

"I'm sure of it." I stretched an arm around her for a hug. "He's been waiting."

Her head rested on my shoulder for a moment and she sighed, long and slow, like a runner finally crossing the finish line.

As her gaze met mine, I smiled. "And so have we."

• • •

A blue jay zipped past, returning my thoughts to the present as the pastor spoke. "Will you promise to love, honor, cherish and protect her, forsaking all others and holding only to her forevermore?"

My dream son-in-law leaned a few inches closer to my child to answer, his voice lowered. "I will."

I believed it then and I believe it still. The wait is over. And this dream came true.

~Heidi Gaul

Matchmaker

A dream you dream alone is only a dream. A dream
you dream together is reality.
~John Lennon

Evan and I had been friends for about ten years, but after an argument we hadn't spoken to each other in more than eight months. We were living more than 1,000 miles apart.

Then one night, I dreamt that Evan and I were ballroom dancing. I had on a gorgeous, sparkly red ball gown and Evan was holding me, looking especially handsome in a tuxedo as we glided across the floor. I was crying into his shoulder because I had missed him and was happy to be with him. Then I woke up.

I called him. I felt an overwhelming desire to talk to him. When he answered, I said, "I had a dream about you."

He asked, "Did it involve dancing?"

Surprised, I said, "Yes, it did. How did you know that?"

He answered, "Because I had the same dream."

He then described the exact same dream I had. I was astonished. I hadn't told anyone the dream. We decided that I would visit him in Pittsburgh the following week.

In Pittsburgh, we had one of those sappy conversations that belong in a romantic comedy, in which he said, "I can't do this without you anymore. You're the missing piece in my life." I, of course, broke down in a mess of happy tears. We spent a week together, and it was as though nothing had changed. I realized how much I missed him, and we managed to move past our argument and past our hurt feelings. I returned to New Orleans knowing that he loved me, and that we were finally reconciled and were going to work as a couple.

We've been married a few years now, and to this day I think about that dream. I can't help thinking it was more than a coincidence. That dream was sent to us, to help us realize that we needed each other. My husband is my best friend, and I'm so grateful for him every day.

~Stephanie Lieberman

73

The Man of My Dreams

So, I love you because the entire universe conspired to help me find you.
~Paulo Coelho, The Alchemist

One morning in July 2012, I woke up remembering fragments of a very vivid dream in which I was having dinner at a restaurant with a handsome, dark-haired man named Marco. As I lay in bed recalling the dream, I thought about how real it had seemed. But I didn't know anyone named Marco, and anyway, it was just a dream. It didn't mean anything.

Besides, it was some years since I had been in a serious relationship and, at the ripe old age of thirty-one, I had given up thinking I would ever be in one again. "It was a nice dream, but it'll never happen," I thought to myself, as I got out of bed and carried on with the rest of the day.

The days went by and I forgot all about the dream.

At the time, I was living in Melbourne, Australia and I began to think of moving to another city. I couldn't explain it, but it was as though something was compelling me to move to Fremantle, a coastal city in Western Australia I had always loved visiting. So I booked myself into a backpackers' hostel until I could find more permanent accommodation and on the 19th September, I checked in to the Sundancer.

While I didn't know it at the time, on that exact same day, a twenty-eight-year-old Italian man had boarded a flight from Venice to Melbourne. He stayed in Melbourne for a few days, did some sightseeing and decided he would prefer the west coast of Australia. So he took a plane to Perth, just sixteen miles from Fremantle.

The flight ended up being delayed by some hours, and by the time the young man arrived at Perth airport, it was well past midnight — too late to go searching for a hotel room. He began to settle in for an uncomfortable night's sleep on the chairs at the airport when, as luck would have it, a flight attendant who had just finished her shift approached him.

He explained the situation to her and she offered to drive him to the hostel that was on the way to her house. He thanked her for her generosity and followed her to her car.

The flight attendant dropped him off outside the backpackers' hostel closest to her house — the Sundancer in Fremantle.

And the name of the handsome, dark-haired Italian man? Marco.

We have since moved back to Melbourne to start our life together, and we have been together for two and a half years. I am not sure if it was fate, premonition or just a strange series of coincidences that brought us together, but I cherish every day with this wonderful man who has restored my faith in love.

And wherever she is, I'd like to thank the flight attendant who, through an act of kindness to a stranger, delivered the man of my dreams straight into my arms.

~Rachel Lee

The Key

It's often the last key in the bunch that opens the lock.
~Author Unknown

The first key dream was not what I wanted. Frank and I had been together for a few years and I was sure that he was "the one." He'd been a friend of my ex-husband, Darrell, and had always been part of our small family.

I had a dream that Frank met me in People's Park — a popular Berkeley hangout spot for hippies and homeless people — to hand over the key to his apartment. For some reason, I didn't take it.

A few years after that dream, Frank announced that he had fallen in love with a woman at his office! I was devastated. In the six years that we had been together we had bought a new house in the Berkeley Hills, had gotten married, and were living a wonderful life with two blossoming careers. I'd had another child and was as happy as I had ever been — I thought.

Frank and I dismantled our lives, sold the house, and separated our finances. I moved back to my old house that I had rented out when we moved up into the hills.

Two years later, I had a dream that my first ex-husband, Darrell, now back in the picture as a sort of savior, handed me a key. I didn't accept that one, either. "It's too short," I told him. That dream helped to settle the uncertainty I had been harboring that we should get back together.

A couple of years passed as my two daughters and I rebuilt our lives. The older one was happy in school, the little one was in full-time day care, and my career as a corporate space planner working with architects and designers was taking off. I was promoted to Business Development Manager, overseeing important company accounts. I was happy again.

I loved my children and my work and my funky 1920s Berkeley home, but still longed for a partner. Over the next two years, I dated a string of unappealing men who had no interest in my children. That was a deal breaker!

Eventually, I abandoned all hope of meeting anyone — at least not while I was raising children. I came to a place of inner peace. I was doing well financially and I was happy at work. I owned my own home and had two wonderful children. I had friends and family. I would learn to live with what I had and stop wishing for what I didn't have.

Soon after that, I met Adam. A successful tech professional, he was divorced with two children close to my older daughter's age. He loved to read, he was an oenophile and gourmet cook, and best of all, he loved my children! He was the most generous, loving man I could have ever conjured up.

The third key dream came after Adam and I were together for three years — right before we were married. In the dream, Adam was digging in the dirt, searching for a key.

About a year later, I decided to change careers. After eight years in my old job, I had done everything I had set out to do. I was ready to commit to becoming a full-time writer. I had two degrees in Creative Writing, had published poems and articles in journals and papers and was now ready to go for it.

I hired Jane, a Life Coach with skills as a therapist and an intuitive. One day, after my second collection of poetry was published, Jane said: "Joan, I searched up and down Union Street for a gift for you. I looked at everything — crystals, jewelry. Nothing resonated. Then my cellphone rang. I dropped it, and when I picked it up this key fell off the shelf."

"A key! Jane you won't believe this!" I was shaking.

I told Jane the three key dreams. And in that moment, I realized what the key dreams were telling me! A partner or lover, no matter how dear, cannot hold the key to me. The key is about my connection with my higher power — and I've had it all along... I just needed to be reminded!

After that pivotal meeting with Jane, I was given a fourth key dream. In that dream, I was hiding a key for my older daughter. I showed her best friend Crystal where the key was hidden. "Make sure you tell Simone where the key is," I instructed Crystal.

Now that I know where the key is, I am in a position to help others find theirs... starting with my daughter.

~Joan Gelfand

Dreams and Premonitions

Personal Transformation

75

From Bully to Best Friend

Bullying is not okay. Period.
~Jim C. Hines

When I was in middle school, I was bullied, and as a result of not having someone to talk to, I became a bully myself. I didn't know how to deal with my problems in a healthy way, so instead I took out all my sadness and anger on other people. I was verbally abusive, and at times I would say hurtful things to those around me without even considering how they might feel. The consequences of me being a bully led to two suspensions and the loss of many friends. But it wasn't until the eighth grade that I began to change my behavior and discover self-love.

During my eighth grade year I had a dream that I was walking around campus listening to all the people I'd bullied talk about how I made them feel. In the dream, I was having an out-of-body experience; it almost felt as if I were a ghost, where I could see and hear them but they couldn't see or hear me. I remember hearing one girl say, "Mariah doesn't understand that I'm suicidal and every time she's mean to me, she gives me another reason not to live on this planet."

"I'm sorry, I'm sorry, I'm sorry!" I shouted, but she couldn't hear me. Feeling sorry was something I wasn't used to. In my waking life the bully part of me wouldn't care, but in the dream I was compassionate, begging to

Personal Transformation | 271

be understood, and wanting to share my story.

Another girl said, "Mariah is the meanest person in the whole universe," and I responded by saying, "I'm so sorry for all the pain I've caused you. Please forgive me." This time I was in tears, thinking, "The meanest person in the whole universe? There are seven billion people on the planet, so I can't possibly be the meanest person in the whole universe, can I? It's not my fault I'm so mean — I'm like this for a reason."

Upon awakening, I sobbed for twenty minutes before I got dressed for school. All I kept thinking was, "I have to apologize for all of the horrible things I have said and done to those I bullied." The dream shook me to my core. I sobbed while I looked at myself in the mirror and saw a stranger. She was not the person I was supposed to be.

That dream changed me. I've learned to be compassionate, to open my heart and to put myself in other people's shoes before I speak, to consider how they may feel. I've also learned to take responsibility for my actions and to not overreact when something doesn't go my way. Most importantly, I've learned the power and importance of forgiveness.

"I need to apologize." That was the first thing that came to my mind when I woke up from the dream, and that's exactly what I did. I apologized to every person I had bullied. I was terrified about how people would react, but I wanted to start a new chapter in my life before I went to high school. Although I apologized, I wasn't expecting to be forgiven. I chose to forgive myself, which allowed me to gain peace of mind and have the courage to let go of the past and adapt to a new way of being in this present moment.

Almost every person that I had bullied accepted my apology. Now I am a senior in high school, about to go to college. I would have never imagined that I would become a youth advocate for different organizations in Los Angeles that do great work regarding the United Nations' Millennium Development Goals. I am passionate about making a difference in the world and using my voice as a tool to empower, uplift and motivate those around me. If it weren't for this dream I don't know where I would've ended up. Being both the bully and the bullied has helped me understand and interact with others more effectively, while getting to know them as individuals. It feels great to have gone from bully to best friend just by paying attention to my dreams.

~Mariah Reyes

Editor's note: To see Mariah talking about her experience, visit https://mariahreyes.wordpress.com and watch her post from August 30, 2014.

76

Wake-Up Call

Which is the true nightmare, the horrific dream that
you have in your sleep or the dissatisfied reality that
awaits you when you awake?
~Justin Alcala

That unique blended scent of funeral flowers overwhelmed me as I walked slowly toward the gleaming oak casket. My husband was dead and I had to say my final farewell.

Mercifully I woke just then, my tears flowing. It was only a dream, I told myself, and yet the scene lingered with me.

I quickly patted the bed beside me and I panicked upon finding it empty. Then I remembered that my husband had gone into work early.

I reached for my phone. "Barry, are you okay?" I asked, relieved when he answered his office phone.

"Of course. I'm fine," he said, sounding pleased that I asked, probably because lately I'd been irritable more often than not.

"What's wrong?" he asked.

"Nothing. Nothing at all," I said. After hesitating, I said, "I love you."

"I love you too," he said.

I said goodbye, knowing that I needed to share more than I could on a brief phone call. I hoped he would be willing to listen when he came home, though I didn't really deserve it. We had been going through a challenging time in our marriage for the past two years. We'd moved to a new state where the work my husband had hoped for hadn't materialized. We had two newly adopted, older children with (understandable) emotional problems that were not only overwhelming for them to deal with, but for our whole family. Even though we ended up returning to Indiana and a secure job for my husband, I fell apart. I hadn't recovered from the years of worrying about money, dreading the mail and phone calls because of bills. I resented my husband for it and I didn't know how to change my attitude. I tried prayer. I tried reading books. I tried talking with friends. It was all to no avail.

I became self-centered: I lost weight, went back to college to finish up my degree, and ignored my husband. By then our daughter was in college and our son was just finishing up his homeschooling. I made a new set of friends, and went out with them nearly every weekend. It was as if I were a teenager again.

My husband lovingly continued to support my choices. He worked overtime to pay for my college classes, while I found part-time work to buy my books. He cooked on the nights I had to study for exams. He drove me in bad weather to lunches with my friends and came back to pick me up afterwards.

The nightmare I'd just had opened my eyes to all the good things about my husband. I was deeply ashamed of my behavior.

I owed this man so much more than an apology, and I quickly got busy, thankful I had a rare day off. First I cleaned the house thoroughly. Time was always short due to my schooling and the subsequent teaching job I took, so I hadn't done more than the basics such as the dishes and laundry in a long time. Now I swept under the cushions and placed the pillows at a jaunty angle I knew he'd appreciate. I filled the air with a lovely apple-scented spray.

I went shopping and bought a new dress that I thought he'd like. Then I stopped by the salon where I used to get my hair done. "Do you have time to flat-iron this mess?" I begged, pointing at my unruly hair. In fifteen minutes I was on my way, smiling at my smooth hair in the mirror.

There was still time to buy the things for his favorite dinner (fried chicken, mashed potatoes, green beans and rolls) and stock up on his preferred snacks, something else I hadn't bothered to do in a really long time.

When everything was ready, I waited anxiously by the door. Finally I saw his Nissan pull in. I barely waited for him to get in the door before holding his face in my hands and kissing him.

"Look at you," he said, touching my hair.

"This is for you." I handed him a blue envelope. The card contained a note apologizing for the bitterness in my heart, for the things (real and imagined) that I hadn't forgiven him for. For complaining and nagging. For exaggerating every bad thing. For downplaying the good.

When he read it, we both broke down in tears and I clung to him the way I had wanted to when I woke that morning after my nightmare. I felt as if I were myself for the first time in a long time.

We talked, really talked, over dinner, and it felt as if no ground had ever been lost in our marriage. I never wanted to take him for granted again, and I told him so.

If I ever think I am beginning to take him for granted nowadays, I stop, close my eyes and think about that dream, that nightmare, and I imagine what would happen if it came true. It changes my attitude every time.

~Drema Sizemore Drudge

77

First Things First

Perpetual devotion to what a man calls his business,
is only to be sustained by perpetual neglect
of many other things.
~Robert Louis Stevenson

My neighbor's two-acre yard is immaculate. And for that I am grateful. It is that yard that saved me from neglecting my children. Or, rather, it should have.

The year was 2004. My daughters were in fifth grade and kindergarten. My husband and I had just started a new ministry. As part of that ministry, we volunteered at an afterschool program. The only problem was that we didn't volunteer one or two days per week, but five days, Monday through Friday, without fail. We were at "the club" from three o'clock until well past closing time, sometimes not arriving home until eight o'clock.

When the opportunity arose for me to become an employee, I welcomed it. Of course that increased my hours. I was then at "the club" as early as one in the afternoon and sometimes stayed as late as nine o'clock. Next came the opportunity for me to become the club's director.

"This is a great opportunity," my husband told me. "You're already making an impact on the kids. Imagine what you could accomplish as director."

"I don't know," I told him. "We're forcing our own kids to be there

Personal Transformation | 277

every day after school and into the late evening."

And even though our fifth-grader was able to do her homework while the other children did theirs, and even though both girls seemed to enjoy "the club," something wasn't quite right. I felt guilty about not being home with them in the afternoons. I was giving so much of my time to the other children and hardly any to my own.

While considering the director's position, I had a dream. In the dream, I saw my neighbor's yard. The once well-cared-for lawn was overgrown with weeds. My neighbor, haggard and worn, said, "I've been so busy taking care of other people's yards, that I haven't had time to take care of my own."

When I awoke, I thought, "Wow, I can't believe how horrible Mr. Jones' yard looked." (Yes, I really live next door to the Joneses.) But then I dismissed the thought.

Later that morning, I randomly opened the Bible to Song of Solomon, and read: "My mother's children were angry with me; they made me the keeper of the vineyards; but mine own vineyard have I not kept."

It took me a moment to make the connection. But still, I did nothing about it.

Then, my older daughter's grades started falling. And my family no longer had time to do more than gobble down dinner before going to bed. And another employee at "the club" began to resent my presence and make my time there miserable, even to the point of mistreating my children.

That's when I heeded the dream and the scripture reading and quit "the club" and began, once again, to spend the evenings tending to my own vineyard. A few years later, when the opportunity arose for my husband to volunteer in an afterschool program, I knew my limitations. We had a third child by then, too. Rather than joining my husband, I continued picking up my children from school, heading home, and taking care of my own vineyard.

~Linda Jackson

78

Transformation

When we quit thinking primarily about ourselves and our own self-preservation, we undergo a truly heroic transformation of consciousness.

~Joseph Campbell

A number of years prior to embarking upon my life as a spiritual teacher I had a series of dreams where three men were chasing me. Each night they would get a little closer. At one point they were very close, and I was going to wake myself up like I normally did.

But this time I turned around and there was a small tent behind me, with a long line of people. The line was so long I couldn't even see the end of it... and I realized I knew everyone in this line. I thought to myself, "These men can't hurt me because I have all these friends here."

I started shouting for help and all the people turned their backs on me. Two of the men grabbed me and held me down as the third man plunged a knife into my heart. It was physically excruciating. I screamed... and I died.

When I woke up from that dream I was surrounded by a presence I could only describe as "Love Beauty." At the time I was agnostic and the word God wasn't a part of my vocabulary.

My whole life changed after that dream. I began to research what had happened to me; I began to study eastern and western mysticism; I began to meditate; I lost all my friends because they thought I freaked out.

They were right. On some level I did freak out...in a good way. Dying in my dream marked the beginning, as an adult, of my pursuit of an awareness of oneness with the Presence.

~Michael Bernard Beckwith

79

Her Final Lesson

If you want to turn your life around, try thankfulness.
It will change your life mightily.
~Gerald Good

On October 19, 2011 I picked up the phone to hear that my best friend since the sixth grade, Pitrice, had died. She was nineteen. She had been in the hospital since August after suffering a brain aneurysm.

On the day of her visitation, I walked up to her open casket with my mom and my friend Kaitlin. We took a long look at Pitrice as I tearfully slid an envelope between her two gloved hands. I had written her a private letter thanking her for the years of friendship and the lessons she taught me. She had always been wise beyond her years, and I asked her to watch over me.

In June 2012, I graduated from an acting program at college and moved back in with my parents. I was a hopeful but nervous graduate as I was thrown into the real world. Not too long after moving home, I desperately began to miss college.

I missed my friends, my student housing, and my roommates. I missed my landlords, my professors, my college fling, and my classes. I missed everything. I discovered that becoming an actress was a lot harder than I anticipated. I wasn't getting anywhere despite my attempts to contact agents and go to auditions.

I was facing a lot of rejection and it started affecting my self-esteem. I avoided seeing my friends because I was embarrassed that they were all doing so well and I was not. My life was going downhill and I had no energy to do anything. Then one night, after spending another day feeling sorry for myself, I went to bed and fell asleep.

I awoke in a room that was completely white. There was no furniture. In the corner of the room, Pitrice stood quietly, staring at me. Her dark skin contrasted with the white walls as she walked toward me. She looked healthy but her eyes were serious.

I immediately began venting to Pitrice about how much my life sucked — my hopeless love life, my nonexistent career, my lack of money, my failing social life, my insecurities, how society had failed me, and so on. I complained about everything. I told Pitrice how much I missed her. I told her that I felt lost and lonely.

Pitrice listened quietly, but then she let out an angry scream. "YOU'RE STILL HERE!" Pitrice shouted. "Move forward."

I froze as I realized that I was bellyaching about my life to a person who longed for the chance to be alive. Pitrice didn't get to graduate from college. She didn't get to pursue any of her dreams. A wave of guilt washed over me as I looked at Pitrice's face. She stared at me as she slowly faded into the white background and disappeared.

I stood there in the white room. "I'm still here."

I gasped as I woke up in my bed from the dream.

"I'm still here. I can still change the things I'm unhappy with."

Since I had that dream, I've been appreciating my life more, realizing it could be taken away at any moment like Pitrice's was. The dream changed me. Simple things like the taste of food and the feeling of the sun on my skin became special as I realized I was still here to appreciate them. I became healthier and looked better. I got in touch with Pitrice's family and to this day we remain close. I found a job, saw my friends and moved on from my heartbreak in college. I found an agent and continued auditioning. I am still taking acting workshops to improve my craft and striving to achieve my dream of becoming an actress.

Now I see the stressful periods in my life as little gifts that help me achieve maturity and growth. Whenever I feel frustrated, I go back to that dream of Pitrice. The dream serves as a constant reminder of the value of being alive and the importance of continually moving forward. Even after death, Pitrice continues to do a wonderful job of guiding me.

~Shannon MacKinnon

Unusual Therapy

Self is the only prison that can ever bind the soul.
~Henry Van Dyke

When I remember a dream, I often ask myself, "Is this one because of stress, random nonsense, hormones, or an emotional battle in my subconscious mind?" I can often pinpoint what type of dream it is, and then I can use the dream to help me to understand and even heal from difficult times. Relationships, divorce, my mistakes, separation from people and places I've loved, and grief — those are what my life-lesson dreams have been about. They have served as a form of therapy for me.

There was one dream I had over and over several years ago. As with many dreams, parts of it were based in reality, parts were clearly symbolic, and other parts were a mystery. It involved my parents, who in reality had divorced about twenty years before these dreams happened.

I'd had such a difficult time dealing with their divorce! We all know that the emotional, financial, mental and spiritual baggage of divorce often has long lasting effects on families.

Here is the dream:

Dad lived in a very large and luxurious home, somewhat mansion-like. He lived there with his new wife. They seemed content.

Mom lived alone in a small, plain, one-room apartment that was inside Dad's house. She was often depressed. She had the basic necessities but not much more.

I would occasionally visit my father and his wife in their mansion. I always felt out of place. I could see my mother in the little room. She never came out. Was she locked in there?

Sometimes I'd see her cleaning. Other times she was just sitting at a table, looking sad.

I began to feel very worried about Mom in that small apartment. I suspected that she was being kept there against her will. I started getting very angry with Dad and his wife! But I was afraid to accuse them of anything because I was trying to determine what was really going on. I felt so confused!

I don't remember talking to Mom, but just watching her through a window. One day, I finally went into her apartment. I saw an open doorway that I hadn't seen before, but it was in plain sight from inside. It had no door, no locks, and it led directly into the gorgeous home. There was also an exit to the outside that I hadn't seen before.

I was shocked! Mom could apparently come and go as she pleased. The situation was not at all what it had appeared to be!

Then I woke up.

I remembered it all just a couple of minutes after awakening. That last scene struck me like a lightning bolt! I started to sob. My mom wasn't a hostage; she chose to stay there! The way out was right there the entire time! Was it possible she just couldn't see it?

I shouldn't have made a judgment call when I couldn't see the entire picture! I asked God, "Why is this in my head now? The divorce happened so long ago. Mom's passing too. Our family has come a long way since then!"

Then I realized. The lesson was for me. The truth is, I still needed some understanding about my parents and their situation. Sometimes, knowing the truth sets you free, or at least brings another level of healing.

I was having my own marriage problems at that time. I was feeling depressed and stuck. The dream showed me that I also had a way out! I wasn't a prisoner or a victim. I had choices! It happened slowly, but I started making progress in baby steps. I started seeing things differently, getting some outside help, and taking responsibility instead of just blaming.

I am very grateful that after much prayer, hard work, counseling and ups and downs, our marriage survived. We are doing well and will celebrate our thirtieth anniversary soon.

I was shown the way out of despair, the exit to hope, in a most unique way. I wouldn't trade my unusual gift for anything.

I think I'll start keeping a dream notebook next to my bed.

~Diana Bauder

81

No One Listened

*If you want to be respected by others the great thing is
to respect yourself. Only by that, only by self-respect
will you compel others to respect you.*
~Fyodor Dostoyevsky

The beds in the upstairs hallway are lined up like the berths on old sleeper trains. I am the only visitor in this dark, creaky mansion, with faded mahogany walls and dusty cherry wood floors. A man comes by before lights out, checking on me as I settle into one of the beds. He asks if all is well. Before I can say that I'm fine, warm liquid drips from my ear. I swipe at the fluid and droplets of blood snake down my fingers, palm, and wrist.

The man is moving on as I reply, "I don't know."

He stops, doesn't seem alarmed, doesn't even come back to check on me. He points to a nurse down the corridor. I climb from the bunk and pad down the hall to show the nurse, who beckons a doctor. He glances up from his clipboard. "Oh, we'll do surgery." He's not concerned or rushed. He turns his back and peruses the file in his hands while the nurse turns away and writes in a folder.

I raise my hand to my ear, but I can't stop the flow. Blood pools around my feet. "Help me," I plead. The nurse keeps writing. The blood rushes out like sheets of water. I slump to the floor. "Please help me." The doctor walks away. I look toward the nurse. She steps over me and follows the doctor from the room, neither giving me another glance.

The problem in my life was clear; no one listened to me, not even those who loved me the most. What's worse, no one realized it mattered because I never spoke up.

At the time I had this dream my husband and I had fallen into a complacent routine. He'd come home from work and I'd unload on him, telling him our to-do list and updating him on things he didn't want to hear.

Later, he wouldn't remember what I had said. Add in children who weren't listening, and various relatives who would either fail to listen or would talk right over me. Tired of repeating myself or vying for attention at the table, I chose silence.

I knew what my dream was telling me: Keeping silent made me invisible, voiceless, with opinions that didn't matter.

I decided to speak up. I speak loud and clear now to those who are hard of hearing. I make eye contact with those who talk over me so they know when they interrupt, I call out my smug in-law, and when I speak to my husband I make sure he isn't absorbed in a project, e-mail, or book. And, if his attention lags, I ask, "Are you listening?"

It wasn't easy to change my behavior. I feared offending people. As it turned out, I didn't offend anyone, my family still loves me, and I gained respect because I spoke up.

My marriage is stronger, my family relationships are sturdier — even when we don't agree with each other — and I'm more confident.

More importantly, I'm heard. I no longer dream of dying while those who are most capable of helping ignore me.

~Diane DeMasi Johnson

82

The Rope

Change always comes bearing gifts.
~Price Pritchett

My life-changing dream happened in July 1984, when I was twenty-nine. A few weeks earlier, my first husband, Ray, had passed away after a long battle with bladder cancer. Ray had been training as a Baptist preacher, and his faith became more vibrant than ever in his last days. I, however, had a very restricted image of God. I believed He was there but that the relationship was based on us acknowledging Him, without much coming the other way.

My dream was incredibly vivid and unlike any I have had before or since. The images in it were accompanied by a background commentary —words that imprinted strongly on my mind and clearly told me their meaning as the dream progressed. If only all dreams were like that!

When the dream began I did not know where I was. It was pitch black. Then I realized that I was standing beside the bed in which my husband was lying. We were at the bottom of what appeared to be a very deep, dark pit. As I looked up I could see light at the top. Every now and then the sun would travel overhead and wide, bright beams of sunlight would suddenly light up the area.

I was informed that the sun represented God, and these beams were all prayers people had been saying for us.

The next moment, I found myself watching as my husband's bed, with him lying in it, started to rise upwards. I watched it slowly ascend, and inwardly expected that once it reached the top of the pit it would end up on the land by its side, with him able to enjoy the sunlight. However, it reached the top and then continued ascending right up into the sun itself. I understood this meant he had been taken into the full light of God's presence, but it also meant I was now apparently completely alone in the bottom of the pit, feeling desolate.

Then I found myself being raised up, travelling up the side of the pit, and hopeful of ascending as my husband had, but in my case I was deposited on the land beside the pit. This was fine with me — I enjoyed the full warmth and light of the sun shining above me. Then something made me curious about the place I had just left. I walked over to the side of the pit and looked into it. To my surprise, I could see a huge number of people in the bottom of the pit; many of them seemed to be rushing back and forth aimlessly.

I felt I had to do something to help them, just as I had been helped. I wanted to reach down and help someone else come up out of the darkness, into the light — but how could I possibly do that? Something made me look up toward the sun/God, and I found myself saying these words: "Oh Lord, give me a rope."

At this point the commentary was most strongly impressed upon my mind. I was told that God would indeed supply me with a "rope" to help others who were in all kinds of difficulty, but I was to remember that only He would know exactly what kind of rope was right for each person. I must always look to Him to supply the rope, according to what He knew that person most needed at the time.

This dream changed my life in that it completely changed my view of God, and set me on the path that would lead to my becoming a Methodist minister. That happened over twenty years ago, and during that time I have frequently found myself in pastoral encounters with all kinds of people. I have lost count of the number of times thinking about my dream has brought me new insight, which in turn has proved a blessing to the other person. And whenever I have felt at a loss to know what words might help them, I have prayed inwardly: "Lord, give me a rope."

~Deacon Sylvie Phillips

Chapter 10

Dreams and Premonitions

Love Doesn't Die

Closure

Angels have no philosophy but love.
~Terri Guillemets

My father passed away when I was in my sixth month of pregnancy. He would never get to see his first grandchild. My overwhelming grief brought on complications in my pregnancy that worried my doctors. To make things worse, my mother and I were not getting along, and she hadn't let me visit my father during his final days. I was consumed by the lack of closure.

However, life goes on and my beautiful baby girl was born on a hot day in August. Motherhood was a great balm for my grief and I poured all my love into my precious little girl. The days went by quickly. Nevertheless, it was the quiet nights when I allowed myself to wallow in my grief. I still held on to an irrational hope that I would have one last conversation with my father.

One night, when my baby was already eight months old, I cried myself to sleep. Then I began to dream.

I was in a gray place. It was not light, and it was not dark, just gray everywhere. All around me I saw shadows of people walking past me. None of them seemed real. Then out of the shadows of people, came my father, and he didn't seem gray at all. In fact he looked good. He seemed so real. When he approached me he was smiling and held out a hand to me.

I automatically took it and blurted out, "I can't believe this is happening. I don't feel like this is a dream. You seem so real."

He smiled just like he used to and said calmly, "For now this is real. And we have to talk. It's very important."

Amazed that his hand felt real and warm and full of life, I couldn't help my excitement. "This is wonderful! You are real. I missed you so much. I don't want to stop holding your hand!" I placed my other hand on top of our clasped hands. It felt wonderful.

"Amy," he said my name very seriously. "We need to talk. I don't have much time and I have to tell you something."

"Okay, go ahead."

"I need you to know that everything is okay between us. There is no reason for you to be upset. I know you love me and I love you. It's all okay. Everything that happened, I understand and it's all okay. You don't have to worry anymore. I love you."

I was crying with relief and I clung to him, saying over and over, "Thank you, thank you, I love you. I really do...."

Then he stood up and said he had to go and that I had to go back. I was angry and I wouldn't let go of his hand. I told him I needed to stay with him a little longer. But he was very insistent that we needed to part ways at that moment. He pulled his hand from mine and again told me he loved me. Then he joined the other shadows that were walking past, and disappeared. I sobbed and sobbed so hard that I woke up.

I was not making any noise, but all of a sudden my husband yelled, "Oh my gosh, what was that? What was that?" He was pointing over my head. When I looked nothing was there.

He flipped on the light and I could see he was really shaken. He told me that something woke him and when he looked toward me he saw a white light glowing over my head. Then it vanished. It really scared him.

I felt the most amazing peace. "Don't worry." I told him. "It was my father. Everything is okay now." And it was.

~Amy Schoenfeld Hunt

84

Gift from Above

*Sometimes you will never know the value of a moment
until it becomes a memory.*

~Dr. Seuss

My grandmother was not in perfect health, but she was managing well at a local nursing home. She did have some dementia, though, and most of the time she did not know who I was. I felt guilty about not visiting as much as I should, but I had a hard time bringing myself to go there.

One night I dreamt that I was running through the doors of my church with my wedding gown on. When I got inside, I found my grandfather, who had passed away about ten years earlier. I was thrilled to see him. I had missed him dearly on my wedding day, but in my dream, he was there! I ran up to him and gave him a big hug. He told me I looked beautiful. I said, "I can't believe you're here after all these years!"

I didn't see my grandfather's face, but I noticed he was wearing a long, purple woman's coat. It was quite noticeable that it was missing two very large buttons at the neck. My grandfather said, "Your Nanny will not be with you much longer." I said, "I can't believe you're here and you've come back after all of these years—you've waited so long!" He hugged me tightly and told me to go and visit my nanny. Then he said. "I love you princess," which was what he always called me.

I woke up crying.

I knew I should visit my grandmother but a few days passed until

Love Doesn't Die | 297

I had a very strong urge to go. I packed up both my boys and headed over to the nursing home. I prayed all the way there that God would give me the strength to handle it if she didn't know me.

As I walked into the nursing home, pushing my baby in a stroller and holding the hand of my other son, I saw my grandmother walking down the hall. She noticed the stroller so she moved over to let it pass, not realizing that I was the one pushing it. I stopped in front of her. She looked up, recognized me and called my name!

She was so happy to see me… it was as though she hadn't seen me in years! She said, "And these are your beautiful boys?" I was so thrilled that I couldn't help but cry. She saw me! She knew me! She got to finally meet my boys and know who they were! I gave her the biggest hug and whispered a thank you to God. We spent the afternoon together. She held my son's hand, she sang him the songs that she sang to me when I was a little girl and we talked like we hadn't talked in years! It was wonderful.

When it was time for me to go, my grandmother made me promise that I would return to visit her again soon. I gave her a big hug while tears filled my eyes. I told her I loved her a lot. I told her I would see her soon. Unfortunately I knew in my heart the truth — that this kind of lucidity often occurs right before the end. And my grandfather had told me in my dream that it was her time.

Two days later we got a call from the nursing home that my grandmother was not doing well. We went again to say goodbye; this time she was unable to respond. She passed on the next day.

The funeral was scheduled for the day of my wedding anniversary, an interesting coincidence since I saw my grandfather in my dream on my wedding day. And more surprising, the morning of the funeral my mother arrived in my grandmother's old purple overcoat — the one my grandfather was wearing in my dream — and there was a large button missing at the neck. Later that morning, at the funeral home, my mother said, "Oh no, look," and sure enough a second button had popped off and was rolling on the floor.

It was then that I realized my dream was not a dream at all. It was a gift from above — a gift to both my grandmother and me. I will always be grateful for that day and I will pay close attention to my dreams from now on.

~Barbara Light-Baillargeon

85

Blue House, Yellow Rose

True love stories never have endings.
~Richard Bach

For two years, I planned our perfect move into the perfect house with the perfect yard. I planned to plant the perfect garden and enjoy long evening walks with my husband. We moved, and I had just brought the last box into our new house when my husband fell ill and passed away.

Our dream was over.

One morning, weeks after burying my beloved, I woke up with an unexplained knowing, a summons to get back into life. I realized that I still had a future waiting for me.

Our perfect house, filled with unpacked boxes, was a constant reminder of what we had lost. I knew, to survive this bittersweet season of my life, I would have to move again despite having spent so much to move there in the first place.

I began looking for a new place to call home. I can't remember how many times I got into my car and drove around looking, but I do remember it brought healing. I got lost over and over again, stopping to ask for directions. It was all part of my journey to find not only a new house, but myself.

One weekend, I had a sudden, strong feeling that this was the day I would find my new home. I grabbed a cup of coffee and scrolled through the list of houses for sale. There was a new posting, and all it said was "Blue House for Sale." This was it. I could feel it. And it was listed for the exact price I was willing to pay.

I called the number listed several times but there was no answer. My son and I left numerous voicemails that were not answered.

I started to question my intuition. It had seemed so certain that this was my new house. That evening, the owner called back. He was a lone cattle rancher with long days, and he was looking for a change in his life, too, thus the sale of the Blue House. He chuckled, almost in delight, about the number of voicemails we had left.

The rancher asked when I wanted to come see his Blue House, and I anxiously blurted, "How about now?" I could hardly believe this was happening, but I knew I would be the new owner of the Blue House.

The sun was setting by the time my son and I got there. The house's blue exterior was actually a pale blue, my husband's favorite color, and there was a large S hanging out front, the first letter of our last name. And most importantly, there was a yellow rosebush under the big letter S. My husband had frequently brought me a yellow rose, just to say, "I love you."

I purchased the house over dinner that night. It all happened so quickly, it was as if something had steered me there, a continuation of our love story, with a yellow rosebush waiting for me under the first letter of my husband's last name.

That yellow rosebush was in full bloom when I bought the house in the summer, and it continued to bloom through the bitter cold winter. It's really quite amazing. The first time my husband gave me a yellow rose and I asked why he choose a yellow rose instead of a red rose, he explained that yellow roses symbolize an immortal love, a union that will never fade, neither through time nor passing of a loved one.

~Diane Schock

A Lesson in Love from the Other Side

*Sometimes the poorest man leaves his children
the richest inheritance.*
~Ruth E. Renkel

The service had been carried out according to my father's wishes — almost. In all likelihood he would have objected to having any service at all, which is why he had insisted on cremation: "so that no one feels like they have to visit my grave and cry over me." But my mother needed that cry. And he wasn't in charge anymore.

As for me, I was pretty sure that the emotion that filled me wasn't grief as much as it was anger. There was a good deal left unsaid at the time of his death — things that couldn't be said because he was so sick. My dad was a free spirit; he had lived apart from us as much as he lived with us.

Two months after the funeral, when life was starting to feel normal again, Dad visited me in a lucid dream.

He was behind the wheel of an old car I used to have, standing still in traffic, as if he couldn't move forward until he had this conversation with me. He smiled, and as I reached over to hug him I could feel the stubble of his beard and the fabric of his shirt against my skin. "Get in, honey, we need to talk."

His words were perfectly clear, but his lips weren't moving. And ready to find fault, I told him in no uncertain terms how much his telepathic communication "creeped me out." He chuckled, and with another telepathic response, said, "You'll get used to it — get in."

"You are dead, right?" I asked.

"Yep… as a doornail," he replied. His face was radiant, as robust and healthy as he had appeared before the heart disease. He flashed the toothy grin that I knew I had inherited from him… the one that only showed itself when we were completely elated (or extremely pleased with ourselves).

"And I assume, since you're smiling, you're in a good place?" I asked.

"A very good place, a beautiful place… that's partly what I came to tell you."

My curiosity got the better of me. "If you feel so at peace, why have you come to me now — I mean, don't you surrender your 'earthly cares' and all that jazz?"

I had to ask. The man was dead. And while it felt very strange — and good — to have this time with him, I couldn't see why he would be so bent on visiting me now.

"Yes, but the great thing… the really wonderful thing… is that you get to keep the love. In fact, it is all that you really do keep. Everything that you are doing in this lifetime, all that you are and all you will become is sifted through at the end and what remains… is just love."

I felt like I'd fallen into a scene from Ghost, and was about to say as much when he leaned in with those intense hazel eyes and made his point. "This is what you must always remember: While you have this time, take every opportunity to generate as much love as possible, fill your heart with it, be a catalyst for it, do good deeds, receive it and give it. It is what we all became human to experience, and it makes the afterlife so much sweeter. I loved you and your mother so much that I never wanted to see you suffer. There is something I would like to give you — to help you understand…."

At that point, in what would equate to a couple of hours of conversation in a physical time plane, I experienced a human "download" of his thoughts, feelings, motivation, fears, and insecurities — all born from an intense love and concern for my well-being that was colored by his own experience and the tragic life he lived.

What I realized was — given the same set of circumstances, the same feelings, the same experiences — loving my child as I did, I would have likely acted in the exact same way. He stayed away from us so that he wouldn't hurt us.

I sensed our time growing short. He felt it too and said he would have to go soon. But I was still curious, and I asked why on earth (and he smiled at that turn of phrase) he had shown up behind the wheel of one of my old clunkers. He said he picked it because I loved this car in particular and would spot it in the line of traffic. And then I would be able to decide whether to talk to him despite my anger.

"How about it?" he asked. The smile had never left his face. "Traffic is starting to move again. Do you want to take this thing for a nostalgic spin before I go? You can drive."

His offer caught me by surprise.

"Daddy!" I hadn't called him that since childhood. "You know my driving always made you crazy!"

I recalled all the times he was my passenger, one hand on the dashboard and the other one gripping the passenger door handle, so that he could hold on tight or bail as the situation called for. He did this well into his later years, up until the last time I saw him.

If possible, his grin became even larger now as he prepared to deliver the greatest line of all time.

"Yeah… but I figure it's different this time."

And he paused for the full effect.

"You can't kill a dead man."

That's when I woke up, sitting straight up in bed, tears rolling down my face, laughing out loud and crying at the same time.

But now — finally — I understood.

~Nancy Herold

From Despair to Peace

*Mother's love is peace. It need not be acquired,
it need not be deserved.*
~Erich Fromm

My mother died at the age of thirty-six, leaving my brother and me, ages seven and six, to be raised primarily by relatives while my father remarried and divorced numerous times. By my early twenties, I had learned that my mother, who had polio as a young child, had not been expected to live past her early twenties.

After the tumultuous upbringing I'd had, I began to question why she chose to have children when she knew she was expected to die young. Why would she knowingly bring us into the world if she knew she would not be able to raise us? Finally, I gathered the courage to ask my aunt, who gave a simple reply: My mother had always defied the doctors' predictions. She had done so well with her health issues that she thought she would live long enough to raise us.

I remained obsessed with this, however, and I still felt profoundly wounded that my mother had left us in such difficult circumstances. And then the dream came:

There were no words spoken and no thoughts exchanged. There were only feelings. I recall no backdrop to the dream — no pastoral field, no heavenly mansion, no clouds — only the vision of my young, beautiful mother walking toward me. She was free of the severe scoliosis that had plagued her in life. She walked straight and came toward me with her arms open, her kind eyes shining even more so than I remembered, a beautiful smile on her face. She wrapped her arms around me and I returned her warm embrace. We held each other tightly and I could feel the softness of her hair against my cheek.

We simply stood, holding each other in that warmth as an overwhelming feeling of deep, unconditional love washed over me. In that dream moment I knew that my mother never intended to bring me into the world and then leave. She loved me then and she had kept loving me. She would continue to do so as long as I lived.

Thirty-five years ago I awoke from that dream with a profound peace. My despair had vanished. I have never since had a single moment of doubt as to my mother's hopes for my life. I have lived with the secure knowledge of my mother's unconditional love. It is the greatest gift she ever shared with me.

~Kimberly Ross

88

Ghost Cat

*I believe cats to be spirits come to earth. A cat, I am
sure, could walk on a cloud without coming through.*
~Jules Verne

I was telling a friend about some of my psychic experiences
when he interrupted me, saying, "Sorry, but I don't believe in
that stuff." I said I didn't blame him. If you have never experienced any psychic stuff why would you believe?

So I changed the conversation to something we had more in
common — cats.

Partway into that conversation he said, sheepishly, "I have a ghost
cat."

"What?" I replied.

"It's true. Twice now couples have stayed in my guest room overnight
and in the morning have reported a cat walked across the bed during
the night. The door was closed and no cat was present in the room.

Then I had to tell him about our own cat, Molly, who we adopted
as a newborn kitten and had for almost seventeen years. When my
wife Sandy and I finally had to take her to the vet for her final visit, we
were devastated. And I couldn't shake my guilt for tricking her into
taking a sedative that last day. She never liked trips to the vet, and I
thought she would be more comfortable and less stressed with the
pills. I hoped she would forgive me.

About two months after Molly's passing I was lying in bed, face
down, early on a Sunday, when I felt Molly walk up my back as she

used to and sniff the back of my head. I thought for a moment how nice it was that Molly had come for a visit. Then, suddenly, I became fully awake and remembered she was no longer with us. I woke Sandy up and told her what had happened and we both had a good cry. Sandy was disappointed she hadn't experienced Molly's visit.

A couple of months later I was laying in bed and I could feel Molly jump on the bed, then come over and knead the mattress beside me as she used to do. This time I wasn't startled and I talked to her. I could feel the vibration of her purr and a sense of complete satisfaction. It lasted several minutes. Again I awoke Sandy and told her of the visit and again she was disappointed to miss it.

Later that summer we had friends visit us and stay in our guest room. The first morning, as we were all sitting around the breakfast table, they looked at each other sheepishly and had a short argument over who should tell us something.

"Tell us what?"

Getting up the nerve, she replied, "A cat walked across our bed last night." Her husband nodded in agreement.

Both Sandy and I burst out laughing.

"We're serious," they both said.

"Oh, we believe you," I replied. "Both of us have had visits from Molly this past year."

Needless to say, they were relieved to hear that, and we told them of other visits from Molly. By the time of Molly's last visit, Sandy had experienced Molly's spirit climb on top of her in bed and lie on her chest, too.

~N. Newell

89

Listen to Your Mother

Mothers hold their children's hands for a short while,
but their hearts forever.
~Author Unknown

Shortly after Mom died, I dreamed she was riding in the car with me. As usual, she was chattering away, and I felt oddly comforted by the fact that nothing had changed.

The dream was a strange blend of fantasy and reality. I was aware that she had died, but I wanted to pretend that she was really there so I could talk to her one more time.

"Mom?" I finally asked her softly. "You know you're dead, right?"

"Of course I'm dead!" she chirped. "You'd have told me to hush up a long time ago if I were still alive!"

I chuckled to myself. That was so like her! So for a while I was content to let things just evolve. I had the feeling we were in a hurry to get somewhere, but since the destination was unclear, I just kept driving.

"Hey!" said Mom, interrupting herself. "Let's stop for pancakes!"

"Pancakes?"

"You love pancakes!" she said. "And we have to have some right away."

"Why?"

"Because it's snowing."

"It's what?" The sky was dark with clouds, but there was no snow in the forecast.

In my sleep, I wrestled with the idea of arguing with her or letting her have her way. Suddenly, a log cabin–style building loomed by the side of the road. The sign said "House of Pancakes," so I pulled into the lot.

We went inside and sat by the window. Mom waved the waitress away. "We'll have pancakes," she said. "Buttermilk pancakes."

I looked deeply into her eyes. I'd never had such a vivid dream. "I love you, Mom."

"I love you, too," she said. "Remember to eat your pancakes."

And with that, the dream faded and I awoke, immediately reaching for my notebook to write down as much about the dream as I could remember.

The following weekend I needed to drive several hours — and across a mountain pass — to get to a class I was teaching. I planned to arrive there a full day ahead of time, but I'd gotten a late start and had skipped breakfast.

Just before the road started the steepest part of its ascent, I spotted a log cabin–style building sporting a sign that simply read "Restaurant." On a whim, I pulled off the highway.

"You're just in time," said the waitress, showing me to a table. "We're about to get slammed."

"Oh? Why is that?" I asked, taking the menu she offered.

"It's snowing heavily at the top of the pass and they've temporarily closed the road. Everyone will be looking for a place to hang out for a few hours until it's cleared."

"Snowing? In late April?"

The waitress smiled and shrugged, then pulled her order form and pencil from her apron pocket. "What'll it be?"

I was deeply grateful I wouldn't be spending the next few hours in a cold car watching the snow fall and waiting for the road to be passable. "Pancakes," I replied, without hesitation. "Buttermilk pancakes."

Thanks, Mom.

~Jan Bono

90

Big Yellow Car

*The tie which links mother and child is of such pure
and immaculate strength as to be never violated.*
~Washington Irving

My mother will always be my closest female friend, confidante, and supporter, even though one Sunday night in July 1986 my dad found her in their home, dead of an apparent heart attack at age fifty-two.

All four of my children had birthdays in July and somehow I got through the "celebrations" that year. In August, I sent my youngest child to first grade and I started on my own long-planned path to becoming a CPA by taking classes in calculus, managerial accounting, and statistics at a nearby community college. In October, without celebration, I turned thirty years old.

With the support of my sister, I muddled through the early fall days. My husband worked long hours and it was hard to keep up with my own schoolwork, my children's activities, and my housework. Eventually, Thanksgiving Day came and my brother, sister, and I went to what had become "Dad's house" and ate a meal that tasted like cardboard.

The Friday after Thanksgiving, relieved that the first holiday without my mother was over, I took my children to the movies with my sister while my husband was at work. We talked and I said sometimes I felt like I needed to just gather my little kids and go somewhere where

I could sleep for about a week and wake up and find the nightmare was over. She said I really needed to talk about my feelings with my husband.

The next day, during the conversation with my husband to discuss my feelings, he told me that in September he had started an affair with a co-worker, and for the first time in his life knew what it meant to be in love. He told me that they were emotionally and physically intimate, but that he didn't want a divorce. Never before or since have I felt like I've been hit so hard. I was numb. I was surprised that I kept breathing.

I fell asleep that night on the sofa in my living room feeling like everything I had ever believed in was a lie and wishing I would never wake up.

I was awoken by the sound of a car in my driveway. It was my mother! She was in my driveway in her big yellow car! I ran outside to greet her and get in her car with her, but she suddenly backed out of my driveway and left. I chased her car for about a quarter of a mile before she finally stopped and got out.

I ran to her and threw my arms around her. I was so happy because I knew she was there to take me home with her!

But instead of inviting me into her car, she put her hands on my arms, looked me straight in the face, and told me I could not go because it was not my time to go. She told me that I had four little kids who needed me. She told me that I was a strong woman and that I could do anything that I needed to do. She told me she loved me, that she would love me forever, and that someday she would come back to take me with her. But she also said that it was going to be a long time before she came back for me because there were a lot of things I needed to do and I had a whole lot of living to do.

It was with mixed emotions that I watched her drive away in her big yellow car.

Shortly afterward, I sat up and realized I was still on the sofa in my living room. However, instead of depression and despair, I had a renewed confidence that I was a strong woman who would survive. I knew there were things I needed to do, just like my mom had told me in my dream. I knew I had living to do.

Yes, there were times over the last thirty years when living was not easy, but when the difficult times came, I always thought back to the visit my mom made to me that night. I often think about the love she has for me and her confidence that I am a strong woman who can do anything I need to do.

The four little children grew up to be four outstanding adults and I have also been blessed with eight little grandchildren. I divorced the man I loved who did not love me, earned a master's degree in accounting, and earned my CPA license. I married a man I love who is faithful to me and loves my grandchildren and me. I do the things I need to do and I live my life.

I will forever be thankful to my mother for coming that night in her big yellow car to remind me to live.

~Lynn Rothrock Westhoff

91

An Otherworldly Visit

Sadness flies on the wings of the morning and out of
the heart of darkness comes the light.
~Jean Giraudoux

Sergeant, our late Chocolate Lab, was a bundle of lovable chaos from the moment he came to live with my family. He abused his privileges, chewed everything he could fit his mouth around, ran away almost every chance he got, and even buried a legion of stuffed animals (mostly brown dogs) in the back yard during a rainstorm. But he was there for me when I didn't have any friends, was always up for spending any length of time with his humans, and loved every single one of us more than we deserved.

After age fourteen, Sergeant's quality of life began to deteriorate. He developed arthritis. He lost weight. His hearing and vision became impaired. He lost control of his bowel movements. He was easily confused, and he was lethargic. He couldn't play anymore.

We all knew that the end was near but no one wanted to accept it. In his final months, I could hardly look at him anymore. I felt guilty and helpless. I got angry when he wouldn't eat his food. I got angry when he pooped on the back deck. I got angry when he stumbled into me or tripped me. I used my anger as an excuse to avoid him. I wanted to be angry instead of sad. I told myself every day that I would feel guilty about my attitude after he was gone, but I couldn't really

hat he would die.

n we had to put him to sleep. I avoided that too, but the first

313

oesn't Die

night after he passed, I was hit hard by grief and guilt. I woke up at four in the morning and sobbed for two hours.

About a month and a half later, I had one of the most vivid dreams I've ever experienced. My dreams usually run together and blend into each other to form a bizarre string of stories and events that have nothing to do with each other, but this dream stood alone.

I was walking by the back window in the kitchen when I glanced outside, like I've done hundreds of times before. To my surprise, I saw Sergeant sitting on the deck. Our other two dogs were casually roaming around and playing as if he had been there all along. In the dream, I was aware of the fact that he was dead yet I simply felt as if he had come back for a visit. I rushed outside to pet him. He still looked old, but he looked happy and healthy again. His vision was back. His energy was back. His "smile" was back. His presence had a tangible and ethereal quality about it. I petted him over and over again, and his fur felt very warm and real. I can still feel it as I write about it.

After a few moments of greeting one another, we walked out into the yard and he did his signature "galloping" run as if he had missed his yard and was happy to be back. After a few moments of running around and playing, he started playfully digging a hole, something he hadn't done in years.

I laughed at him and asked what he was digging for as the other dogs ambled over to see what he was doing. As I stumbled back to avoid the dirt flying behind him, I stepped into an ant bed. I was wearing flip-flops, so amid my panic and struggle to brush the ants off my feet, I was jolted awake.

It's hard to describe the feeling I had upon waking. For the first few seconds, I couldn't even move. I was sad that it was just a dream, but at the same time, I couldn't shake the feeling that it was more than that. I felt grateful and at peace. I was certain that Sergeant was okay and happy wherever he was — that he forgave me, even though I was struggling to forgive myself.

I broke down in tears before attempting to Google what I had just experienced. It was so powerful that I was eager to see if anyone else had similar stories. They did. Not only had people had similar dreams about deceased pets, but loved ones too. In a matter of minutes able to define what I had experienced as a "visitation d

I'm as big a skeptic as any, but it's hard to deny the validity of something when you personally and powerfully experience it yourself. Maybe it was just an elaborate dream. Maybe it was just a message from my subconscious telling me to forgive myself and move on. All I know is that I was so deeply affected that I cried for the better half of the following morning and didn't really want to do anything except wrap myself in a blanket, drink hot chocolate, and let my soul finish doing whatever it was trying to do. I believe that in some way, shape or form, Sergeant came to say goodbye.

And I haven't dreamt of him since.

~Madison Sonnier

92

The Reunion

When you are sorrowful look again in your heart, and
you shall see that in truth you are weeping for that
which has been your delight.
~Kahlil Gibran

I did not question why I was walking in a meadow with my grandmother or even how we had gotten there. I just lived in the moment, enjoying a perfect spring day. The grass had just turned green, and the sweet smell of the new foliage combined with the clean smell of the air after a thunderstorm.

The sun washed over her face, and she had a glow that most people would not expect from a woman in her eighties. I was sure I had not seen this side of my grandmother since I was a small child, if I'd ever seen it at all. I did not question that either. The rosiness of her cheeks, the firmness of her skin, and her upright, almost regal posture was exactly what I somehow expected.

When I complimented her on accessorizing her polka-dot print dress with simple pearls, she objected. "Clothing doesn't mean a wit and you know it, Cathy."

"I do, Grandma, but still I can't get over how pretty you look. I've never seen that dress before."

"Let's not waste precious time with trivialities. Tell me about your children, your husband, what makes you happy."

"You do, Grandma. Being with you makes me happy."

"A fleeting moment. Invest yourself in what will last. The children are *what really matter. They're our future."*

"Oh boy, are we in trouble!"

My grandmother chuckled. "Maybe, but how would I know since you never bring them by to see me anymore."

"You don't know how lucky you are. They're a real handful these days — worse than when they were small and got into everything."

My grandmother stopped walking and turned to me. "Nonsense! They're great kids."

"Not so much lately. Take Billy for example. You can't tell him anything. He thinks he knows it all."

"Knows what he thinks and isn't afraid to express it. It'll be a great trait later on."

"Scott's the exact opposite. Can't get him to talk about anything. Spends all his time either playing sports or with his nose in a book."

"Work hard, play hard. Nothing wrong with that either. And Tim?"

"Still a character," I replied shaking my head.

"He is so cute. Makes me laugh."

"Yeah, he's funny, but it isn't so cute anymore."

"The ability to laugh is insurance against adversity."

"You make things seem so easy, but I tell you some days they wear me out. I leave them home so I can enjoy our visit."

"Someday you'll even miss the squabbles."

"You may be right."

"Oh look, here comes Pop now."

I shielded my eyes from the bright sunlight in the direction she pointed. "Grandpa? He's here?" I wanted to bolt in his direction, but my grandmother had a firm grip on my hand, forcing me to be patient.

As he approached, I couldn't help but notice that he too looked years younger than he did when he died, and he had a spring in his step of a much younger man. Nevertheless, the sweet smell of the pipe he held tight in his teeth filled my heart with memories long past, and I began to cry.

I threw my arms around his neck and kissed his smooth-shaven cheek. "Grandpa, Grandpa, it's really you! I missed you so much."

He lifted me off my feet and spun me around like he had when I was little. As he put me down, he said, "I can't say I missed you."

| Love Doesn't Die

I was crushed. "Didn't miss me? I thought I was your favorite."

My grandfather lifted my chin and put his forehead against mine. "Don't you know I'm always with you?"

I barely noticed that despite the continued sunshine, it had started to rain. Drizzle mixed with my tears, making it hard to see.

Finally, Grandpa broke the silence and turned to my grandmother. "Now I wish I could stay longer, but we have an appointment. Time to go, Mae."

"No, no, you can't leave yet! So soon? You just got here!" I cried.

"Sorry, Kickity Cat, we have to go, but remember what I said."

"Have a good life, dear," my grandmother interjected as she took my grandfather's hand.

Somehow instinctively I knew that there was nothing I could do or say to stop them. Just as I knew that I couldn't follow them, no matter how much I might have wanted to at the time. So instead, I just stood and watched them leave, returning their wave as they crested the hill from whence my grandfather had come. The hill that was now topped by a magnificent rainbow.

It was at that moment that I awoke to find myself in my bed. Dark shadows replaced vivid color. Stillness replaced life. The only thing remaining of the dream was my tear-stained face. The bedside alarm clock read 3:15. I knew at that moment that it was more than a dream. My grandmother had gone to join my grandfather. At nine o'clock that morning the phone rang. It was my mother confirming what I already knew.

A week after the funeral I went to visit my aunt. As we pored over personal possessions and photographs, I gasped. Among the pile of pictures was one I was sure I had not seen before but at the same time was beyond familiar. It was a photo that my grandfather had taken. On the back were his studio stamp and the notation Mae, 1956. On the front was my grandmother, wearing the same dark blue and white polka-dotted dress she had worn in my dream. I figured she'd think I was crazy, but I told my aunt about my dream. By the time I was done, we were both crying.

"Thanks so much for telling me, Cathy. I'm so relieved. It killed me to think she died in the hospital alone. Even though the nurses insisted it was okay to leave her, I should've been there. Now I know you and Daddy were there."

During the rest of the afternoon, we both laughed and cried through our memories. As I drove home reliving that cherished afternoon with my beloved aunt, a stray thunderstorm blew through and cleared in minutes, leaving in its wake a rainbow as breathtaking as the one in my dream.

~Catherine Mayer Donges

Dreams and Premonitions

Miracles Happen

93

Two Feathers

Courage is being scared to death… and
saddling up anyway.
~John Wayne

"Y ou're planning to leave your husband," Emily blurted out on the phone. I should have known that Emily would have picked up on my dilemma, yet I was still shocked to hear her say what I'd been keeping to myself for months. I had gone to Emily for psychic card readings during my early twenties, but after I moved away to college and got married I lost contact. It wasn't until I was desperate that I decided to call her.

With the phone cradled on my shoulder, I stood near the large window overlooking the side yard of our recently purchased 1940s-style bungalow. Frigid air seeped through gaps of the weathered sash as I watched a fluffed-up sparrow scratch at the frozen earth below the snow. It was late February, and I had just turned thirty-one.

"If you don't leave your husband now," Emily said, "then things will get worse and you'll end up leaving further down the road when it will be harder."

How could things get any worse? My marriage had disintegrated into a silent war. It had become so uncomfortable that I had started sleeping on the beat-up hand-me-down couch.

And then there was the depression. It had plagued me off and on for several years, but now I was losing a lot of weight. On top of that,

Miracles Happen | 325

I still suffered from panic attacks, a leftover from the agoraphobia that gripped me in my late teen years. I decided to see a therapist, who helped me uncover a painful truth: I had married a man who was domineering and angry and who didn't know how to love me.

I was devastated, but I stubbornly continued to believe that somehow he would change. I also didn't want to leave the home we had just purchased or the friends I had made or the nursery school our child was attending. I had also gotten involved in the local art community, something that I thoroughly enjoyed. Yet deep down I knew that I was building my life on the wrong foundation.

I said my goodbyes to Emily with a promise to call her in a few weeks.

That night, I had a startling dream.

I was in a woodland park standing by an old footbridge that spanned a deep, clear-running stream. I wanted to cross the bridge in the worst way, but the other side was dark and hazy, so I hesitated. I was terrified of what lay beyond it. I noticed two feathers on the ground near my feet. The feathers were big and brown, like eagle feathers. When I bent down to pick them up, I discovered that I was wearing Native American clothes: a pair of buckskin pants and matching shirt. I had a medicine bag around my neck and realized I was male. But the most incredible part of the dream was the unbelievable self-confidence coursing through me. I had never felt that way before, without any fear or hesitation, and I willingly crossed the bridge to the other side.

I realized upon waking that this man, whomever he was, wanted me to know what it felt like to be him, to be confident and sure of myself. I'd never had such an incredibly vivid and peaceful dream before. I lay in bed and wondered who this man was and why I had become him.

Later that same day my husband and I got into a huge fight. I had quit my part-time job as a cashier in a department store to start an illustration business, and he wanted me to get my old job back. I refused. This made an already unbearably tense atmosphere in our home even worse. I was angry and had to get away to clear my head, so I hopped in my car and drove to the bay, which was on the other side of town. I parked the car and stared at the dark, choppy water trying to summon up the courage to leave my marriage. But as I drove home an hour later I confronted two fears. I was afraid of being alone and I had serious doubts about my ability to support myself financially.

Walking up to the house, I found two crow feathers lying side-by-side on the front steps. I picked them up, just like in my dream. My hand was shaking. Was this a dream? Déjà vu? Was there such a thing? It couldn't be a coincidence. An image flashed through my mind of hands outstretched on the other side of the bridge, and I felt a surge of confidence flow through me. As I went through the front door, I knew what I had to do.

I called my mom that night and finally told her everything that had been going on. She knew that my relationship wasn't in a great place, but she didn't know the extent of my suffering or that I had been thinking of ending my marriage.

"You can stay with us," she said finally. My great-aunt Amy had passed away that year and left my mom a small inheritance. She offered me some of that money to go back to school so that I could get a better-paying job. I knew it wasn't going to be easy living with my parents again, but it would be a lot better than staying in the marriage.

During the next two weeks, I saw a lawyer and secretly began packing my things. I was collecting the artwork I had stored in the attic when I came across a small painting I had made as a teenager. I had forgotten all about it. The painting was of a Native American man sitting on a horse. I couldn't take my eyes off the two feathers in his hair. Could this be the same man whose clothes I wore in the dream? Was he responsible for the two feathers on the front step? Chills ran down my spine. I had heard about spirit guides before, but I never thought it would happen to me — and certainly not like this.

As I walked down the stairs with the painting in my arms, I didn't feel as alone. I was getting help from above, and it made a world of difference.

On a windy, rain-soaked March day, I left my husband and my miserable life behind. With my child in the back seat and my belongings stuffed into my little VW Rabbit, I headed for my parents' home seventy miles away. I hung the painting above my bed as a reminder to have courage and confidence no matter how bad things got. I named my guide Two Feathers, and I still find feathers to this very day.

~Shelley Szajner

Over the Edge

*God's promises are like the stars; the darker the night
the brighter they shine.*
~David Nicholas

I wasn't stressed out. I was a contented wife and grandmother enjoying a happy retirement. Then the dreams began.

Three nights in a row, the same dream invaded my sleep. Three nights in a row, I walked down a dark and unfamiliar road until I crested a slight incline, where the road dropped abruptly off the edge of a towering cliff that spilled into a bottomless pit. Three nights in a row, I backed away from the edge in fear and awoke trembling.

The fourth night, I dreaded bedtime. Would the dream invade my sleep again? It did, and this time, instead of backing away from the edge of the cliff, I inched forward and stepped over the edge. And I floated, hovering like a hummingbird. I surveyed the world in wonder as it peacefully revolved beneath me: majestic mountains, flowing rivers, bustling cities — everything in order. "Trust God," said a comforting voice, "and you will not be afraid." I awoke relieved.

But I was also puzzled. What did these nightmares mean? Why did they show my life careening frightfully out of control before it settled down and became routine again? My life was good. My marriage was solid. Paul and I were happy, healthy, and financially comfortable. Our children were thriving, our grandchildren blossoming. Why was I getting this "trust God" advice? I already did trust God!

The next night, Paul and I were watching TV when he left the room.

Moments later I heard a crash and then a thud.

"Paul?"

Silence.

I hurried to the bathroom and found him lying on the floor. He was still. He was quiet. Was he dead?

Stifling my panic, I fumbled for his wrist — his pulse was weak but it was there. Then his chest rose. Oh, thank God! He wasn't dead, but he wasn't coming around, either. I ran to the phone.

By the time the ambulance arrived, Paul was conscious and not in pain. Now the paramedics connected him to a heart monitor, strapped him to a gurney, and rushed him to the ER while I followed in our car.

At the ER, technicians in green scrubs wheeled Paul from room to room for various tests. Throughout the long night, he felt no discomfort and the tests revealed nothing to explain his collapse. His doctor had recently praised him for being fit and in good health. No news is good news, even when it baffles the mind. I happily drove us home.

But soon, life became anything but routine. First, Paul's occasional sleeplessness morphed into nightly sleeplessness. Next, he experienced fatigue, anxiety, and depression. Paul's face took on a haunted, tortured look. Formerly an avid reader, he now spent hours staring grimly into space, his books unopened, his laptop untouched. Prescription medications didn't help. His doctors seemed helpless and I felt hopeless. Something was dreadfully wrong and I knew it.

My series of fearful dreams had been a forewarning. I was now walking the dark and unfamiliar road I had seen. How many other bad things were still to come? Where was the edge of my cliff? Trust God and you will not be afraid, I reminded myself, playing and replaying in my mind the dream message that would become my mantra.

Paul's dysfunction increased. I dispensed his medications when he forgot them, did his household chores when he neglected them, and took over our finances when he overlooked them. I stopped leaving him alone when he became confused, chauffeured him to medical appointments when he stopped driving, and promised him we'd face it together when, two months after his collapse, he received a diagnosis of Alzheimer's disease.

Trust God and you will not be afraid, I reminded myself, as Paul greeted this progressive, incurable, mind-stealing brain disease with unflinching courage. I listened when he shared his end-of-life concerns, accepted when he offered me his power of attorney, and consented when he named me his health care surrogate.

Trust God and you will not be afraid, I reminded myself as Paul became delusional in the death grip of the rapidly advancing, merciless Alzheimer's. I spoon-fed him when his appetite waned, agonized when he stopped eating, and despaired when I admitted him to a hospital. I wept when I signed his do-not-resuscitate order, grieved when I transferred him to a hospice care center, and surrendered when, four months after his collapse, I met with family and planned his funeral.

Trust God and you will not be afraid, I reminded myself, as I approached the edge of my cliff.

And then Paul rallied!

"Where am I?" he asked, entirely lucid. "And how did I get here?"

The hospice doctors had prescribed a medication intended to keep Paul comfortable during his few remaining days. Instead, it had restored him to sound mind, rekindled his appetite, and spared his life. He remembered little of the prior few weeks. His weight was down to 112 pounds on his 5'11" frame. Too weak to manage his personal care, he wasn't ready to return home.

"I flunked hospice," Paul announced cheerfully as an aide rolled him into the wheelchair transport van transferring him to a rehab facility.

"No," she disagreed, smiling. "You graduated. You beat the odds — because we don't get many graduates."

Happy to be one of the few, Paul worked on his physical therapy and weight gain while I drove back and forth for daily visits and kept our household running. Eleven months after his collapse, with his mind sound, his walk steady, and his weight at 145, I welcomed him home. God, who knew our future when we didn't, had met our need when we couldn't.

Three years later, life is back to normal, just as I dreamed. Paul shows no signs of Alzheimer's. Did he ever have it? If not, what made him ill? His doctors haven't said. But here's what matters.

One eventful year, Paul waged war with death and won, and I didn't go over the edge during the war because I had gone over the edge in my dream.

~Carole Harris Barton

Tested, Not Arrested

It is a good divine that follows his own instructions.
~William Shakespeare

"Ma'am, I will need you to blow into this, please," said the burly Honolulu police officer matter-of-factly. He had eased out of his patrol car and was holding a small device out to me. I was bright red with embarrassment. Why did he want me to take a Breathalyzer test?

I hadn't been drinking. I had been driving just fine. But it was apparent that my new police officer friend's request was more than that; it was a command.

I put the device to my lips and blew. My attempt was slow and shallow, and it didn't register. The contraption was difficult to blow into. It was tight, like a balloon that had yet to be stretched. I wondered how people, especially those under the influence, were able to produce anything on this handheld machine. The next try, however, proved more fruitful. The police officer seemed pleased with this second performance, and the blowing episode was complete.

The police officer stepped away and leaned into his car. Soon after, he produced a small but thick handheld machine that resembled a calculator. It looked like the ones delivery people use to obtain our signatures.

"You are most definitely lactose intolerant," stated the police officer.

What? It was a lactose test? Why would a police officer test my lactose tolerance, and why test it on that machine? How did he know to test my lactose tolerance anyway?

It was surreal. As I stood there facing the officer, perplexed by the whole ordeal, my dream suddenly ended. Day had broken, and I was awake.

Could that dream hold the solution to my abdominal problems? What if I *was* lactose intolerant?

Slipping downstairs to the computer, I investigated. It didn't take long before the trusty search engine produced answers. The lactose intolerance test seemed to be similar to blowing into a balloon-type instrument. The gases from the participant's breath were contained in this contraption and were then tested. The level of certain gases determined whether the person was lactose intolerant.

I was astounded. This information was all new to me, but it was remarkably similar to the dream, and it deserved my attention. Was God trying to tell me something?

Afterward, it seemed natural to limit my intake of dairy products. The numerous symptoms that I had endured over the years quietly disappeared. I felt good once again.

Who would expect a dream about a Hawaiian police officer to help a person regain health? I certainly didn't, but the results have spoken for themselves. The only test I ever had was the one in that dream, but I thank God for that Hawaiian police officer and for the good health that came as a result of his roadside test.

~Kristi Woods

96

Drill Here

*Dreaming permits each and every one of us to be
quietly and safely insane every night of the week.*
~William Dement

At the first hint of a midlife crisis, I gave away all the stuff — furniture, clothes and treasures — that filled my four-bedroom house. I tossed in my comfortable professional job for good measure, but tucked the money from the sale of the house into a savings account and set off for the wilds of New Mexico to discover myself. Secretly, I harbored a desire to use the money to build a healing center, but I kept that to myself; I wasn't interested in giving my friends the final evidence they needed to commit me. That I was clueless as to what a healing center actually entailed was beside the point.

I managed to get invited to occupy the spare room at a friend-of-a-friend's house while I searched for a decent country rental. On day two, during my first daylight adventure to pick up a local paper, I drove past a magnificent property with huge rock outcroppings, set in jagged hills with a scenic landmark sign proclaiming "Garden of the Gods." I was awestruck and totally enchanted. I had fallen in love. Minutes later I burst into my hostess's home and sealed my fate. "That Garden of the Gods place is the most gorgeous hunk of earth I've ever seen. If it were for sale, I'd buy it." Of course, I didn't exactly mean it. I needed time. I needed to find myself. Instead, I had impulsively blurted out this crazy thought that was met with equal enthusiasm.

"It is for sale, isn't it amazing? It was a power site for the Pueblo people. It was used for sacred purposes for millennia. There is a cave and a bed of quartz under it and rumors of hidden treasure," she said, looking back over her shoulder as she dialed the owners.

Any hope my friends held of my reunion with common sense evaporated with that phone call. Within the hour I was braving a sudden snowstorm and walking the land with its uninhabitable forty-five-year-old Airstreams and crumbling adobe- and dirt-floor buildings. Yet, instead of these things registering as deterrents, it felt as though I'd popped through some mystical veil and landed in a wintry Shangri-La. I was a goner. So when details arose about the cost (four times the estimated value) or the "seep" that passed for running water, the information didn't compute, and for a while, at least, this city girl stayed blissfully in denial.

My first nod to reality came four days after I signed the mortgage papers, when the redwood tank that held the water pumped from the seep sprung a leak. Unbeknownst to me, an inadequate supply of water had caused the boards to shrink. I was so green I had no idea what to do, so I selected a familiar option, assumed my victim stance, and became quite hysterical. It was as if the skies had parted and a booming voice had cried out "Well, then, you want to start a healing center on sacred land? Let's start with you!" My dance with my inner victim and the scarcity of water in the high desert had begun.

Following the advice of neighbors, I had the redwood tank replaced with a metal one. With time, I got my mountain woman on. I learned to gage the gallons of available water and run the pump with exactness. Over the years of the extended building process—with Murphy's Law as the honorary ranch motto—every step forward depended on water, be it falling from the sky, filling up the seep from below, or being hauled in from town. My own healing moved forward, but the dream for a center lay dormant in the sandy, parched stretches of the power spot I was stewarding.

By the summer of the ninth year, my inner work had paid off, and I no longer defaulted to a victim stance when things went wrong. I was deep in my peace. I had a lovely home, and a first guesthouse formed from the original stone walls of a large chicken coop. I used the land to host sweat lodges, fire walks, and meditations, yet something wasn't quite right.

A dawning realization led me to admit my seep was failing, not even able to produce the 100 gallons a day I needed to sustain the life I had carved out of the rocks. I had witnessed neighbors drilling expensive dry holes, so I never considered taking the risk of digging a well. When I prayed for divine intervention, I was imagining my water request, if answered, would fall from the sky. If not, I saw a part-time job in my future funding the tankloads of water needed for survival.

As fall approached that year, I distracted myself from my water woes by directing my attention to a journey I was getting ready to lead to Peru. I was excited to be returning to Machu Picchu and, with a short time to go, fell asleep thinking of final details. The dream arrived on the edge of my awakening. It was startling in its intensity but, more than that, it had a very particular feeling to it that I had experienced once before when I had dreamed the subject for a friend's book that became a huge bestseller. However, this powerful dream was not a gift for someone else. It was all mine. I was shown with precise clarity where I would find water if I dug a well.

I had no doubt.

I found a water witch on referral who confirmed, with the aid of some crazily animated dowsing sticks, the location of an underground artesian spring in the exact position indicated in my dream. Soon I was placed on a waiting list by a reputable driller who, with yet another change in plans, showed up unannounced with his rig as I was loading my luggage about to head to the airport. I showed the driller the spot we had marked for the well and told him I had to leave. He told me they usually get fifty percent up front, but I replied there was nothing I could do as I was literally on my way to Peru. I would trust him to stop when he got to the right depth if he would trust me to pay him when I got back. I left for Peru in complete knowing. I returned several weeks later to witness a profoundly generous well flowing in excess of fifty gallons of water per minute. The miracle dream had led me to water — a thought I'd never previously dared to indulge.

With the gift of water I was able to create the Garden of the Goddess Retreat Center so I could share the magic of possibility with others. Over the years since, many folks have visited and been touched by the grace that seems to emanate from the rocks. It is with abiding gratitude I affirm the flow of water birthed from a dream sustains it all.

~Gini Gentry

97

On the Wings of Eagles

Faith is putting all your eggs in God's basket, then
counting your blessings before they hatch.
~Ramona C. Carroll

I was a lonely only child. While some children thrive being an only child, I didn't. I was shy and found it difficult to make friends. When I was five years old a neighbor gave me a blue ball for Christmas. I burst into tears, saying, "I have no one to play ball with and if I throw the ball, no one will throw it back to me." I must have made the neighbor feel terrible and I always regretted that I didn't just thank her.

My greatest dream was to grow up and get married and have a dozen children. None of them would ever be lonely and I would never be lonely.

Because I was shy and spent most of my childhood alone I had no social skills. I was nineteen before I had my first date; it was a disaster because I don't think I said five words all evening.

Fortunately, I finally overcame my shyness and when I was twenty-five I met a very nice man and got married. We were eager to start a family.

We weren't too concerned when the first year passed without a baby. We were both healthy and there was no reason we couldn't have a baby, but then the second and third and fourth years passed and still no baby. People kept asking me why we were waiting so long to start a family. I felt like a failure. I felt cheated. And I was depressed.

When the fifth year of marriage came and went I accepted that I was never going to have children, despite my constant prayers. I began avoiding friends who had children because it was too painful.

My husband and I had agreed we would not seek medical treatments to become pregnant; we would leave it in God's hands.

Then I had a dream different than any other dream I'd ever had. *It didn't even feel like a dream. It was as if I were watching a movie. The colors were brilliant and beyond description. There was music I had never heard before. I was high in the mountains standing on a rocky ledge with a deep canyon below me, but I wasn't afraid of falling. There was a large eagle's nest near me. The eagle spread its powerful wings and flew away and I could see four eggs in the nest. The eagle came back with food and the eggs suddenly hatched and four baby eaglets struggled out of their shells. The mother eagle fed her babies, spreading her wings over them protectively and then, in the dream, the eagle looked straight into my eyes and I knew it was not just a dream; it was a sign. It was a promise.*

When I woke up I was filled with joy and peace. I knew in my heart I was going to have four children.

I didn't tell anyone, not even my husband, because I believed so completely in my dream that I couldn't risk anyone laughing at me or trying to explain it away. It was my own secret message.

The next morning I went shopping and bought baby clothes. I felt like dancing down the aisles in the infant section of the store. Each little outfit, each soft blanket, each pair of booties was a precious treasure.

Instead of asking God to give me a baby, I thanked God for the four children I knew he had promised to me.

I put the baby clothes in my dresser and every day I got them out and held them against my heart.

I bought a book of baby names and began picking names I liked.

A month later I was pregnant. I was delighted but not surprised.

Nine months later we had a beautiful, healthy son.

The next year we had another beautiful healthy son.

The next year we had another beautiful healthy son.

The next year we had a beautiful, healthy daughter.

We had four children in less than five years.

The dream had come true. The promise had been fulfilled.

Although I even hoped for one or two more children, that wasn't part of the dream. The dream — the promise — was about four baby eagles; I couldn't ask for more.

I never had another dream that compared to the dream about the eagle. I've had thousands of dreams since then but no other dream was so clear, and no other dream carried a message or a promise.

I've only shared my dream with a handful of people. One or two said it was just a dream or a coincidence or luck or fate. Those closest to me knew it wasn't just a dream; it was a prophecy.

We live in an area where there are bald eagles and I never watch one flying overhead without feeling a tug at my heart and tears in my eyes.

Just a dream? All I know is I tried to have a baby without success for five years and after that dream I was pregnant in a month and had four children in five years.

I believe the dream was a message from God that he had heard my prayers and was going to answer them. No, it wasn't just a dream.

~Linda Davison

98

For the Greater Good

All that I have seen teaches me to trust God
for all I have not seen.
~Author Unknown

My son's friend had just gotten his driver's license and had been given a car. He arrived with some other friends to pick up my son and go out for the night. I went out to the car to congratulate him but when my son opened the door to get in I had a sudden, intense feeling of fear and dread. I was stunned and stood there holding the door open to keep them from leaving.

I had conflicting premonitions—one that I shouldn't let him in the car, and the other that I needed to let him go with his friends. I stalled as long as I could. But I finally let him go, if only to spare him the teenage embarrassment of his mom not letting him go, not to mention that I would sound absolutely insane if I told him about my premonition. When I went in the house I had a one-sided chat with God telling him that I trusted that they were in his hands but seriously he had better not mess up.

I got the call at midnight: There was an accident—get to Northern Westchester Hospital. It wasn't my son who called so I spent the thirty-minute drive wondering if the woman on the phone was lying when she told me that he was okay.

When I arrived at the hospital a couple of teens came running up to me saying Paul just had a small injury to his hand and was being treated. Everyone else had minor injuries, too. My stomach was churning as they described the accident—the car had gone off the road and flipped over. I was so shocked that it barely registered when I heard someone say "and Paul saved everyone's life." The EMTs said that the only reason they all survived was because everyone had their seatbelts on—front and back. Paul had made everyone put on their seatbelts and wouldn't let the driver go until everyone was buckled in. Paul's young cousin had been killed in a car accident—thrown from the back seat while not wearing a seatbelt.

It was then that I understood my conflicting premonitions—if I hadn't let my son go and suffer that minor injury, the rest of his friends might have been killed that night.

~Geri Moran

99

The Green Dream Machine

A generous heart, kind speech, and a life of service and
compassion are the things that renew humanity.
~Buddha

The bedroom curtains danced in the breeze as I woke up. I had just had the same dream that I'd been having for several weeks now.

In the dream, I'm driving down the road when I come across a parked green van, sporting a neon "For Sale" sign taped on the windshield.

What could it mean?

Rubbing the sleep from my eyes, I hurriedly dressed, eager to begin the day. I'd been volunteering with my social worker friend Mary for a year. We spent our days helping abused women "begin again." These remarkable women were learning how to write résumés, dress for job interviews, and balance checkbooks. If that weren't enough, they were also learning parenting skills and how to prepare healthy food for their children.

Over coffee at a nearby Starbucks, Mary and I discussed the "wish lists" the women had given us the previous week, trying to figure out ways to fulfill as many wishes as possible.

"Gracie needs a vehicle to get back and forth to her new job. She has four children, so it's going to have to accommodate a large family,"

Mary confided. We ended our coffee break with prayer, asking God to be with each family he'd sent our way.

The following week I spent countless hours searching for an inexpensive vehicle large enough for a family of five, but when Friday rolled around, I was forced to admit defeat. Sighing, I reached for my cellphone to call Mary, pulling off the highway to make the call.

That's when I spotted it… A green van sporting a neon "For Sale" sign parked in someone's front yard.

I unbuckled the seatbelt and hurried over to read the asking price.

"There's no way our lady in need can afford this van, Lord."

A tall woman, the owner of the car, approached. I shared our dilemma with her, explaining that we didn't have enough money to pay the asking price. I thanked her for taking the time to speak with me. She shook my hand with a smile, promising to keep her eyes open for a cheaper vehicle. Impulsively, I jotted down my cellphone number for her.

Later that evening I was gathering materials for our weekly session when my cellphone jingled.

"Mary, this is Marge White. I'm the woman with the green van… I'm calling to let you know that I'd like to donate the van to the mother and children in need."

As the sun disappeared behind the horizon hours later, I stood at the kitchen window staring out at the vehicle that would soon bring security, hope and independence to a courageous family of five.

It wasn't until I slid beneath the cozy quilt that night that I remembered the dream I'd had for weeks… or had it been a vision? A heavenly vision of a "green dream machine…."

~Mary Z. Whitney

Momma Knows Best

*Being a mother means that your heart is no longer
yours; it wanders wherever your children do.*
~Author Unknown

The phone rang at 4 a.m. It was never good news when I got a call that early, especially on a Saturday morning. Afraid to pick it up, but more afraid not to, I fumbled for the receiver in the dimly lit bedroom as my husband grumbled next to me.

"Hello," I whispered, afraid that if I spoke any louder, the news would be worse.

"Sis, we're leaving for the hospital!" Mom was beside herself. "I'm so afraid! Bob is dying!"

"Did the hospital call you?" I asked, trying to remain calm.

"No, but Dad and I are leaving right now!"

"Mom, wait just a minute, please," I begged. "Why do you think he's dying if they didn't call you?"

"Because Grandma was holding her arms out for him! She had a beautiful, welcoming smile on her face as she beckoned him to come. I know she is going to persuade him that he'll be better off with her!"

"Mom, please go back to sleep for a couple of hours and check with the hospital in the morning. I'm certain you must have had a bad dream. They would have called you if Bob was really dying!"

"No, you don't understand Sis! He doesn't want to go! He was calling out to me. 'Momma, Momma,' he cried over and over!"

"Grandma is dead, Mom," I pointed out, hoping to snap her out of the hysteria.

"I know that! Why do you think I'm so worried? We'll call you when we get there," she retorted, and hung up the phone.

I was too sleepy to think clearly but too upset to sleep. I slipped out of bed and went to the kitchen to make a pot of coffee.

I knew it was conceivable that Mom was correct. She was very intuitive and usually sensed when something was wrong—especially when it involved one of her three children. Hopefully, I consoled myself, my brother was just having a bad night.

As I sat down with my much-needed cup of hot, strong coffee, my husband stumbled into the kitchen. "What's going on?" he asked with a muffled yawn.

"Mom thinks my brother is dying," I answered with a sigh. "She woke up from a dream in which my grandma was coaxing Bob to go with her. I think Mom took it as a sign that he's dying. She's really upset, so she and Dad are driving to Seattle to check things out."

"Isn't it kind of silly to put so much credence in a dream?" he probed. "She should've at least called them first."

"Normally, I would agree with you. But, Mom is usually pretty accurate with her premonitions.

"Do you feel like we should go to the hospital then? If we left within the hour we'd probably get there soon after your parents."

It was a good three-hour drive from our home in Portland to the hospital burn center in Seattle where my brother was taken after he was severely burned in a house fire about a week earlier. He had initially escaped from the fire, but ran back inside to retrieve some items that were of particular importance to him.

He had burns over half of his body, many of which were third degree. I'd driven to the hospital with my parents just two days earlier and the doctors cautioned us that this was a very critical time in his recovery. Although we hoped for the best, and tried to remain optimistic, we knew his condition was fragile.

My husband and I both agreed it would be good to make the trip up to Seattle. Mom could very well be right, and we'd feel terrible if we weren't there.

As we drove along the freeway, I thought about what Mom had said on the phone. It gave me an uneasy feeling that Bob had called her Momma in the dream. He hadn't called her that since he was a little boy, and most of the time it was when he was crying because he was hurt or sick. I was glad we would be there soon.

We arrived at the hospital well before noon. I was grateful that my parents greeted us before we asked to see Bob. Mom looked worried, but not completely devastated, so I knew there was hope.

In an attempt to relieve some of her anxiety, I smiled bravely and proclaimed, "I've come to hear some good news!"

"He's a little better right now," Mom responded nervously as she twisted a tissue in her hands. "The nurse said they almost lost him last night, though!"

Before Mom could finish her story, a doctor stepped up and asked if he could talk with us. "It looks like Bob is out of the woods for a while at least. The stronger antibiotics are starting to work, and we've managed to get his fever down. His condition is still very critical, but stable for the moment. We're fairly optimistic that he will continue to improve slowly. Please make sure that only two of you visit him at one time, and keep the visits short.

We thanked him for his update, and he shook hands with each of us. As he started to walk away, he turned back suddenly and confided, "I don't know if someone has already shared this with you, but when Bob was in trouble last night and we didn't think he was going to make it, he repeatedly cried out for his Momma. It was one those moments that tugs at our heartstrings; the emotional side of saving lives that we can't escape."

He looked at my mother with a warm smile and said, "I was so pleased to see you folks here early this morning. Everything was happening so quickly, I wasn't certain if anyone had been able to make contact with you."

"If he only knew," I chuckled. "If he only knew!"

~Connie Kaseweter Pullen

Stella Sky

The sixth sense is at the core of our experiences. It is
what makes experiences out of events.
~Henry Reed

I was spending a week at a friend's lake cabin in northern Minnesota. It was a trip I made almost every year — I would visit family in Minneapolis and then head north to spend some time off the grid on a lake in the woods.

This particular year, my friend Janet and her daughter Stella joined me for a few days. I had been friends with Janet for many years, and while I had known Stella since she was a baby, our encounters had always been brief, mostly hellos and goodbyes, sometimes with years in between.

It was wonderful having both of them there, and by the end of our second day of swimming, canoeing, exploring and telling stories, I was struck by how ten-year-old Stella saw the world as a mix of fantasy and reality. She was at that amazing age where she could simultaneously inhabit the child's world of fairy tales and make-believe and the adult's world of mundane everyday life. For Stella, the forest and the lake, while obviously just trees and water, were also full of magic and mystery, and that mix fascinated me.

On their last night at the cabin, Stella was in the bedroom loft, brushing her hair before bed, and she asked me to hand up the small kitchen mirror. When she was done, she leaned over to hand the mirror down to me, but it slipped from her fingers. The mirror hit the floor

Miracles Happen | 349

with a crash.

As I swept up the pieces, Stella started to cry. I did my best to convince her it didn't matter, but the tone of my voice betrayed me, I was actually really annoyed. Now I would have to hike three miles out to the car and then drive fifteen miles into town to find a replacement. As a guest I felt it was up to me to see that things weren't broken, or if broken, then at least replaced.

When I woke the next morning I was still annoyed about the shattered mirror, and that seemed so ridiculous it annoyed me even more. I was annoyed about the mirror and I was even more annoyed with myself for being annoyed.

I made coffee and then Stella and I went down to the lake for a pre-breakfast swim. Stella plunged into the water, and I stood on the shore for a few minutes, sipping coffee, looking at the pine trees and listening to the calling loons.

I was still brooding about the broken mirror when something strange happened. I had never felt anything like it before nor have I since. It was like a flash of light in my mind that was coming out of the sky. My skin felt electrified as if energy was being fed into my body from some source outside of me. One second I was sipping coffee and watching Stella swim, the next second an entire story had crystallized inside my mind, a kid's adventure story that would take place in the north woods with a main character named Stella, inspired by the real Stella who was swimming in the lake. This was definitely more than an insight or inspiration; this felt more like a visitation or a vision. Wherever it had come from, now it was inside me, and while I didn't actually hear a voice, the message was clear: *Here's a story — now write it.* I actually looked up at the sky and nodded. I would write the story. I felt transformed.

That afternoon, the three of us went into town, and after we bought a new mirror at the general store, Stella and her mom headed south to Minneapolis and I returned to the cabin to finish my stay. When I got there I began to outline the story, writing notes from my morning vision with a black Sharpie on a legal pad. The next day everything felt different. There seemed to be a lot of magic in the forest. I went down to the lake for a morning swim and when I got out of the water I found a dozen Admiral butterflies fluttering and landing on my towel. I watched them, and then approached and picked up the towel but they didn't fly away. They fluttered around me and landed on my hands and arms. They looked beautiful in the morning light.

Two hours later I sat on the deck making notes for the story that would become *Stella Sky*. A fawn, still in spots, leapt onto the path and quietly approached and stopped no more than seven feet away. It watched me for a while and then it slipped into the forest. A few more hours passed. I was still making notes and sipping my now cold coffee when a black bear loped out of the woods and approached. It sniffed and squinted, and then it stopped at the foot of the deck stairs less than four feet from where I sat. When the bear began to move even closer, I whispered "No" and startled it. It shook its head and snorted as if it hadn't seen me, and then it rambled off, disappearing into the shadows between the trees.

While I had always thought of myself as a writer, I had never thought of myself as a writer of children's books. Nevertheless, when I returned to Los Angeles I knew I had to write the story that had been given to me; weeks had passed since that crazy lakeside morning vision, but my memory of it hadn't faded at all.

A few months later, when I had finished the first fifty pages, I got in touch with Janet and asked if she and Stella would consider reading along as I wrote. I would send them story installments, and they could tell me if they thought it was any good.

The writing went well, and during the next year, I sent them chapters and they read *Stella Sky* aloud together before bed. Then, toward the end of the first draft, something happened that I couldn't explain. I was writing a scene in which Stella and her friend George were in trouble; they were dying of exposure, adrift on a raft on Hudson Bay, and as I wrote it, I started to cry. By the time I finished writing those paragraphs my face was wet with tears. It didn't make any sense to me. I knew how the story ended. I was the one writing it. In the end

Stella lives. The story has a happy ending. The spontaneous crying seemed so strange that I even told a few friends about it. I wanted to know what they thought.

In June, I finished the first draft of *Stella Sky* and sent the final installment to Stella and her mom. Then one morning several weeks later, while working on the second draft, I came to the part toward the end where Stella and George are adrift and dying, and once again, as I read those paragraphs, I started to cry. The crying seemed even stranger this time; it was completely involuntary. I had accepted my tears while I was writing those scenes the first time, but to cry while I was editing them? That didn't make any sense.

Later that same day I called Janet to see if they had finished reading *Stella Sky*. I wanted to know if they liked the ending. Janet told me they had about fifty pages left, and then she said, "Maybe we'll read it this afternoon. Stella just got home from a sleepover birthday party. She's not feeling that good and she went up to bed." When I heard that, I almost responded with, "I'm not surprised, she almost just died," in reference to the part of the story that I had just finished editing. I thought it but didn't say it. Instead I said, "I hope she feels better soon," and then we said goodbye.

Three days later, I called again and Janet told me Stella *had* almost died. That night, after she came home from the birthday party, a streptococcal infection had spread through her body and become lodged in her shinbone, ultimately causing toxic shock syndrome. Her kidneys had stopped functioning and Stella had been put on life support. It had been a very close call.

Like *Stella Sky*, this story also has a happy ending. Ten days later Stella was out of the ICU, and after four weeks of intravenous antibiotics her strep infection was cleared. Today, Stella is a happy, healthy teenager, and the story she inspired — the one that seemed to come out of the sky — is also out in the world.

The question I ask myself sometimes is this: Can writing a story about someone where they are saved from dying save that person from dying? I don't know the answer, and I would never claim to even understand how that might work, but the part in the story of *Stella Sky* where Stella almost dies... no matter how many times I read it... that part still makes me cry.

~C.A. Strand

Dreams and Premonitions

Meet Our Contributors
Meet Our Authors
Thank You
About Chicken Soup for the Soul

Meet Our Contributors

Monica A. Andermann lives and writes on Long Island where she shares a home with her husband and their adventurous tabby Samson. Her work has been included in such publications as *Guideposts*, *Woman's World*, *The Secret Place* and many other *Chicken Soup for the Soul* books.

Mary Ellen Angelscribe is author of *Expect Miracles* and *A Christmas Filled With Miracles*, and an international pet columnist. Animal Planet featured her swimming cats performing the kitty paddle! Her stories and cat videos can be seen on Facebook under Angel Scribe and Pet Tips 'n' Tales. Learn more at www.AngelScribe.com.

K.S. Bair is a mother of three children living in Ohio.

Carole Harris Barton, author of *Rainbows in Coal Country* and *When God Gets Physical*, is retired after a career in public service in Washington, DC, and Fairfax, VA. Her stories have appeared in *Kentucky Humanities* magazine and Tim Russert's *Wisdom of Our Fathers*. She lives with her husband, Paul, in Dunedin, FL.

Diana Bauder studies elementary and special education. She worked with all ages of children and adults with special needs. She's married and has two adult children and one grandchild. Diana loves blogging and writing, gardening and league bowling. She just started her freelance writing career. E-mail her at diana.bauder96@gmail.com.

Dr. Hayley Bauman is a licensed clinical psychologist, specializing in psycho-spiritual relief. She has written two books, *Serendipity and the Search for True Self* and *The Write to Heal*. Dr. Bauman lives in the mountains with her husband, two children, three cats, and countless butterflies.

Dr. Michael Bernard Beckwith is the founder and spiritual director of the Agape International Spiritual Center and host of the Revelation Conference. He is a sought-after meditation teacher, conference presenter, and originator of the Life Visioning Process. His three most recent Nautilus Award–winning books are *Life Visioning*, *Spiritual Liberation*, and *TranscenDance Expanded*.

Walter Berry, M.A. is a dreamworker, writer and artist. The weekly dream group he conducts has been featured in the *Los Angeles Times* and *The New York Times*. He conducts dream workshops internationally, lectures on dreams, and has appeared on radio shows and in publications on dreams. E-mail him at Myth2u@verizon.net.

Jan Bono's specialty is humorous personal experience. She has published five collections, two poetry chapbooks, nine one-act plays, a dinner theater play, and written for magazines ranging from *Guideposts* to *Woman's World*. Jan is currently writing a mystery series set on the southwest Washington coast. Learn more at www.JanBonoBooks.com.

Michele Boom turned in her teacher chalkboard to be a stay-at-home mom. While juggling two toddlers and a traveling husband, she began to write. Today, her work appears in regional magazines across the U.S. and Canada. She is also a regular contributor to the *Chicken Soup for the Soul* series. E-mail her at mammatalk@gmail.com.

As the CEO and founder of Vision Quest Consulting, **Wendy Capland** is an award-winning and internationally recognized leadership development expert, bestselling author of the book *Your Next Bold Move for Women*, and the leading authority on "Stepping into Leadership."

Wendy lives in New England with her family.

Jane E. Carleton, M.A. G.G., specializes in dreams as a personal advisor, educator, workshop leader, and adjunct university professor. She holds two graduate degrees in the studies of Dreams, and Consciousness. She lives in Northern California, enjoys teaching in Bali, and is also a professional gemologist. Learn more at www.yourdreamingself.com.

Eva Carter has worked in finance and has been an aerobic instructor. She enjoys going out to dinner with her husband Larry and friends, as well as traveling to different countries. E-mail her at evacarter@ sbcglobal.net.

Barbara Chepaitis is the author of several published novels and two books of nonfiction. Her works include *Feeding Christine*, *Saving Eagle Mitch*, and *Jaguar Addams and the Fear* series of science-fiction novels, available through Wildside Press. She earned her doctorate in creative writing from University at Albany–SUNY.

Kim Childs is a life and career coach with a certification in Positive Psychology, the "science of happiness" and meaningful living. She is also a writer, singer, drummer, Kripalu yoga teacher and facilitator of Boston-area workshops on The Artist's Way and Positive Psychology. Learn more at www.KimChilds.com.

Dr. Sam Collins has been named one of the Top 200 Women to Impact Business & Industry by Her Majesty the Queen of England. Sam founded Aspire in 2001, a global organization that empowers women. Its programs work in eighty countries and have made a positive difference in the lives of more than a million women.

Judy Davidson is a retired educator and social worker. She would like to thank her husband Jeff for sharing in her premature excitement, her late girlfriend Natalie Cohen who was her partner in pink and godmother to Marti and Joshua, and, most of all, thank you, Marti and Joshua.

Linda Davison is an artist and enjoys painting pictures of wildlife. She writes poetry and collects antique postcards. Linda is currently writing a book about not growing old gracefully.

A teacher of adjudicated youth by day, **Catherine Mayer Donges** earned her MA/MFA from Wilkes and MSEd from Capella University. She has authored two yet-to-be-published novel-length works, in addition to many nonfiction articles available online. She lives with her husband, Sheltie, and two cats in south-central Pennsylvania.

Paul Dragu is a freelance writer from Atlanta, GA. He's been published in *Thoughts About God* magazine, is a frequent contributor to RedState. com, and the collaborative writer of two memoirs. Paul is a member of Free Chapel Worship Center in Gainesville. He loves all things outdoors, especially hiking and fishing.

Drema Sizemore Drudge is a Spalding University MFA graduate. She is an agented author who primarily writes fiction about art. Drema and her husband Barry live in Indiana. You can read more about her at dremadrudge.com.

Deborah Dutilh is a theatre artist from Los Angeles, CA. She lived in France for nearly thirty years before relocating to Los Angeles. A visitation dream warning her of a serious illness saved her life in 2013 and also inspired her solo show, *Into The Panther's Cage*.

Cheryl Elise has a diverse background, from alternative medicine to law enforcement, and weaves her knowledge into her stories. Recently, she completed a Creative Writing program in Arizona. When she's not writing, you just may find her at a comic book convention. Cheryl currently lives near the red rocks of Sedona.

Marcia Emery, Ph.D., is a psychologist, intuitive consultant, professor and author of *Intuition Workbook*, *PowerHunch!*, and *The Intuitive Healer*. She was a board member of the International Association for the Study of Dreams and an expert on the *Dream Decoders* TV series. She lives in Kensington, CA. E-mail her at PowerHunch@aol.com.

Jane A. Foley, prophetic dreamer, has served as "Ask Ms. Ultrasound/ Dreams" expert on www.Pregnancy.org for more than ten years. Jane has found her ultrasound lab and her ability to see the future in her dreams to be the perfect laboratory for the study of dreams about pregnancy. Look for her book on predictive dreams coming soon.

Daisy Franco received her Bachelor of Arts degree from the University of Illinois at Chicago and her Master of Arts degree from DePaul University. She works in the communications field and is a former schoolteacher. Daisy enjoys traveling and exploring Chicago with her husband Epi. She is working on her first novel.

Rus Franklin was born in the West, raised in the South, grew up in the jungle and now lives in the Arizona desert. After military service, twenty-two years of living and three children, he earned B.S. and M.S.L. degrees. He has written extensively for in-house journals and travel websites. E-mail Rus at rus.franklin@cox.net.

Laura Fredrickson is a "fulfillionaire specialist" and founder of the Institute of True Wealth whose global mission is to promote our self-worth beyond our net worth. Laura has enriched the lives of countless individuals through coaching, consulting, speaking, workshops and her online programs. Learn more at www.LauraFredrickson.com.

Pamela Freeland is a medium, psychic, energy healer, Faery Reiki master and shaman. She holds a degree in liberal studies and is completing her degree in English. Pam has been writing from an early age and has a completed manuscript she hopes to publish soon and another one in the works.

Susan Friel-Williams is a licensed private investigator in Florida who specializes in family search and reunion. She has appeared on *Oprah*, *CBS This Morning*, the *Today* show and most recently as a cast member on *The Locator*. She and her husband Lane Williams just celebrated their twenty-fifth wedding anniversary.

Patricia Garfield, a renowned expert in dreams, has a Ph.D. in Clinical Psychology. She's written fourteen books on dreams, including bestseller *Creative Dreaming* (called a classic, it appears in fifteen languages). Her honors include the 2002 Parent's Guide to Media Award and the 2012 IASD Lifetime Achievement in Dreamwork.

Heidi Gaul lives in Oregon's Willamette Valley with her husband and four-legged family. She loves travel, be it around the block or the globe. Active in Oregon Christian Writers, she is currently writing her fourth novel. Contact her through her website at www.HeidiGaul.com.

Joan Gelfand received her MFA in Creative Writing from Mills College in Oakland, CA. A contributing blogger for *The Huffington Post*, Joan is the author of three collections of poetry, and an award-winning chapbook of short fiction. Her CD, *Transported*, may be found on iTunes. Learn more at www.joangelfand.com.

Gini Gentry is the bestselling author of *Dreaming Down Heaven*, the former teaching partner of don Miguel Ruiz, author of *The Four Agreements*, a principal in the documentary *Dreaming Heaven* and steward of the Garden of the Goddess Retreat Center near Santa Fe, NM. Contact her through her website at www.ginigentry.com.

Gloria Gonzalez, born in New Britain, CT, for such a time as this, is Puertorriqueòo and now lives in Daytona Beach, FL. She is the mother of Gea and Jovan, has come through great tragedy and loves to sing, dance, study the Bible and ride her bike on her beautiful beach. Thank you to Donna Tinselly for help in crafting her story.

V. Grossack is the "Crafting Fabulous Fiction" columnist at www.Writing-World.com, the author of *The Highbury Murders* and the coauthor of several Greek mythology-based books in the *Tapestry of Bronze* series.

Rebecca Gurnsey holds an A.A.S. degree in Business Technology and has worked many years in business, as well as teaching. She is now a full-time author and speaker. Rebecca has published five faith-based novels. Rebecca enjoys her children and grandchildren, as well as camping, traveling, and gardening. She resides in Texas.

Rob Harshman has been a social science teacher for over forty years. Rob has also travelled widely to over forty countries. He is married with two married daughters and a grandson. Rob enjoys photography, reading and gardening. He plans to continue writing short stories.

Best known under her former professional pseudonym of Adrianna Larkin, **Nancy Herold** is a holistic coach and motivational performer, crafting original music and programming to help others facilitate change. She and her husband own Sacred Fire Farms, a spiritual artist retreat in rural Missouri. Learn more at www.sacredfirefarms.net.

Rebecca Hill feels even the best wordsmith in the world could not describe her grandfather's aura. In her lifetime, Rebecca has only met one other person like Papu, so rare and special were his unique gifts for life.

Bob Hoss retired from industry to fully embrace dream studies. He is an officer and past president of the International Association for the Study of Dreams, a Haden Institute staff member and directs the DreamScience Foundation for research grants. He authored *Dream Language* and *Dream to Freedom*. Learn more at www.dreamscience.org.

David Hull was a teacher for twenty-five years before retiring, which has allowed him even more time to read, garden and spoil his triplet niece and nephews. He has had short stories published in numerous magazines and newspapers and several *Chicken Soup for the Soul* books.

Amy Schoenfeld Hunt is a freelance writer for newspapers and magazines, the author of three published books, and a regular contributor to the *Chicken Soup for the Soul* series. She's also a costumed historical interpreter at Old World Wisconsin, a museum that depicts life in the 1800s. E-mail her at Shaynamy@aol.com.

Linda Jackson enjoys life with her husband Jeff and their three children. As an author, she enjoys spinning stories with small-town settings. Her debut novel, set in fictitious Stillwater, MS during the summer of 1955, is forthcoming from Houghton Mifflin Harcourt. Learn more at www.jacksonbooks.com.

Diane DeMasi Johnson enjoys writing articles, short stories, and suspense/mystery novels. She is blessed with a horde of boys and loves exploring trails, ghost towns, and rundown places with them. Diane loves to connect with people. E-mail her at Diane@DianeDeMasi.com.

Vicki Joseph shares her "Then There Was Light" dream at speaking engagements. She writes and speaks about hope and reflects on her dreams to remind others tough times do pass. Originally from Chicago, Vicki now calls home Encinitas, CA, where she golfs year-round. Her pride and joy is her daughter. E-mail her at vickijoseph1888@gmail.com.

Jenny Karns loves her work as a CASA, especially with the teens! She is also an avid dreamer, healer, animal and nature lover, and author of the book *Baby Boy Phoenix: A Tale of Rescue, Love, and Second Chances*. Her favorite thing is to tell stories that encourage, enrich, uplift, and inspire.

This is **T. Jensen Lacey's** tenth story to be published in the *Chicken Soup for the Soul* series. In addition to these stories, Lacey has fourteen books and more than 800 articles in newspapers and magazines to her credit. She is available for speaking engagements. E-mail her at TJensenLacey@yahoo.com or learn more at www.TJensenLacey.com.

Mary Ellen Langbein has been writing short stories and poetry ever since her grade school days. It is one of her favorite hobbies. She also keeps busy playing golf, paddle tennis, decorating and traveling with her husband. She resides in New Jersey, is married, and Mom to Lauren and Logan.

Stephanie Lieberman is a teacher and freelance writer who possesses a Master of Arts degree in British literature from the University of New Orleans. Originally from New Orleans, LA, she currently resides in Pittsburgh, PA with her husband Evan and her German Shepherd, Cosette.

Barbara Light-Baillargeon has been happily married to her best friend Darren for the past fourteen years. They have three beautiful children: Eric, Kyle and Megan. Barb enjoys her nursing career, writing short stories, camping and spending time with her family. She is dedicated to her family and to God, who continues to guide her path.

Susan L. Lipson writes stories for children and young adults, as well as poetry, songs, writing lesson materials, and two blogs. She also teaches and coaches writers of all ages. Before becoming a mom of three kids, Susan worked as an associate literary agent with the larger-than-life subject of "Connections."

Lavina Litke completed a writing course at the Institute of Children's Literature. She is a married mother of four children and grandmother of sixteen grandchildren. She enjoys writing short stories.

Shannon MacKinnon graduated in 2012 from Seneca College's Acting for Camera and Voice Program. She aspires to be a working actress and writer. She believes she was born to create, to heal, to entertain and to help people with art. She lives in Mount Hope, ON, Canada and enjoys baking and spending time with her family.

Julie Mac Lellan is a working wife and mother who writes in her spare time. She found her passion for the literary arts in her teenage years and continues to pursue her dream of becoming an accomplished writer.

Elena Mankie enjoys watching her happy little girl explore the world. A full-time pet groomer and grooming instructor, she doesn't really have "spare time." But she enjoys family time at the zoo, museums, movies, and visiting the dog park with her dog, Chico. E-mail her at kidsbookwrighter@gmail.com.

M. Kate McCulloch began writing an Op-Ed column for *The Metropolitan* on a dare, then graduated to speculative fiction, and the occasional true-life essay. She lives in Colorado with her husband, children, dogs, cats, peony bushes, and a linden tree. The future is undetermined, but she plans to continue writing.

Judy M. Miller considers herself a storyteller. A married mother of four, she is an author of two books, a part-time freelance writer, and an adoption educator. Her articles and essays appear in parenting magazines and anthologies. She enjoys yoga, tennis, traveling, and time with family and friends.

Jann Mitchell enjoys life with her dear Eric, who has lovingly nursed her through cancer treatment and a stroke. Read more about their love story in her *Where Love Leads* trilogy on Amazon.com. E-mail her at jann.m.mitchell@gmail.com.

Cate Montana is author of *Unearthing Venus: My Search for the Woman Within* and *The E Word: Ego, Enlightenment and Other Essentials.* She is a freelance editor and journalist specializing in consciousness studies, alternative health, quantum physics and feminism. She lives in the Pacific Northwest.

Joanne Moore received a degree in photography in Cincinnati and then spent many years as a restaurant manager in North Carolina. She recently moved to Tennessee and is inspired by the Smoky Mountains. Joanne has two dogs and a deep love for all animals and outdoor activities. She is working on a young adult novel.

Geri Moran is a technical writer and craft artist who lives in New York. She loves to make people smile with her handcrafted products, cartoons and writing. She has a shop on Etsy.com named Emerald Greetings. Geri is thankful daily for her wonderful friends and family, and especially grateful for her son, Paul.

Marya Morin is a freelance writer. Her stories have appeared in publications such as *Woman's World* and Hallmark. Marya also penned a weekly humorous column for an online newsletter, and writes custom poetry on request. She lives in the country with her husband. E-mail her at Akushla514@hotmail.com.

Robert Moss is the creator of Active Dreaming, an original synthesis of modern dreamwork and shamanism. He is a novelist, poet and independent scholar. His many books include *Conscious Dreaming*, *The Secret History of Dreaming*, *Dreaming the Soul Back Home*, *The Boy Who Died and Came Back* and *Sidewalk Oracles*.

Beki Muchow lives in Sherwood, OR with her family and a growing collection of four-footers. Her stories can be found in *The Storyteller* magazine, *The Writers' Mill Journal Vol. 3*, the *Chicken Soup for the Soul* series, and others. She is currently working on a collection of short stories and a novel. E-mail her at BekiM@WritersMill.org.

Val Muller is the author of the kidlit mystery series *Corgi Capers*, the young adult novel *The Scarred Letter*, and several other works. She lives with two Corgis and a human in Virginia, where she teaches English. Learn more at www.ValMuller.com.

Kirsten Nelson enjoys life with her three children. Following a rewarding career in nursing, she teaches high school medical science courses in Colorado. She shares her passion for writing through freelance, health and education ezines, and works to help students discover the power of reflective journaling. She's on Twitter @MommaKat.

N. Newell, a longtime skeptic, discovered his own psychic ability at age forty-seven—since that "awakening" he has helped several people with messages from the spirit world. He considers himself a reluctant psychic.

Sara Nolt is a dedicated Christian, a happy wife and a stay-at-home mom of two preschoolers. While this defines most of her world, she also takes time for short-term mission work and freelance writing for Christian publications. Recently a first-time author, she is working on her second book.

Kathleen O'Keefe-Kanavos is an international, multi-award-winning author, TV/radio host/producer of *Wicked Housewives on Cape Cod* and a three-time breast cancer survivor whose dreams diagnosed her illness. She believes dreams can diagnose your life. She enjoys tennis, cooking, horses, scuba diving and mentoring women.

Susan Allen Panzica works with her rock star chiropractor husband, is a mom of two, a speaker for women's groups, Bible teacher, writer of the devotional blog *Eternity Café*, and co-founder of Justice Network, which educates and advocates about human trafficking. Learn more at www.susanpanzica.com and www.justice-network.org.

Sharon Pastore is a forty-one-year-old entrepreneur and avid dreamer whose purpose is to help people "wake up," follow their dreams and believe in the magic. She now runs a dream circle, called Dreamgirls, which uses night dreams to help daydreams come true. She lives in Havertown, PA with her super cool husband and two precious girls.

Sylvie Phillips has been a deacon in the British Methodist Church for twenty-two years. In 2011 she received a Master of Arts degree in Mission from University of Manchester (UK) with a dissertation arguing the case for a new Methodist culture of dream-sharing. Sylvie is a pastoral counsellor and trainer. She is a widow with a grown son.

Connie Kaseweter Pullen lives in rural Sandy, OR, near her five children and several grandchildren. She received her Bachelor of Arts, *cum laude*, from the University of Portland in 2006, with a double major in Psychology and Sociology. Connie enjoys writing, photography and exploring the outdoors.

As a professional writer, **Deborah Quibell** contributes to various online publications, including *The Huffington Post*. She is a senior instructor of Pranic Healing, teaches yoga and meditation in Europe and the U.S., and is a Ph.D. candidate in Depth Psychology. She believes passionately in breathing enchantment into everyday existence.

Mariah Reyes received the ABC7 Cool Kids award in 2014, worked for the U.S. Forest Service in the summer of 2015, and is currently a Youth Social Media Correspondent for the World Peace Caravan. Mariah loves to hike, sing and volunteer.

Mark Rickerby is a writer, screenwriter, singer, voice actor and has contributed multiple stories to the *Chicken Soup for the Soul* series. His proudest achievements are coauthoring his father's memoir, *The Other Belfast*, and releasing *Great Big World*, a CD of songs for his daughters, Marli and Emma. Learn more at www.markrickerby.com.

Gale Roanoake received her Ph.D. from Pacifica Graduate Institute (California), where she wrote on muses, memory, and personal story. She is married with three adult children, young twins, and three grandkids, all of whom mean everything to her. When not writing, she is a global executive coach and leadership trainer.

Kimberly Ross holds a Master of Divinity degree from Saint Paul School of Theology. In her former work as a chaplain and pastor, she served in a homeless shelter, VA hospital, hospice, retreat center, and churches. She is a writer, Reiki master, proud mother of three wonderful young adults and an adoring grandma of one.

Diane Schock received her nursing license and graduated with honors from the University of the Pacific in Stockton, CA. She has three sons and three granddaughters. Diane enjoys gardening, fishing and helping others refurbish antiques. In the future, Diane plans to continue writing both fiction and nonfiction stories, for all ages to enjoy.

Stephanie Sharpe is a trained lay minister. She studied TV production in college and directed live TV. She is a mother of four, living in Fond du Lac, WI with her partner and five cats. Stephanie currently works as a professional driver, and is pursuing a career as a full-time published author.

Gail Small is a Fulbright Memorial Scholar. She is the author of six books and speaks internationally on her Joyful Living series. Travel is her passion and she has visited all seven continents. Learn more about Gail at www.GailSmall.com. E-mail this motivational speaker and educational consultant at JoyforGail@aol.com.

Madison Sonnier is a freelance writer who has appeared in various online publications, including TinyBuddha.com and mindbodygreen.com. Her work was featured in *Tiny Buddha's Guide to Loving Yourself* by Lori Deschene. Madison currently resides in Alabama and is working on her first novel.

Joyce Stark is retired from Scottish local government, loves to travel, especially in the USA and Europe, and writes about the many things she encounters.

C.A. Strand is the author of the Stella Sky fantasy series, including

Stella Sky — The Shattered Mirror. He attended The Cooper Union for the Advancement of Science and Art in Manhattan, where he received a BFA in painting. He currently lives in Venice, CA and skis Mount Baldy when it has snow.

Lynn Sunday is an artist, writer, and animal advocate living in Northern California with her husband and two senior rescue dogs. Her stories have appeared in several *Chicken Soup for the Soul* books, and numerous other publications. E-mail her at Sunday11@aol.com.

Shelley Szajner has a B.A. degree in Illustration and is currently writing and illustrating a mystical fantasy for middle grade kids. She also writes inspirational stories for adults. In her spare time she teaches workshops on dreams, symbolism and spiritual art.

Tina Tau is a teacher, artist and writer in Portland, OR. She is a member of the International Association for the Study of Dreams (IASD), and one of her passions is helping people tap into the surprising wisdom of their dreams. She loves to sing, cook, and fall over laughing. Learn more at www.tinatau.com.

Dr. D.L. Teamor is a pastor, author, and founder of Calvary House, a 501(c)(3) established to support U.S. veterans. She is a proud daughter, wife, mother, and grandmother. She is a member of ACF Writers, the National Writers Union, Indie Author Network, Amnesty International, and the Military Officers Association of America.

Jean Tennant was first published in fifth grade, when a teacher submitted her poetry to *Highlights* magazine. Since then she's had several books published, as well as short stories, articles, essays, and collections. This is her third story in the *Chicken Soup for the Soul* series.

Ashley Thaba lives in Botswana, Africa. Her desire to be obedient to whatever God calls her to do has taken her on a journey of adventures across the world. She wrote an amazing book about the near-death experience of her son and his miraculous recovery. If you would like to read her book, e-mail her at ashleythaba@gmail.com.

Anneke Towne lives in coastal Florida where she writes web content for a variety of clients. She enjoys sporting activities, live music, and photography.

Pat Wahler will soon retire from grant writing to focus on writing essays and fiction. She is a proud contributor to many publications, including nine previous *Chicken Soup for the Soul* books. Visit her at www.critteralley.blogspot.com.

Debbie Spector Weisman has been a young adult author and film production executive. She credits her work on the groundbreaking film *What the Bleep Do We Know!?* as inspiring her to become a Dream-Life Coach. She is a wife, mother and author of *101 Dream Dates: How to Say I Love You to the Most Important Person in Your Life... You!*

Lynn Westhoff received a B.S. in Financial Accounting in 1988, a B.S. in Business Education in 1994, and an M.S. in Accounting from Illinois State University in 2004. A Chief School Business Official for a PK-12 public school, she has four adult children and eight grandchildren. She enjoys traveling with her grandchildren.

Mary Z. Whitney has been featured in over twenty-two *Chicken Soup for the Soul* books. She often writes for publications like *Guideposts* and *Angels on Earth* magazine. Mary has written the children's inspirational book entitled, *Max's Morning Watch*, as well as the adult fiction, *Life's A Symphony*.

Dallas Woodburn is a writer and teacher living in the San Francisco Bay Area. She is proud to have contributed stories to more than two-dozen *Chicken Soup for the Soul* books. Learn more about her youth literacy organization Write On! at www.writeonbooks.org and visit her blog at daybydaymasterpiece.com.

Kristi Woods loves a sunny day and clicking words of encouragement onto the screen of www.KristiWoods.net. She, her retired-from-the-military husband, their three children, and several rescued pets survived the nomadic military lifestyle and have set roots in Oklahoma. Kristi writes Christian nonfiction.

Meet Amy Newmark

Amy Newmark was a writer, speaker, Wall Street analyst and business executive in the worlds of finance and telecommunications for thirty years. Today she is publisher, editor-in-chief and coauthor of the *Chicken Soup for the Soul* book series. By curating and editing inspirational true stories from ordinary people who have had extraordinary experiences, Amy has kept the twenty-two-year-old Chicken Soup for the Soul brand fresh and relevant, and still part of the social zeitgeist.

Amy graduated *magna cum laude* from Harvard University where she majored in Portuguese and minored in French. She wrote her thesis about popular, spoken-word poetry in Brazil, which involved traveling throughout Brazil and meeting with poets and writers to collect their stories. She is delighted to have come full circle in her writing career — from collecting poetry "from the people" in Brazil as a twenty-year-old to, three decades later, collecting stories and poems "from the people" for Chicken Soup for the Soul.

Amy has a national syndicated newspaper column and is a frequent radio and TV guest, passing along the real-life lessons and useful tips she has picked up from reading and editing thousands of Chicken Soup for the Soul stories.

She and her husband are the proud parents of four grown children and in her limited spare time, Amy enjoys visiting them, hiking, and reading books that she did not have to edit.

Follow her on Twitter @amynewmark and @chickensoupsoul.

Meet Kelly Sullivan Walden

Kelly Sullivan Walden is on a mission to awaken the world to the power of dreams. She is a bestselling author who has written nine books, including *I Had The Strangest Dream*, *It's All In Your Dreams*, *Dreaming Heaven*, *Dream Oracle Cards*, and the upcoming *Love, Sex & Relationship Dream Dictionary* (2016).

Kelly began her fascination with dreams at age five, sparked by a special "tandem dreaming" connection she shared with her younger sister. Since those early years Kelly has grown into a trusted advisor, coach and consultant, enriching the lives of countless individuals, including Fortune 500 executives, UN ambassadors, celebrities, entrepreneurs, inner-city kids, and stay-at-home moms.

She is the founder of Dream-Life Coach Training and The Dream Project, a non-profit organization inspiring young people to solve global issues described in the United Nations Millennium/Sustainable Development Goals.

She captured the attention of the media at age twenty-one when she was featured on an episode of *Lifestyles of the Rich & Famous* as "Miss Public Nuisance of Beverly Hills" (a publicity stunt for an art gallery she worked at on Rodeo Drive). Twenty years ago she upgraded her crown and has since become known as the dream queen (or in some circles, "doctor dream") — a dream ambassador who, over the past two decades, has reached millions of people on national talk shows, such as *The Dr. Oz Show*, *The Ricki Lake Show*, *The Real*, *Bethenny*, *Huffington Post Live*, *Coast to Coast AM*, and FOX News. Kelly is known for saying, "Don't take your dreams lying down," "There's no such thing as a bad dream," "Redirect your dream, redirect your life," and "Our dreams can be our greatest wake-up call, illumining the path for us to live the life of our dreams."

To download your free dream gifts, go to: www.KellySullivanWalden.com.

To receive your free fifteen-minute Dream-Life Coach Training inquiry call, go to www.DreamLifeCoachTraining.com.

Find Kelly on Twitter @KellySWalden or on Facebook at www.Facebook.com/KellySullivanWaldenDoctorDream.

Thank You

In most kitchens more than one cook might compromise the soup. But not in this case! In the *Chicken Soup for the Soul: Dreams and Premonitions* kitchen we've culled spices from more than one hundred people in order to create its life-affirming, spirit-uplifting, soul-enhancing flavor. It's my joy to express my gratitude to the following chefs for rolling up their sleeves, opening their hearts, sharing their personal stories, editing, reading, curating, and stirring the pot in their unique way to move this book from dream to reality, a true feast for the soul.

Thank you from the bottom of my heart to the entire Chicken Soup for the Soul publishing dream team. My coauthor Amy Newmark, who is also the publisher and editor-in-chief of Chicken Soup for the Soul has been such a dreamy partner, and we couldn't have done it without the amazing VP and assistant publisher D'ette Corona, who worked tirelessly with all our story writers to make their own writing dreams come true.

My incredible husband, Dana Walden, supported me in birthing this book (as he has so many projects). He was very understanding about my need to read Chicken Soup for the Soul stories on planes, trains, and automobiles throughout our European excursion to get this in on time. Meesha Walden and Julie Sullivan provided invaluable feedback in helping me to select the stories for this book.

There were several thousand stories submitted for this collection, and even though we could only publish 101, all of the stories were read and had an influence on how we chose our themes and the finalists. I want to thank all the authors who have courageously laid their soul on the line in contributing their stories to this book. In particular, I'd like to thank my friends and colleagues in the dream community: Debbie Weisman, Mariah (Diamond) Reyes, Wendy Capland, Joan Gelfand, Sam Collins, Vicki Joseph, Robert Moss, Patricia Garfield, Walter Berry, Deb Dutilh, Jane Carleton, Nancy Herold, Laura Fredrickson, Jenny Karns, Kathleen O'Keefe-Kanavos, Diane Schock, Cate Montana, Christian Gustafson, Gini Gentry, and Michael Bernard Beckwith.

Julie Isaac deserves very special accolades for being the Twitter queen who was our angel and matchmaker, putting Amy and me together. She is the godmother of this book.

And last but not least, a very special thank you goes out to the International Association for the Study of Dreams (IASD) for being instrumental in the creation of this book, with a particular thanks to my hero, Bob Hoss, and reviewers Laura Atkinson and Joy Fatooh. Their expertise was invaluable. IASD is the premier international, non-profit, multidisciplinary organization dedicated to the pure and applied investigation of dreams and dreaming. We were honored to have stories in the book from IASD members Bob Hoss, Marcia Emery, Tina Tau, Sharon Pastore, and Deacon Sylvie Phillips, as well as several IASD members already listed above, including Patricia Garfield, Robert Moss, Walter Berry, Debbie Weisman, and Jane Carleton. For more information about the IASD, please go to www.asdreams.org.

~Kelly Sullivan Walden

Sharing Happiness, Inspiration, and Wellness

eal people sharing real stories, every day, all over the world. In 2007, *USA Today* named *Chicken Soup for the Soul* one of the five most memorable books in the last quarter-century. With over 100 million books sold to date in the U.S. and Canada alone, more than 200 titles in print, and translations into more than forty languages, "chicken soup for the soul" is one of the world's best-known phrases.

Today, twenty-two years after we first began sharing happiness, inspiration and wellness through our books, we continue to delight our readers with new titles, but have also evolved beyond the bookstore, with super premium pet food, a line of high quality food to bring people together for healthy meals, and a variety of licensed products and digital offerings, all inspired by stories. Chicken Soup for the Soul has recently expanded into visual storytelling through movies and television. Chicken Soup for the Soul is "changing the world one story at a time®." Thanks for reading!

Share with Us

We all have had Chicken Soup for the Soul moments in our lives. If you would like to share your story or poem with millions of people around the world, go to chickensoup.com and click on "Submit Your Story." You may be able to help another reader, and become a published author at the same time. Some of our past contributors have launched writing and speaking careers from the publication of their stories in our books!

We only accept story submissions via our website. They are no longer accepted via mail or fax.

To contact us regarding other matters, please send us an e-mail through webmaster@chickensoupforthesoul.com, or fax or write us at:

Chicken Soup for the Soul
P.O. Box 700
Cos Cob, CT 06807-0700
Fax: 203-861-7194

One more note from your friends at Chicken Soup for the Soul: Occasionally, we receive an unsolicited book manuscript from one of our readers, and we would like to respectfully inform you that we do not accept unsolicited manuscripts and we must discard the ones that appear.

Chicken Soup for the Soul

Hope & Miracles

101 Inspirational Stories of Faith, Answered Prayers & Divine Intervention

Amy Newmark
and Natasha Stoynoff
Foreword by John Edward

Good things do happen to good people! These 101 true stories of wondrous connections, divine intervention and answered prayers show miracles and good happen every day, giving hope whenever you need it most. You will be amazed and uplifted as you read these inspiring stories. Great for everyone — religious and not — who seeks enlightenment and inspiration through a good story.

978-1-61159-944-2

More amazing stories

Chicken Soup for the Soul®

Touched by an Angel

101 Miraculous Stories of Faith, Divine Intervention, and Answered Prayers

Amy Newmark
Foreword by Gabrielle Bernstein

Seen or unseen, angels are in our midst! These divine guides, guardian angels, and heavenly messengers help and guide us when we need it most. In this collection of 101 miraculous stories, real people share real stories about their incredible, personal angel experiences of faith, divine intervention, and answered prayers. You will be awed and inspired by these true personal stories from religious and non-religious, about hope, healing, and help from angels.

978-1-61159-941-1

to open
your heart

Chicken Soup for the Soul.

Think Possible

101 Stories about Using a Positive Attitude to Improve Your Life

Amy Newmark & Deborah Norville

It's always better to look on the bright side. The 101 personal stories in *Chicken Soup for the Soul: Think Possible* will inspire you to follow your heart and make your dreams reality. The book is filled with stories about optimism, perseverance and strength from people who have reached higher and accomplished more than anyone thought they could. You'll be inspired!

978-1-61159-952-7

Inspiration & entertainment

Chicken Soup for the Soul

Merry Christmas!

101 Joyous Holiday Stories

Amy Newmark
Foreword by Santa Claus

Jumpstart your own holiday spirit with these 101 heartwarming and entertaining stories of holiday traditions, family, and goodwill. You'll be entertained and inspired, and you'll want to share these stories with your family and friends. And like all our Christmas books, *Chicken Soup for the Soul: Merry Christmas!* is "Santa-safe!" We keep the magic alive for younger readers, too!

978-1-61159-953-4

to brighten your days

Chicken Soup for the Soul®

Volunteering & Giving Back

101 Inspiring Stories of Purpose & Passion

Amy Newmark
Foreword by Carrie Morgridge

Volunteers and people who give back choose hope over despair, optimism over cynicism, and caring over indifference. By serving others, they also help themselves, reporting that the biggest beneficiaries of their charitable activities are themselves! In this inspiring collection of 101 personal stories you'll read about how volunteering can change your life and improve your relationships, give you new perspective, and teach you new skills.

978-1-61159-951-0

Change your life